Great Events in the Story of the Church

Great Events in the Story of the Church

Geoffrey Hanks

CHRISTIAN FOCUS

ISBN 1 85792 383 9

Published in 2004
by
Christian Focus Publications, Ltd.
Geanies House, Fearn, Tain,
Ross-shire, IV20 1TW, Scotland

www.christianfocus.com

Cover Design by Alister MacInnes

Printed and bound by
Bell & Bain, Glasgow

CONTENTS

ACKNOWLEDGEMENTS

Many of the illustrations in this book are the authors but there are a few he got from other sources and wishes to acknowledge them.

Athanasius - Evangelical Library
St Sophia - Turkish Tourist Office
Waldensian Preachers - Prescot Stephens (Waldensian Church Missions)
Domus. - SPCK (Society for Promoting Christian Knowledge)
Hus - Evangelical Library
Luther - Evangelical Library
Calvin - Evangelical Library
Baptist Chapel, 1701 - Revd Brian H Keyworth (Friends of Monksthorpe)
Breeches Bible - The Bible Society
Penn - Evangelical Library
Wesley - Wesley Chapel Museum
Edwards - Evangelical Library
Kay Family - OMF (International) UK
Harper - Christian Communications Partnership
Graham - Evangelical Library

PREFACE

This is the third volume written to give an overview of the story of the Church, from the first century down to the present day. Together with its two companion volumes – *70 Great Christians* and *60 Great Christian Founders* – the growth of the Church is followed through the lives of leading men and women who have contributed towards the shaping of Church history, and aims to present in a readable format some account of the events that are recognised as landmarks in the story of the Church.

The present book, like its two predecessors, has been written for teh lay-man and woman interested in furthering their understanding of the development of the Faith, from its origins up to the end of the last century. It is impossible to fully comprehend where we as Christians stand today unless we have some grasp of the significant events that have determined the course of the history of the Church. To gain an insight into the lives of those who have gone before us and laboured, often at great personal sacrifice, to build the Church of Christ, leaves us with a sense of awe and admiration. Through these real-life dramas we can trace the hand of God in the progress of the Faith and can more easily understand the reasons for what we believe.

Dr Martin Lloyd-Jones, formerly minister of Westminster Chapel, London, and probably the most outstanding preacher of the last century, offered further reasons for such studies. He made the following comment about the value of reading the lives of Christian people and past events: 'The real value of looking to the past and to history is that it should help us to face the problems and difficulties of our own age and generation. I am not interested in that which is merely antiquarian and historical; (we) turn to these men (and women) in order that we might learn from them.'[1]

---

1. From the Annual Lecture of the Evangelical Library for 1962, published by the Evangelical Library, London.

1

AD 30 THE DEATH OF JESUS THE MESSIAH

The Road to the Cross

In the year AD30, at the Jewish festival of Passover in Jerusalem, three men were led outside the city walls to be executed by the Romans. Two of them were brigands who had taken part in an insurrection. The third man was innocent. Accused by the religious leaders of claiming to be 'the Messiah, the Son of God', he had been condemned to be crucified by the Roman procurator on the grounds of being King of the Jews. The death and subsequent resurrection of Jesus proved to be the most awesome events the world has ever known and form the foundation rock upon which the Christian Church is built.

First century Israel was gripped by a messianic expectation that excited the hopes of the whole nation. Especially since the Roman occupation of the land, the people had been looking for a Deliverer, a prophet whom it was believed God would send to save them from their enemy and set up his kingdom. When Jesus preached the kingdom of God and confirmed his message with miraculous signs, many ordinary people acknowledged him to be 'the one who was to come' – the Messiah. It was mainly the religious leaders who rejected his claim, for he failed to conform to the popular image of a victorious military leader.

The concept of the Messiah has its origins in the Old Testament, where there are numerous passages regarded by the rabbis as prophetic of the special person who would one day be revealed by God.[1]

---

1. Edersheim lists 456 OT passages which ancient rabbis applied to the Messiah or messianic times. See *Life & Times of Jesus the Messiah*, Vol 2, p.710.

The term 'messiah' (Hebrew, 'anointed') is rendered in Greek as *christos*, which is used for the New Testament designation of Jesus. It was not until the first century, however, that the term was first applied in a technical sense, when it appeared in Jewish apocryphal works such as the Similtudes of Enoch and the Psalms of Solomon. By the time of the Lord's appearance the term was generally recognised as a reference to a future Redeemer whom God would send to restore the kingdom of Israel.

Further ideas of the Messiah can also be gleaned from a study of the non-canonical literature, rabbinic writings and synagogal prayers of the time of Jesus. In some references the messianic person was spoken of as a priest or a prophet, whereas other sources suggested he would combine the two functions in one role. It was also assumed that he would have supernatural powers, as foretold by the prophet Isaiah (Isa. 35:5ff).

The main idea to emerge, however, was that of a descendant of King David, a warrior-king who would bring victory over the Roman conquerors and usher in an age of peace, righteousness and justice. Anyone speaking of a Messiah during the New Testament period would have had in mind this picture of 'Messiah son of David', a person endowed with military prowess who would establish the messianic kingdom.

There are also references in rabbinic literature to a slain Messiah, designated 'Messiah son of Joseph', one who would be 'pierced for our transgressions' (cf. Isa. 53:5; Zech. 12:10-12). Just as the patriarch Joseph had suffered at the hands of his brothers, so would the Messiah also suffer. One consequence of these diverging portraits was the development within Judaism of the notion of two Messiahs, one from the royal line of Judah who would bring peace ('son of David') and the other from the priestly tribe of Levi who would suffer vicariously and die for Israel ('son of Joseph'). This is in contrast to the Gospels which speak of one Messiah coming twice.

Messianic Claim

Although Jesus never openly claimed to be the Messiah, he clearly portrayed himself as the one spoken of by the prophets. Because of his apparent silence on the matter, the idea was put forward, known as the 'messianic secret',[2] which proposed that Jesus deliberately refrained from making such a public declaration. Yet the Gospel accounts clearly portray Jesus' claim to be

---

2. The term was coined in 1901 by William Wrede, a German scholar who proposed that Jesus deliberately kept secret his claim to be the Messiah (cf. Mk. 8:27ff).

Israel's Messiah. The earliest indication of the awareness of his vocation was given at his baptism, when he was designated by the heavenly voice as Messiah and Suffering Servant of the Lord (Mark 1:9ff). While both these concepts were spoken of in the *Tanakh* (Old Testament) by the prophets, the Jewish rabbis had never previously linked them together.

Throughout the Gospel accounts there are allusions by Jesus to his identity as the messianic person, both in his teaching and by his miracles. Many of those who followed him, grounded as they were in the Scriptures and rabbinical teaching, recognised his claims. More than this, however, Jesus also showed himself to be the Divine Messiah which filled the concept of the Messiah with an altogether new content and was in opposition to Jewish expectations.

One of Jesus' most revealing actions was the healing of the demon-possessed man who was blind and dumb (Matt. 12:22ff). Though rabbis were also known to perform healings and cast out demons, by the first century they had listed seven miracles which they judged only the Messiah would be able to perform, one of which was the kind of healing in question. When Jesus healed the man, enabling him to both see and speak, people asked, 'Could this be the Son of David (i.e., the Messiah)?'

As the healing was in public, the Pharisees had either to reject the implication of his action or explain how else Jesus could have performed a messianic miracle. Their answer (v. 24) was that he cast out demons by the prince of demons, an argument Jesus showed them to be absurd. So, on the grounds that he was said to be demon-possessed the Pharisees rejected his messianic claim; as a false prophet, therefore, he should be put to death (Deut. 13:1-5).

When from time to time Jesus spoke of himself in terms of the Messiah, he did so by his self-designation as 'the Son of man'. The title, derived from Daniel 7:13ff, appears to have been readily understood and accepted by the crowds who followed him. However, this passage has an even wider implication, for it speaks of a heavenly King, one who would 'come with the clouds of heaven' and whose kingdom would be everlasting; in other words, the Messiah would be of divine origin. When, for example, Jesus forgave the paralytic his sins (Mark 2:1-12), the teachers of the law who were present were indignant, declaring that only God had such authority. To which Jesus responded by healing the man and affirming his divine prerogative, that 'the Son of Man had authority on earth to forgive sins...'

SON OF MAN

The title 'Son of man' occurs over sixty times in the Synoptic Gospels where it is used exclusively by Jesus to refer to himself. It is a Greek translation of a Semitic phrase meaning 'man' (Hebrew, *ben adam*). Whilst some scholars deny that the title has messianic implications, many suggest otherwise. Brad H. Young (*Jesus the Jewish Theologian*, p.244) discerns three meanings in the use of the term and argues that the context should be allowed to determine the interpretation:

(1) In some instances Jesus used it as a generic term, to refer to a human being or as a substitute for the personal pronoun 'I' (e.g., Matt. 12:32; 13:37).

(2) On occasions, the Son of man is conceived of as a supernatural being, spoken of in Jewish apocalyptic teachings, and was an elevated way of referring to the messianic task (e.g., when Jesus spoke about the final judgment, Matt. 25:31-36).

(3) Then, a combination of the two previous usages, employed by Jesus when speaking of his Passion and his future return to complete the messianic task during the last judgment (e.g., Mark 8:31; Luke 17:30).

This title of the Messiah is based on Daniel 7:13ff, and more than any other reflects Jesus' claim to be the one of whom the prophets spoke.

Divine Messiah

The pivotal event of the gospel story is the incident at Caesarea Philippi, when Peter declared Jesus to be 'the Messiah of God' (Luke 9:18ff). Straight away Jesus warned his disciples not to tell anyone, possibly from fear of a premature arrest that would have hindered his mission. Having acknowledged his identity, Jesus began to teach the Twelve what kind of Messiah he was to be: he must suffer, be rejected and be killed, but would rise again the third day. This was in complete contrast to the popular expectation of a military leader who would lead the nation to victory.

It is clear the disciples did not fully appreciate Peter's insight. Nor, either, did Peter understand Jesus' prophecy concerning his death and resurrection, for he was offended by the thought of his master's mission ending in apparent failure. Only when the Lord had been raised from the dead did the disciples begin to understand the meaning of this prophecy.

From here Jesus set off for Jerusalem, knowing that the time of his death was approaching (Luke 18:31). If there was any lingering doubt about his Messiahship, then his entry into Jerusalem at Passover, a time when messianic expectations ran high, convinced even his enemies. For here was a clear declaration by Jesus, deliberately fulfilling a messianic prophecy (Zech. 9:9). Pilgrims going up for the festival recognised his action and acclaimed him with shouts of 'Hosanna to the Son of David!'

The incident in the Temple, when Jesus rebuked those who were using it for purposes of profiteering, was an open challenge to the Temple authorities. The chief priests and elders consequently looked for an opportunity to arrest him, in order to have him killed. The Sanhedrin (Jewish Council) had also become fearful of his popularity and determined to have him silenced. Following the raising of Lazarus, one of them had protested, 'If we let him go on like this, everyone will believe in him, and then the Romans will come and take away both our Temple and our nation' (John 11:48). It was better, the high priest argued, that one man should die rather than the whole nation be put at risk.

Arrest

The opportunity to arrest Jesus came when Judas, one of the twelve disciples, went to the chief priests and discussed how he might hand over his master to them without attracting public attention (Luke 22:1ff). The following evening, as Jesus shared the Last Supper with his disciples, Judas was able to slip away from the upper room and begin to put the plan into action. From then on, events happened at great speed.[3]

It was late at night, in Gethsemane – a grove of olive trees on the lower slopes of the Mount of Olives – when Jesus was arrested. From here he was taken across the Kidron Valley to the house of the high priest in the upper city, where he was awaited by Caiaphas and certain members of the Sanhedrin. By now it was nearly midnight. Normally, any trial involving a capital charge could only take place in daylight, but Caiaphas was anxious to have the matter dealt with before news of Jesus' arrest became public. In this and several other matters the trial would appear to have been illegal.

At this preliminary hearing, held to determine the charge, the high priest introduced false witnesses in an attempt to produce a conviction. But despite this ploy he was unable to find any grounds for a case against Jesus. Finally, in exasperation, he applied the most solemn form of oath in Jewish law and asked a direct question: 'Are you the Messiah, the Son of the Blessed One?'[4] As a law-abiding Jew, Jesus was bound to give an answer. 'I am,' he replied. He then went on to speak of himself as the 'Son of Man sitting at the right hand of Power[4] and coming on the clouds of heaven' (Mark 14:61ff). In

---

3. The following outline of the arrest and trial of Jesus is based on the traditionally accepted chronology.

4. One of a number of terms employed by Jews to avoid using the name God. See also the use of 'Power'.

saying 'I am', Jesus used the same expression given by *Adonai* when he revealed himself to Moses at the burning bush. Thus Jesus put himself on equality with God and identified with the LORD of Exodus 3:14. His answer clearly demonstrated his claim not only to be the Messiah, but also that he shared the nature of God.

Death Sentence

The gathering was in no doubt about the significance of Jesus' answer. Alarmed at his profession, the high priest accused him of blasphemy and the Council condemned him as deserving death, the penalty for profaning the sacred name. There was no further need for witnesses, they argued, as the prisoner had convicted himself by his own words. At daybreak a further gathering was held in the Council chamber (situated in the Temple Court) to legitimise the decision reached during the night. It only remained to persuade Pontius Pilate, the Roman Procurator of Judea, who alone held such jurisdiction, to pass the death sentence.[5]

To successfully carry through this schedule of events must have involved a degree of preparation on the part of Caiaphas. Having judged the right moment for making the arrest, it was then necessary to ensure that an execution order was confirmed and carried out before sundown, the eve of Sabbath. This would have meant consulting with various officials, including Pilate, to ensure there were no hitches. To secure a death sentence, however, it was necessary to change the accusation from a religious to a political one, for the Romans were not interested in Jewish religious squabbles. Of the three charges brought by the religious leaders against Jesus (Luke 23:2), the most serious one was that of treason, that he claimed to be a king.

Pilate did not accept the charges against the prisoner and made several attempts to have him released. But to no avail. Backed by a crowd that had gathered outside the Procurator's residence (formerly the palace of Herod the Great, near the present Jaffa Gate) the religious leaders[6] put pressure on Pilate for a 'guilty' verdict. Normally suspicious of any messianic pretender and faced with continuous disorders throughout the land, Pilate could not afford to ignore any threat to his authority (John 19:6).

---

5. Authority to execute a death sentence had been withdrawn from the Sanhedrin shortly after AD6, when Judea became a Roman province.

6. Strangely, the Pharisees – Jesus' most outspoken opponents – are not mentioned as being involved in either the trials or the crucifixion. It could be because they regarded handing over a Jew to a foreign power as a sin that could not be forgiven.

Reluctantly, he yielded to the demand. He had Jesus flogged, and on the basis of his admission to being 'king of the Jews' sentenced him to be crucified (Luke 23:24ff).

Crucifixion

It was shortly before nine o'clock in the morning when Jesus was led away to his death. Forsaken by his closest friends, with only John and a group of loyal women watching from a distance, he was taken to Golgotha, the 'Place of a Skull',[7] a plot of rising ground outside the city wall. The Gospel writers give no details of the execution; they simply say 'there they crucified him'.

Paradoxically, the crucifixion clearly witnessed to Jesus' twofold claim, that he was the Divine Messiah.[8] On the cross, over the head of the prisoner, the Romans nailed a board on which the charge was written in Hebrew, Latin and Greek: 'Jesus of Nazareth, the king of the Jews' (a messianic title). Then the religious leaders who had engineered his death challenged him to display his divine powers: 'He saved others; let him save himself if he is the Messiah of God,' they jeered (Luke 23:35).

Jesus hung on the cross for six hours, during which time he spoke only briefly. At three o'clock in the afternoon he called out with a loud voice, 'Father, into your hands I commit my spirit'. And with these words, he bowed his head and yielded up his life. This prayer is a quote from Psalm 31:5 and is still the prayer of a dying, observant Jew (cf. Acts 7:59).

Burial

Under Jewish law it was forbidden for the bodies of criminals to remain on the cross overnight. As the next day was the Sabbath, it was especially necessary to hasten their deaths so that burial could take place before the day of rest. In which case, the prisoner's legs were broken with a mallet (or similar instrument). No longer able to sustain the weight of their body, the victims soon died of suffocation. Jesus, however, was already dead, but to make sure one of the soldiers plunged a spear into his side, just below the heart.[9]

---

7. Alternatively known as Mount Calvary.

8. The Jewish Talmud speaks of Jesus as a '*mesit*' (an inciter to idolatry), who was stoned and hung up for practising magic, and not just for claiming to be the God-Messiah.

9. This action resulted in a gush of blood and water from Jesus' body. Medical opinion has it that while suffering on the cross Jesus' heart swelled until it burst, resulting in an effusion of blood and water serum. This evidence supports the Gospel account that he died from crucifixion and from a ruptured heart. The idea that Jesus only swooned on the cross and was later revived in the tomb simply does not hold.

The church of the Holy Sepulchre, Jerusalem,
built over the probable site of the crucifixion

The burial was a hurried affair, as the Sabbath was only an hour or so away. But Jesus' body was not released until Pilate had checked that the prisoner really was dead. Joseph of Arimathea, a secret disciple of Jesus and a member of the Sanhedrin, made his own nearby tomb available and, accompanied by Nicodemus, another secret disciple, carried out the burial according to standard Jewish practice. Two women watched where the body was laid, in order to return after the Sabbath to complete the task of embalming the body.

For the disciples, it seemed an end to their hope that Jesus would redeem Israel. While some of them returned to their homes in the country, others hid behind locked doors in the city. It was not until after the resurrection, when the disciples met with the risen Lord, that they began to understand who he really was. Fifty days later, at the Feast of Pentecost, the disciples were confidently able to declare in public that Jesus was both 'Lord and Messiah'.

FALSE MESSIAHS

Throughout the history of post-biblical Judaism there have been many petty 'messiahs' who have claimed the title, as foretold by Jesus (Matt. 24:5). The earliest messiah of significance was Bar Kokhbar ('son of a star', cf. Num. 24:17). In 132 he gathered an army of about 400,000 men, captured Jerusalem and forced the Romans to evacuate the Holy Land. His Jewish army was eventually overcome. Jerusalem, left in ruins, became a Gentile city, and many Jews fled to Arabia.

The most remarkable and influential of all the claimants was Shabbathai Sebi of Smyrna (western Asia Minor) who lived in the seventeenth century. He believed he had magical powers; he was a member of a mystical sect called Kabbalah, which taught that only a privileged few were able to enjoy direct communication with God. Learning of the belief of some English sects that the year 1666 would be the opening of the millenium, in 1648 he declared himself to be the messiah.

Excommunicated by the rabbinical authorities, he wandered the Middle East until 1665 when he arrived in Jerusalem. He announced himself as messiah and was publically hailed as such in the synagogues. His reputation reached as far as Europe, where some Protestants even began to doubt the claim of Jesus. In 1666 Sebi moved to Constantinople, only to be arrested. To save his life he converted to Islam and died in disgrace ten years later.

2

AD 35 SAUL OF TARSUS CONVERTED

Apostle to the Gentiles

The spread of the gospel from Jerusalem to Rome during the first century was largely due to the missionary zeal of Saul of Tarsus, a converted Jewish rabbi. His avowed intention was, initially, to search and kill the members of the breakaway Jewish sect which claimed that the crucified Jesus was the Messiah. Such was the brutality of his campaign that it struck terror into the hearts of believers not only in Israel but beyond its borders as well. His search ended abruptly on a journey to Damascus, when he met with the risen Lord. Saul the persecutor became Paul the Apostle, and more than any other was responsible for establishing the early Church on a firm footing.

Saul was a native of Tarsus,[1] the capital of the Roman province of Cilicia (a region in south-east Asia Minor, present-day Turkey). Tarsus was a busy river port and an important trading centre, with a population of about a half million inhabitants. Standing some ten miles inland on the River Cydnus, it was situated at the meeting-place of the Eastern and Western worlds, of Semitic and Greek civilisations. The city was a melting-pot of religions and cultures, and boasted a university whose scholars and philosophers were known all over the ancient world. Such an environment brought Saul into contact with Gentiles and opened his eyes to the wider world around him.

Among the nationalities represented in the city was a considerable number of Jews, for Jews were to be found in all the major cities of the Roman Empire.[2] Saul was descended from a long line of Pharisees, a factor central to his religious upbringing. At the heart of Jewish life and culture

---

1. The date of his birth is unknown, though tradition places it two years after Jesus.
2. It is estimated there were some two million Jews scattered around the Empire.

was the synagogue, where as a boy Saul received his early education. In addition, he received religious instruction at home, for the duty of every Jewish father was to bring up his sons according to the demands of the Torah (the law of Moses). When in later years he was at pains to establish his Jewish identity, he was able to claim that there was no one more Jewish than he was: a descendant of Abraham, belonging to the tribe of Benjamin, born of Hebrew parents and a member of the strictest sect of the Jews – a Pharisee, and 'faultless' in his adherence to the Jewish law (Phil. 3:5ff).

However, it was said in Israel that, 'To be solely concerned with the Torah, to the exclusion of following a trade, was to act like a man who knows not God.' Hence his father, following the time-honoured Jewish custom, taught his son a trade, that of tent-making, which would one day enable him to make a living. The Greek term used to describe this occupation more correctly means 'leather-worker', and was connected with the manufacture of a goat's hair material called cilicium, used for making cloaks, curtains and the like.

Jerusalem

That Saul's father prospered in Tarsus is apparent from his rank as a Roman citizen, which gave him (and Saul) certain rights, and from the rabbinical training he was able to afford for his son in Jerusalem. Soon after Saul became a 'son of the law' at the age of thirteen, he went up to Jerusalem where he studied under Rabban Gamaliel,[3] the greatest rabbi of his day. Gamaliel was a doctor of the law and grandson of the famous Hillel, the leader of a school of disciples that flourished just prior to the time of Jesus.

Here, Saul received his rabbinical training 'in every detail of the law', and could later boast that he had advanced in the Jewish religion more than many Jews of his age. He became 'extremely zealous for the traditions of (the) fathers', that is, for the Jewish oral law (cf. Mark 7:1-4), and was especially observant in carrying out its religious and ethical demands.

THE ORAL LAW

The word 'law' (Hebrew, *Torah*, meaning 'instruction'), is used of the 613 commandments of the Old Testament. It can also refer to the first five books or even to the whole of the Old Testament. The Torah is divided into two branches: the written and the oral Law, both of which were said to have been given to Moses by God at Mount Sinai. The oral law – which in the Gospels is referred to as the Traditions of the Elders – consists of legal opinions and interpretations of doctrines and practices, as well as traditions, delivered over the centuries by the Scribes (teachers of the law) and rabbis. Some rabbis placed the authority of the oral law above that of the written law of Moses.

The reasoning behind the oral law was that the commandments given to Moses did not always give adequate directions for putting the written laws into action, as certain of them seemed unclear. It was the task of the Scribes to interpret the intent of the law, so that it might be more closely followed. In so doing, they put a 'fence' of secondary laws around the Torah. Whilst people might break the laws of the fence, they would not (hopefully) violate the 613 commandments and thereby bring down the wrath of God upon them. Their hope was that by keeping the law they would bring in the Messiah.

The oral law, also known as the *Mishnah* ('study'), was not committed to writing until the beginning of the third century AD. It is divided into six main divisions, consisting of a total of sixty-three volumes. To give one example, the commandment governing the Sabbath is covered by some 1,500 further laws that serve to define what types of work are forbidden.

The first mention of Saul in the New Testament is at the trial of Stephen (Acts 6:12–7:60), who had been arrested and brought before the Sanhedrin for 'speaking against (the) holy place and against the law'. Stephen's accusation, that the people had persecuted the prophets and even killed 'the Righteous One', seemed nothing short of blasphemy. Without waiting for a death sentence to be passed, Stephen was seized and dragged out of the Temple precincts to the place of execution, close to the northern gate of the city, where they stoned him to death.[4]

The two witnesses, whose duty it was to cast the first stones, placed their clothes in the safekeeping of Saul, who had 'given his approval' of the action and who may also have been one of the disputants in the original controversy.[5] Stephen's death was the signal for a systematic assault upon the Church, for Saul felt it his duty to stamp out this heresy before it spread to Jews of the Dispersion. The text of Acts gives occasional hints of the ferocity of his campaign, which can be gained from the three accounts of Saul's conversion.[6] With a band of Temple officials and acting upon the authority of the high priest, he set about a programme of 'religious cleansing', beginning with Jerusalem. He combed the city, house by house, to seek out and arrest any man or woman who was a disciple of the Lord, and throw them into prison; some were even put to death.

---

3. Rabban was a title meaning 'our master' or 'our great one'.

4. Though only the Roman governor had power to pass the death sentence, the Sanhedrin was allowed to stone a prisoner for violating the Temple court. Stephen's death, however, has the appearance of being a lynching.

5. Saul's role suggests he was actually a member of the Sanhedrin, further borne out by his admission that he 'voted' to have believers put to death.

6. Acts 9:1-22; 22:3-16; 26:9-18.

Persecution

Instead of stamping out the new movement, however, his actions served only to advance the cause of the gospel. A large number of the believers – more probably the Hellenists (Greek-speaking Jews of the Diaspora) – left the city and were scattered throughout the provinces of Judea and Samaria, and even beyond Israel. As they went, they preached the gospel and many came to faith in Jesus as Messiah. Saul stepped up his campaign of persecution and spread his net beyond the capital, visiting synagogues throughout the whole land of Israel. He found many followers of Jesus here, for Jewish Christians continued attending synagogue after their conversion, as well as meeting with the believers, a practice that continued until at least the end of the first century.

When believers were arrested he attempted to force them to blaspheme the name of Jesus (i.e., to call Jesus accursed and thus repudiate his claims), probably by having them scourged. The punishment of scourging could be inflicted by the local judicial court (Deut. 25:3) and prisoners received up to thirty-nine lashes to their back. Others who persisted in refusing to deny their Lord were condemned to death, presumably by stoning and with the authority of the Jerusalem Sanhedrin. Later he was to admit that he acted against the Christians 'ignorantly, in unbelief', and out of a sincere zeal for God.

The Temple (model), where the Hall of
Hewn Stone was the meeting place of the Sanhedrin.

When Saul heard there were disciples in Damascus (Syria)[7] he obtained letters of extradition from the high priest to the rulers of the city's synagogues. With permission to arrest disciples and take them back to Jerusalem, he vented his fury by threatening to have them put to death. But on his journey, as he neared Damascus, he had an encounter with the risen Lord which brought about a radical change in the direction of his life. The significance of this encounter is often referred to in his letters, as though to remind himself – as well as his readers – of the awesomeness of his calling. In fact, such was the reality of his experience that in later years he listed it as one of the Lord's resurrection appearances, alongside those to Peter, the Twelve and others (1 Cor. 15:8).

When he entered Damascus, it was not as a persecutor but as a disciple of Jesus. The Lord went before him into the city, where he was welcomed by Ananias, an observant Jewish believer, who prayed with him and then baptised him in water. It was at this point that Saul learned from Ananias that the Lord had chosen him to take the gospel of Jesus, not to his Jewish brethren but to the Gentiles.

Meanwhile, Saul was determined to publicly acknowledge his new-found faith. His baptism in the name of Jesus the Messiah was his 'crossing the Rubicon'; it was his declaration of commitment to his Lord. When he visited the synagogues in Damascus, he astonished the congregations by declaring Jesus to be the Divine Messiah, the fulfilment of Jewish expectations. The persecutor had turned traitor!

Search

The biblical text gives little idea of what brought Saul to faith in Jesus. It may well be that when Luke introduced Saul into the account of Stephen's trial, he was giving a hint that the process leading up to his conversion started at this point. Stephen's speech before the Sanhedrin and his firm testimony as he faced death may have impressed Saul; for instead of cursing the perpetrators of the crime, Stephen called upon God to forgive them. Possibly the manner of his dying deeply disturbed Saul and raised doubts in his mind: Could it be that Jesus really was the Messiah? Had he truly been raised from the dead? Was there a more direct way to God than that prescribed under the law of Moses?[8]

On the other hand, it may be that Saul's conversion followed a period

---

7. Israel was part of the Roman province of Syria (cf. Luke 2:2).
8. Augustine of Hippo (354–430) was probably right when he wrote, 'The Church owes Paul to the prayer of Stephen.'

of 'incubation' that began before the death of Stephen. That his mind had been in turmoil for some while is suggested by Jesus' words to Saul, 'It is hard for you to kick against the goads' (Acts 26:14), as though an inner conflict had been raging over a period of time. Despite his learning, he had not recognised that the prophecies concerning the Messiah were fulfilled in Jesus. Could it also have been that he had a growing sense of a failure to find peace with God, and that his attacks on the Church were an attempt to convince himself of the rightness of his stand?

Who Was Jesus?

There were two issues concerning Jesus which had plagued Saul's mind. First, the disciples preached that the crucified Jesus had been raised from the dead and was indeed the Messiah spoken of by the prophets. Saul had considered Jesus to be disqualified by the fact that he had been crucified like a common criminal, for the Scriptures declared that anyone who was hung on a tree was under God's curse (Deut. 21:22ff). Yet not only did he discover that Jesus was alive, but the Lord spoke to him – and by name. Further, he recognised that the cross was no longer a stumbling-block, for Jesus through his death had redeemed all mankind from the curse of the law.

His second concern was equally disturbing. The disciples claimed Jesus to be the Son of God and spoke of him as 'Lord'. But like all Jews, Saul believed there was only one true God,[9] for God had no 'Son'. To believe Jesus was divine would be idolatry; and the penalty for deifying a human being was death by stoning, a punishment of which Saul was well aware. Yet when he met with Jesus on the road to Damascus Saul had addressed him as 'Lord' and even recognised that the Lord had a call upon his life.

By calling Jesus 'Lord',[10] Saul was using the title by which God was addressed in the Scriptures (where the name Yahweh is translated 'LORD'). As he made this confession, which later became the earliest Christian creed (cf. Phil. 2:11), he crossed over from unbelief to faith. Contrary to what some suppose, he did not abandon his Jewishness and become a 'Christian'; rather he began to discover the fulfilment of all that was written of Jesus in the Law and the Prophets.

---

9. See Deuteronomy 6:4: 'Hear O Israel: the LORD our God, the LORD is one'. This is the *Shema*, the opening statement of the Jewish chief declaration of faith.
10. The term 'Lord' can also mean 'sir'; its interpretation here depends to what extent it is thought Saul had recognised the identity of the voice.

JESUS AND PAUL

There is no mention in the New Testament of Paul having met Jesus or of hearing him preach. Nevertheless, his letters reveal a considerable knowledge of the Lord's teaching which he used as an authority for some of his pronouncements. In his pre-conversion days, such was Paul's anger towards the Nazarene sect that his fury must have been based on what he had heard or learned. He may, of course, have had a written source upon which to draw; either way, there is no sure evidence.

In certain passages of his letters, however, Paul uses the sayings of Jesus, though without quoting his words verbatim (except one saying, 'It is more blessed to give than to receive', Acts 20:35). In his teaching on marriage and divorce, Paul is careful to distinguish between what is the Lord's command and what are his own instructions (I Cor. 7:10-12). In another place he declares that 'those who preach the gospel should receive their living from the gospel' (cf. Luke 10:7). And when speaking of the Coming of the Lord, he writes, 'According to the Lord's own word...' (I Thess. 4:15).

There are echoes of Jesus' words in other places: his teaching on a Christian's duties towards his neighbour (Rom. 12:14ff) mirrors that given in the Sermon on the Mount; the Lord's words concerning the true inwardness of religion (Mark 7:15) is paralleled by Paul's declaration in Romans 14:14, that he was convinced 'in the Lord Jesus' that 'no food is unclean in itself...'; and his affirmation that 'You cannot drink the cup of the Lord and the cup of demons too', reminds us of the Lord's dictum, 'No man can serve two masters...' (Matt. 6:24).

Apostle

For the next ten years or so Paul[11] laboured for the gospel, yet without leaving any account of his work during this period. From Damascus he first withdrew to the Nabataean territory of Arabia, to the south-east of Syria. Whether it was a quest for solitude in order to seek the mind of God, or for purposes of evangelism – or both – is not known. Returning to Damascus (Acts 9:23) he was confronted by Jews who had not forgotten his defection, and planned to kill him. When knowledge of their plot was discovered, the disciples organised his escape and he made his way to Jerusalem from where he had originally begun his journey. His purpose here was to get acquainted with the leaders of the Church.

But he was not initially welcomed by the disciples, fearful of his past record, until Barnabas – who may have heard of his testimony from the believers at Damascus – introduced him to Peter and James (the Lord's brother). By now Paul had apparently formulated the gospel which he felt God had called him to preach (Gal. 1:11ff). The two apostles approved of

---

11. Whether he was given the Roman name Paul at birth or conversion is not known.

his doctrine, and with their blessing the way was open for him to fulfil his calling to the Gentiles.

He returned to his native Tarsus to begin his mission on home ground, where he appears to have established churches, particularly in Cilicia and Galatia (Gal. 1:21). It was several more years before he was invited by Barnabas, probably in the year 44, to help build up the thriving church in Antioch (Acts 11:25), which brought the apostle back into the mainstream of Christianity and led to a more widespread mission among the Gentiles.

St Paul's-outside-the-wall, Rome, the possible site of Paul's martyrdom.

Mission to Gentiles

Paul was singularly fitted to fulfil his calling to be the Apostle to the Gentiles. As a Jew he was thoroughly grounded in the Scriptures, and being brought up in a Greek city enabled him easily to cross the religious and cultural divides of the first century to take the gospel to heathen nations. During his three pioneering missionary journeys he founded more churches throughout Asia Minor and then ventured onto the continent of Europe, perhaps even reaching as far as Spain.

Although he never failed to testify to his compatriots, his mission to the Gentiles led to a vast influx of non-Jewish believers into the Church. His occasional letters, which contained teaching on matters of doctrine and conduct, and which were regarded as having the same authority as (Old Testament) Scripture, were eventually incorporated into the Church canon. In fact, his letters were the starting point of his teaching, and no doubt – like many Jewish converts today – as soon as he experienced a spiritual birth 'the eyes of his understanding were opened' and he could grasp the meaning of the prophetic words.

Paul's role in the early Church has been a matter of considerable dispute amongst scholars. Some have argued that he was not truly a disciple of Jesus, in that he changed the character of Christianity from that set out in the Gospels, that he was the founder of the Church, and not Jesus, and that he taught a new doctrine based on the Lord's ethical teachings. But the case is rather the opposite; for he drew upon both the Tanakh (Old Testament) and the life and teachings of Jesus to further the cause of the gospel. His writings were a means of preserving the essentials of the Faith for future generations.

Though he appears never to have met the Lord, his writings reveal an outline knowledge of the earthly Jesus, from his birth through to his resurrection. Not only was he able to quote the Lord's sayings, but some of the passages in his letters strongly reflect Jesus' teachings. And Paul's great doctrinal themes are a reflection of those expressed in the Gospels: among them, the Fatherhood of God, the fallen nature of mankind, the death and resurrection of Jesus, justification by faith, forgiveness, and of the new birth.

Whilst recognising Paul's contribution towards establishing the Faith and his work in spreading the gospel among Gentiles, it should also be remembered he was the one who stood against the threat of false teachings that assailed the early Church. His letter to the church at Colossae, for example, included a strong attack on the Judaic-Gnostic heresy which, unchecked, later threatened to overwhelm the Church in Asia Minor. J. S. Stewart wrote, 'it was Paul, more than any other, who kept the new religion pure and uncontaminated and faithful to its great original object, in days when danger and corruption were threatening it on every side'.[12]

---

12. *A Man in Christ*, Hodder and Stoughton (1935).

3

AD 48 THE COUNCIL OF JERUSALEM

Gentile Believers Welcomed into the Messianic Community

A controversy arose in the early Church which, unless checked, would have divided the believers and hindered the progress of the gospel. At stake was the need for an agreed definition of the terms of salvation, which came under attack when a large influx of Gentile believers threatened to swamp the Jewish Church. The immediate problem was resolved at the Council of Jerusalem and a major crisis defused, though by the second century the relationship between Jewish and Gentile believers had experienced a serious reversal.

The dispute centred upon the rite of circumcision and the on-going validity of the law of Moses, and to what degree, if any, should Gentile believers be subject to it. To Jews, circumcision was the sign of the covenant God made with Abraham and was therefore still binding; and belonging to the people of God meant obedience to the law. When Gentiles came to faith in Jesus, the question was raised, should these non-Jews have to undergo circumcision and conform to the law of Moses in order to be saved?[1] Putting it another way, could a Gentile become a Christian without first becoming a Jew?

The earliest Christian community, in Jerusalem, was exclusively Jewish; it included both Hebrew and Greek-speaking Jews who believed that Jesus was the Messiah. Some of them were native-born Jews, others were from among the Dispersion. Counted among their number were proselytes, that

---

1. Gentiles had so far not been expected to be circumcised, only to be baptised (cf Cornelius and household, Acts 10:47ff).

is, Gentiles who by obedience to the Mosaic law had been totally accepted as Jewish. (Judaism was a missionary religion and proselytes formed an important group within the synagogues of the Dispersion.)

During the early days, the number of believers in Jerusalem grew rapidly. For a while they were simply regarded by the Jewish leaders as a new sect within Judaism. But at the trial of Stephen (Acts 6–7) the differences between the Messianic Jews and mainstream Judaism began to emerge, resulting in a great persecution against the Church. Many believers, especially the Hellenists (Greek-speaking Jews), who easily identified with Stephen, fled the city. The apostles and the Hebrew-speaking believers were among those who stayed behind.

LANDS OF THE NEW TESTAMENT

Benefit

While some took refuge in Judea and Samaria, others travelled to more distant places – Phoenicia and Cyprus, and to cities such as Caesarea, Antioch (Syria) and Damascus. In the providence of God the attack turned out to the benefit of the gospel, for wherever the disciples went they shared the good news of Jesus with both Jew and Gentile alike.

It was some ten to fifteen years after the birth of the Church before the first Gentiles came to faith in Jesus. It happened at Caesarea when a Roman centurion, a God-fearer[2] by the name of Cornelius, heard the gospel from

---

2. A Gentile attracted to Judaism, who worshipped in the synagogue yet without submitting to the ceremonial law required of proselytes.

the apostle Peter. As he and his household listened to him preach, without making any outward profession of faith they received the Holy Spirit and began to speak in tongues (Acts 10).

When the apostles heard that Gentiles had believed, Peter was recalled to Jerusalem to explain what had happened. After hearing his account the leaders raised no further objections. 'So then God has granted even the Gentiles repentance unto life,' was their response. It seemed that without any undue argument the matter of non-Jews entering the Church had been settled; the question of circumcision or having to obey the law of Moses was not raised.

Antioch

Some 300 miles to the north, in Syria and the provinces of Asia Minor, more Christian communities were being established by those who had fled Jerusalem. At Antioch, the third city of the Roman Empire, later to become one of the leading centres of Christianity, a great number of Jews and Gentiles believed and turned to the Lord, again without any reference to keeping the Mosaic law. Barnabas, later joined by Paul, was sent from Jerusalem to supervise the work there, and a thriving church was established. It was here that the believers were first called Christians. When, later, the young church at Antioch decided to launch its own missionary outreach, Barnabas and Paul were sent to evangelise the people of Cyprus and Asia Minor.

Among the new believers was a large number of God-fearers who, with their attraction for synagogue worship and life, formed the nucleus of many of the new Christian communities and soon constituted a majority within the Church. Trouble arose, however, when a group of believing Pharisees from Jerusalem visited Antioch, claiming to have been sent by James. Without authorisation from the apostles they taught the Gentile believers that they should submit to the law of Moses: 'Unless you are circumcised according to the custom taught by Moses, you cannot be saved,' they argued.

When Peter visited Antioch (Gal. 2:11ff) some time after the conversion of Cornelius, he and other believing Jews felt at ease in taking meals with Gentile Christians. But fearful of the party of Pharisees from Jerusalem, the Jewish believers withdrew from the Gentiles and only sat at the table with the circumcised; this created the threat of a division in the church. Paul took Peter to task over the matter for not being true to the gospel.

The problem needed to be resolved before it led to a rift, not only in the church at Antioch but also between Antioch and the mother-church in Jerusalem. It was therefore felt necessary to consult with James and the other apostles who were the recognised leaders of the church. Paul and Barnabas were sent to Jerusalem at the head of a deputation to clarify the situation (Acts 15:2ff).

The Council

During the initial meeting to welcome the brothers from Antioch, some of the believers from the party of the Pharisees repeated their insistence that Gentiles should be circumcised and required to obey the law of Moses. A gathering was convened to consider the question, at which the delegation from Antioch met with the apostles, elders and other members of the Jerusalem church. It opened with a lengthy discussion between the leaders of the two churches, no doubt reviewing the problem, and Luke's report suggests that the question of the law was fully debated.

Peter reminded the gathering of his experience at Caesarea when Cornelius believed and the question of Gentiles entering the church had been settled. He pointed out that God had made no distinction between Jews and Gentiles, for he had accepted non-Jews by giving them the Holy Spirit as they had received at Pentecost; God had responded to their faith just as he had to the Jews who believed. They should not, therefore, now put the 'yoke of the law'[3] upon them, by prescribing conditions laid down by men, that neither they nor their forefathers had been unable to bear. It was 'through the grace of our Lord Jesus that we are saved, just as they are,' he concluded (vv. 7-11).

Quietened by Peter's appeal, the assembly listened as Barnabas and Paul related what God had done among the Gentiles on their mission to Cyprus and south Galatia. They spoke in support of Peter, describing the miraculous signs and wonders God did through them (v. 12). The inference was that they, too, had witnessed God's blessing upon Gentiles, as Peter had at Caesarea.

It fell to James, the Lord's brother, as leader of the Jerusalem church to make a final pronouncement. Convinced by the testimony of Peter and Paul, he recognised the hand of God in calling non-Jews to faith in Jesus, and spoke of God's concern 'by taking from the Gentiles a people for himself' (v. 14). This was in agreement with Scripture, for centuries before the prophets had spoken of the ingathering of the Gentiles (Amos 9:11ff).

---

3. Proselytes who undertook to fulfil the law were said to 'take up the yoke of the kingdom of heaven' (cf. Matt. 11:29ff).

'It is my judgment,' he concluded, 'that we should not make it difficult (i.e., by insisting on conditions God had not required) for the Gentiles who are turning to God.' Thus it was settled that the terms of salvation were to be the same for Jews and non-Jews alike, and salvation was by faith alone; there was no need for Gentiles to be subject to the Mosaic law.

Jewish conscience

There remained, however, one other aspect of the problem to be resolved. Many Christian communities contained Jewish believers, brought up under the law of Moses. Gentiles, through their contact with Jews as well as hearing the Torah read in the synagogue, would know the sensitivities of their Jewish brothers concerning the ceremonial law. James, therefore, felt it right that they should respect their Jewish conscience by giving attention to certain commandments. He suggested they should write, urging the Gentiles 'to abstain from food polluted by idols, from sexual immorality, from the meat of strangled animals and from blood' (v. 20; cf. v. 29). Whilst on the one hand James was pressing the council not to put obstacles in the way of Gentile believers, he was also urging them to consider various matters which were offensive to Jews.

The wording of James' exhortation, however, is not fully clear. The first two items obviously related to idolatry and to sexual liaisons outside marriage; the third appears to refer to eating meat from animals not slaughtered in the traditional Jewish way (i.e., by killing the animal with a single stroke across the neck, then draining the blood). In which case, this latter command was probably felt essential in order to allow Jewish and Gentile believers to continue sharing food together, for Jews could only partake in kosher meat.

But does 'the meat of strangled animals and from blood' constitute one or two prohibitions? Does the reference to 'blood' refer to drinking animals' blood, or, metaphorically, to murder? David Bivin of the Jerusalem School for Synoptic Research has concluded that it refers to murder, and that the commandment not to eat meat with blood was added by a Greek copyist who did not understand that '*shefichut damin*' (shedding of blood) referred to murder, but thought that it related to kosher laws. F. F. Bruce concluded differently, arguing that the Council's resolution stipulated that Gentile Christians should only eat meat prepared according to Jewish food laws, with the blood properly drained from the animal, an injunction which it is claimed is still incumbent upon all believers.[4]

---

4. F. F. Bruce, *The Spreading Flame*, p.109.

Interestingly, some ancient manuscripts omit 'from the meat of strangled animals'. If this is correct, then James' direction could be to three of the orignal Noachide laws, laid down in the Talmud. These laws were said to have been given by God and were binding on all mankind from the time of Noah. In which case it is possible that James based his judgment on this tradition and that the apostolic decree was a Christian version of the Noachide code.

> ## THE NOACHIDE LAWS
> As Jews treated foreigners living in their midst with kindness, in return they expected them to fulfil certain demands to avoid giving offence. These were laws given before Moses' special revelation at Sinai which the people of Israel believed were binding on Jews and non-Jews alike. The rabbis taught that these laws were considered to be a minimum moral duty enjoined by God on all the descendants of Noah – all mankind – hence the term 'Noachide Laws'.
>
> The prohibitions set out by the Jerusalem Council are closely similar to the Noachide Laws. Of the seven commandments, six were said to have been given to Adam, and a seventh added after the Flood. They were, 1) not to worship idols, 2) not to blaspheme the name of God, 3) to establish courts of justice, 4) not to commit murder, 5) not to commit adultery, 6) not to steal, and 7) not to eat flesh with the blood of life in it. The rabbis taught that to save life a Jew might break any of the commandments except those relating to idolatry, adultery and murder. By the third century the list had grown to thirty, though the original seven were the most important. Any Gentile living according to these laws was reckoned by Judaism to be among the righteous.

The whole assembly – including Paul – readily accepted James' decision. A letter was written to the church at Antioch, addressed also to Gentile believers in the provinces of Syria and Cilicia, setting out their proposals and condemning the Judaizers who had caused the trouble. Two believers from Jerusalem, Judas and Silas, accompanied the delegates on their return journey to personally witness the contents of the letter. The news from Jerusalem was received gladly and it gave the church at Antioch much encouragement. Gentile believers were released from observing the law of Moses, and the way was reopened for the work of evangelism among Gentiles.

Watershed
The Council at Jerusalem marked a watershed in the book of Acts; from then on the focus of attention was no longer on the Jewish Church, but on Paul's mission to the Gentiles. Meanwhile the face to face meeting had

helped sort out the problem between Jewish and Gentile believers that threatened the gospel, and an agreement was reached on a fundamental point of doctrine. What was centuries later to be the great issue of the Reformation was settled; for Jews and Gentiles alike there was only one gospel: salvation through faith in Jesus, alone. A split was avoided and Paul's mission to the Gentiles could continue, fulfilling the calling given him at his conversion.

From this point there emerged a Christianity that enjoyed a greater freedom and wider vision, and potential proselytes found it easier to join the church than the synagogue. As an increasing number of Gentiles came to the Lord, Jewish believers found themselves a minority group within the Church; soon, Christianity was being expressed more in Greek rather than Jewish terms. This was noticeable, for example, in the rejection of food laws and the eventual adoption of the Lord's Day as the day of worship.

In Israel the gospel continued to attract new believers, and when Paul visited Jerusalem around AD58 James disclosed that there were 'many thousands of Jews' who had believed and were 'zealous for the law' (Acts 21:20). Although the Jewish church in Israel continued to flourish, it was dealt a severe blow by the two wars fought against the Romans (AD66–70 and 132–135). Jerusalem, previously the stronghold of Jewish Christianity, was destroyed and a Roman city built on the ruins from which Jews were excluded. A Gentile church was established, and it was to be another 1,700 years before a Jewish bishop was appointed in Jerusalem.[5]

Writing of the Jerusalem Council, F. F. Bruce observed that the decision to allow Gentiles into the church without conforming to the ceremonial law 'must be considered one of the boldest and magnanimous in the annals of church history'.[6] For in refusing to impede the growth of Paul's mission to the Gentiles the Jewish Christians had thrown wide open the door of the church to non-Jews, though paving the way for a church that was soon to deny its Hebraic roots.

THE JEWISH CHURCH

By the middle of the first century the Jewish Christians could be divided into three distinct groups: (1) The more conservative Jewish believers, which included the Pharisees (the circumcision party), and were closely linked to the Jewish Law; they were probably the ones that fled to Pella in AD66 and were later

---

5. See the story of Michael Solomon Alexander, Bishop in Jerusalem in the author's *70 Great Christians* (CFP).

6. F. F. Bruce, *The Spreading Flame*, Paternoster Press.

known as Ebionites. (2) The Hellenists, whose cultural background was Greek and were possibly more liberal in outlook. (3) The Hebrews, a centre party, who were quite likely in the majority; they supported James at the Council and included Peter and Paul.

In various places the Acts of the Apostles gives an indication of the number of Jewish believers in the early Church: from 3,000 on the Day of Pentecost (2:41) to the 'many thousands of Jews who have believed' (21:20). The Greek word used in this last verse is *muriades*, literally meaning 'tens of thousands', which suggests a minimum of 20,000 believers, though the inference is that the figure should be greater.

Before the fall of Jerusalem in AD70 there could have been as many as 400,000 Jewish believers in Israel and throughout the Dispersion.[7] According to a nineteenth century Jewish historian (August Neander) by the end of the first century the number had risen to nearly a million, indicating the significant impact the gospel had made among the Jews. Today the worldwide total of Messianic Jews (as Jewish Christians are now known) is thought to be more than 350,000.

---

7. Jewish New Testament Commentary, David H. Stern, p. 301

4

AD 70 THE DESTRUCTION OF JERUSALEM

Breech between Church and Synagogue Widens

In 63BC the pagan general, Pompey, conquered Israel and brought it under the power of Rome. But the presence of a Roman army, especially in Jerusalem, caused widespread dissatisfaction and continual agitation. Despite Caesar's favourable treatment of the Jewish people, the seeds of rebellion were sown that a hundred years later led to a vain attempt to overthrow the Roman yoke. The revolt that began in AD66 was a result of years of Roman misrule; and though the uprising was initially successful, it left Jerusalem in ruins and the Temple destroyed.

After the death of Herod the Great (37–4BC) the country was governed by a series of Roman procurators who almost without exception were notorious for their avarice and corruption. It was said of Pontius Pilate (AD26–36) that 'his day in Judea was a reign of bribery and violence, robbery, oppression, misery, executions without fair trial and infinite cruelty'. And procurator Gessius Florus (AD64–66), who loved money and hated Jews, was said to have spoiled whole cities so that their inhabitants fled to foreign provinces. It was his misrule that led directly to the start of the revolt.

Of equal importance was the widespread poverty and social distress caused by the heavy burden of taxation imposed by the Romans. As well as the two main taxes – poll tax and land tax – there were numerous other taxes, plus customs dues and duties on all that was bought and sold in the towns. It was mainly for this reason that there was extreme poverty and distress especially among the peasantry, who were generally exploited for the benefit of the townspeople.

Breakdown

The two decades before the start of the revolt witnessed a breakdown in law and order, with frequent riots and further economic decline. There was an increase in the activities of the extremist freedom fighters, now a feature of life in Judea. The most active party was the Zealots, which dominated Jewish political activism in the 60s. They reckoned subjugation to a Gentile power was contrary to the Torah and believed no Jew should pay tribute to Rome. Claiming to look for the kingdom of God, they held it could only be brought in by overthrowing the foreign ruler.

Although there were numerous religious sects in Jerusalem ready to challenge the might of Rome, the upper classes generally preferred the status quo. The moderates in Israel – the Sanhedrin, the Sadducees and Pharisees, plus well-to-do farmers – were prepared to accommodate themselves to the political reality and tacitly supported the Romans.

As the conflict between Jews and Romans intensified, it led in May AD66 to open war. It was finally provoked by procurator Florus when he confiscated seventeen talents from the Temple treasury to cover arrears in tribute money. Rioting broke out; Florus sent in his troops to put down the disturbance and 3,600 Jews were arrested and put to death by crucifixion.

ISRAEL OR PALESTINE?

In the first century AD the land in which Jesus lived was known as 'the land of Israel' (Matt. 2:20), or alternatively by the regional names of Judea, Samaria and Galilee. After the Romans crushed the second Jewish revolt in 135 it was renamed 'Syria Palestina' (it was part of the Roman province of Syria), a term formerly used by the Greeks. The intention was to sever Jewish connections with their ancient homeland. The name 'Palestina' refers to 'Philistia', meaning 'rolling or migratory', the coastal strip of the land of Canaan where the Philistines settled in the twelfth century BC. After the Romans, the Muslim caliphs retained the name until the tenth century but it appears to have been little used by later invaders and was usually referred to as Southern Syria. The Ottoman rulers in the nineteenthth century called the area the Sanjak of Jerusalem.

Britain appears to have resurrected the use of the name in 1917, when the Balfour Declaration proposed 'the establishment in Palestine of a Jewish homeland'. Jews living in the land called themselves Palestinians until 1948, when they became Israelis. The Arabs declined to use the term and following Jordan's illegal annexation of Judea and Samaria in 1950 became Jordanians. The formation of the PLO in 1964 was aimed at eliminating Israel and replacing it with a 'secular democratic State of Palestine', though it was not until after the 1967 Six Day War that the Arabs began to describe themselves as Palestinians.

Sacrifices Stopped

King Herod Agrippa II (cf. Acts 25:26), ruler of Galilee and Peraea, endeavoured to bring about a peaceful settlement with the Romans, but he was driven out of Jerusalem and the Zealots took control of the city. All sacrifices on the behalf of Gentiles were stopped, including the one for the emperor. This was tantamount to a rejection of the emperor's authority and a declaration of war against Rome. Strongholds in Jerusalem were seized by Zealot forces, the Roman garrison massacred and a provisional government set up. It was a signal to the nation, and rebellion flared up throughout the whole land. Roman troops led by Gallus, governor of Syria, marched on Jerusalem, but they were heavily defeated.

The emperor Nero could no longer tolerate the situation and despatched a powerful force to Judea under the command of Vespasian, a brilliant soldier who had distinguished himself during the conquest of Britain. Accompanied by his stepson, Titus, he reached Israel in the spring of AD67 with three legions (about 60,000 troops). He quickly put down the opposition in Galilee, where over 6,000 prisoners were taken. Among them was the Jewish commander, the historian Josephus, whose prediction that Vespasian would one day become emperor of Rome earned him a reprieve.

By summer AD68 Vespasian had conquered most of Judea and was marching on Jerusalem when news of Nero's death reached him. He returned to Rome to claim the title of emperor. Titus assumed command of the army, and in April AD70 advanced towards the capital with a large force of foot soldiers, plus cavalry and engineers. The Jews appeared unperturbed by the threat of a renewed war, for at Passover thousands of pilgrims gathered for the festival. The city was tragically overcrowded when Titus appeared at the walls; the siege lasted until September, by which time thousands of Jews had died or been killed.

Seige

The Roman general hoped that a show of force would dispose the rebels to surrender; it was said that Titus wanted to avoid further loss of life and to prevent the holy city from being destroyed. But the rebel leaders refused the offer, even though the general twice sent their own countryman, Josephus, to plead with them. Determined to starve the city into subjection, the Romans built a rampart around the entire perimeter to prevent supplies reaching the city. They launched their attack from the north, the weakest point in the defences, even though it was defended by three walls. By the beginning of May the Roman battering rams and stone catapults had bulldozed a large hole in the outer north wall; five days later they penetrated the second wall.

Conditions inside the city deteriorated rapidly. People died from famine and plague, friends fought each other over the smallest scraps of food, and even the high priest's wife scavenged the streets in search of crumbs. Large numbers of people took a chance in slipping out of the city to forage for food, but each day as many as 500 of them were caught, tortured and then crucified before the walls. On 24 July, at the cost of considerable losses on both sides, the Romans recaptured the Tower of Antonia, the fortress which guarded the Temple's northern wall. The rebels retreated into the Temple area itself, ready for a valiant last stand.

Although Titus is said to have given orders that the sanctuary should be spared, the soldiers were possibly carried away by their fury towards the Jews. Josephus describes how one of them threw a piece of burning wood through a window, immediately setting alight the interior of the holy place. Titus' order to quench the flames went unheard – or unheeded – by the soldiers, and so the sanctuary was destroyed. The date was 10 August, the anniversary of the destruction of the first Temple by the Babylonians in 587 BC. Josephus ruefully concluded that 'God had for certain long ago doomed it to the fire'. From here the rebels withdrew into the upper city on the western hill and took refuge in the strong towers of Herod's palace. Early in September they were finally overcome. The seige had lasted 143 days.

The Western Wall of the Temple Mount,
left standing after the destruction of Jerusalem.

Control

As the victors took control of the city, the Roman soldiers went on the rampage; thousands of Jews were robbed and then slaughtered. Titus ordered that the whole city, including what remained of the Temple precinct, be destroyed. He left standing a section of the Temple mount supporting wall on the west – the 'Wailing Wall' – and, to provide quarters for the Roman garrison, the three towers of Herod's palace and part of the city wall on the west side.

The loss of life was tremendous. On Josephus' reckoning around one million people died in the war (the Roman historian, Tacitus, suggests 600,000), and 97,000 were taken prisoner in Jerusalem. Titus celebrated the victory by having 2,500 Jewish prisoners killed at Caesarea, either in the amphitheatre or by being burnt to death. About 700 Jewish prisoners, the finest of the young men, were taken to Rome for a triumphal procession before being executed.

The last pocket of resistance was at Masada, the rock fortress built by Herod on the shores of the Dead Sea, where a band of Zealots held out for a further three years. When the Jewish defenders finally realised there was no hope left, 960 of them committed suicide. Two women and five children escaped death by hiding in the conduits.

Turning – Point

The destruction of Jerusalem and the Temple was a turning – point in Jewish history, for it marked the emergence of a reconstructed Judaism and the end of the Jewish state until modern times. The rabbis attributed the disaster to Israel's failure to live faithfully by the precepts of the Torah, while Christians interpreted the event as God's judgment upon Israel for the nation's rejection of the Messiah.

Of the twenty-four religious groups and sects in Jerusalem, only the Pharisees survived the disaster. The problem was, how were they to maintain the religious identity of Israel? Not only had the daily sacrifices ceased to be offered, but with the destruction of the Temple the whole priestly system was brought to an end.

The man responsible for leading the reorganisation of Judaism was Rabbi Johanan Ben Zakkai. Under his direction an academic Sanhedrin and a religious school were established at the coastal town of Jamnia (Jabneh). The synagogue and the home replaced the Temple as the focus of Jewish religious life, and the rabbi rather than the priest became the religious authority. Though the Torah was still the rallying force of the Jewish people, an emphasis was placed on teaching the oral law, which ultimately led to the rabbinical Judaism known today.

THE TEMPLE MOUNT

Following the destruction of the Jewish Temple in 135, the emperor Hadrian built a pagan temple on the Mount as a deliberate insult to the Jewish people. It was demolished in 326 by the Christian emperor Constantine. An attempt to rebuild the Temple was made by the pagan emperor Julian (361–363), though the work was interrupted and then abandoned.

When the Muslims conquered Jerusalem in the seventh century, over the rock Moriah where Abraham had offered Isaac (and from where Mohammad was said to have ascended to heaven on a horse) they built a shrine known as the Dome of the Rock (691–697). The El Aqsa Mosque was also erected close by, probably on the site of a sixth century Christian basilica. Today the site is sacred to both Jews and Muslims.

Since 1967, when the Old City was recaptured from Jordan, Jews have not been allowed onto the Mount for fear of treading on the place where the Holy of Holies once stood. The Muslim Wakf (the religious authority), which was given control of the area, has also denied them access.

Investigations have thrown into doubt the actual spot on which the Temple stood. One claim is that it was located 330ft to the north of the Dome, in which case should the opportunity arise there would be space for both a Muslim and a Jewish shrine. But more recent research suggests that foundational trenches cut into the rock Moriah align exactly with the known dimensions of the Holy of Holies.

For several years a group called the Temple Faithful has been making plans to build a third Temple, while the Temple Institute has been reconstructing the vessels needed for worship (including sacrifices) in readiness for such an event.

Jewish Christians

As for the Jewish Christians of Jerusalem, they refused to fight against the Romans. A great many of them left the city and took refuge in the city of Pella, situated in the foothills across the Jordan, where there was already a small Christian community. According to Eusebius, the Church historian, this exodus was in obedience to a warning from Jesus to 'flee to the mountains' when Jerusalem was surrounded by armies (Luke 21:20-24).

Others, among them leaders such as the apostle John, emigrated to Asia Minor and were assimilated into the Gentile Church. Some were scattered around Judea and Galilee and found a home among the small Christian communities already established there. There was one such group at Nazareth and another at Capernaum, where the traditional home of the apostle Peter had become a house church. It continued as a Christian meeting-place until early in the seventh century when Muslim invaders overran the land.

A number of Jewish Christians returned to Jerusalem after the revolt and re-established a church there. Eusebius lists no less than fifteen Jewish bishops who served in Jerusalem between the years AD70 and 135, after which time the Romans excluded Jews from the city. Prior to the wars with Rome the Jewish Christians had been considered a sect with Judaism, albeit an heretical one, but still part of the Jewish community. Tension between the two groups, however, increased and the process of separation accelerated.

The remains of Peter's house, Capernaum, where an octagonal church building was superimposed over the ruins in the 4th century – a shrine has now been built over the site.

The main issue was the rejection of Jesus by the religious authorities as the Divine Messiah. Another reason for the widening breech was the Christians' changing attitude towards Sabbath worship. Although many Jewish believers continued to attend synagogue, by the beginning of the second century they observed Sunday as the Lord's Day. To the Jews this was tantamount to rejecting Israel and the Mosaic law, thereby abandoning the faith of the Fathers. The recognition by Nero in Rome (AD64) that Christians were not, in fact, a Jewish sect, may also have hastened the split.

When Jewish Christians refused to take up arms against the Romans they were branded as traitors. This accusation was repeated again at the time of the second revolt (132–135), following the declaration that the Jewish leader, Bar Kokbah, was the Messiah. Unable to accept his claim, many Christians refused to join the nationalist cause and were put to death. After the revolt was put down, Jerusalem was declared to be a Gentile city. It was renamed Aelia Capitolina, while the land was called Palestina. The church there became a Gentile church and it was not until the nineteenth century that a Jewish Christian was once more appointed bishop in Jerusalem.

From this time on the church became separated from the synagogue and from its Jewish roots, abandoning the Hebrew heritage into which it had been born. The historian F. F. Bruce wrote, 'It is to be regretted that Jewish Christianity was not more completely integrated into the catholic Church; the valuable contributions that it could have made to the life and thought of Christendom would have been a healthy corrective to certain tendencies, as the contribution of Jewish Christianity in more recent times has been.'[1]

---

1. *The Spreading Flame* by F. F. Bruce.

5

C AD 150 JUSTIN MARTYR'S FIRST APOLOGY

In Defence of the Gospel

By the second century Christianity had spread throughout many parts of the Roman Empire and was becoming firmly established as a serious alternative to paganism. The Jews, following a series of failed revolts around the empire, had fallen under the imperial displeasure and their accusations against the Christians carried less influence. Though Christianity was still a *religio illicita* – an illegal religion – and was liable to extreme penalties, the Church was left undisturbed for considerable periods. Nevertheless, a number of writers felt it important to put forward a defence of the Christian religion, the foremost of whom at this time was Justin Martyr (c100–165).

The rejection by Christians of the pagan gods frequently led to the charge of 'atheism' (that is, they had no gods), and their refusal to join in emperor worship appeared as treason against the state. Unsavoury rumours were rife and they were charged with horrors of all sorts – incest, cannibalism, sacrilege. Though never convicted on these grounds, they were invariably punished for their confession as a Christian.

For the next century, however, even though the systematic oppression of believers was discouraged, they were often treated with suspicion and hostility which led to local outbreaks of persecution. Nevertheless, believers maintained their stand and continued to share the gospel with their pagan neighbours, and their bravery in face of death won for them a new respect and admiration. Those who confessed Christ when brought before the magistrates did not escape the sentence of death. Among the more famous martyrs of the second century was Ignatius, Bishop of Antioch (put to death c110–117) and Polycarp, Bishop of Smyrna (156).[1]

---

1. See the author's *70 Great Christians.*

There was at this time an increasing number of intellectuals and men of literary ability coming to faith, men who took up the pen in defence of Christianity. Known as 'apologists', the aim of these writers was not to win converts but to give a reasoned defence of the Faith against popular accusations by their pagan neighbours. These addresses, called *apologia* ('written defences'), were in circulation from c120–220 and issued mainly from the Greek-speaking part of the empire.

Among the early apologists the most significant contribution was made by Justin – later surnamed the Martyr – in the middle years of the second century. A Greek philosopher from Samaria, his work stands as typical of the whole movement and he is an excellent example of a number of philosophers who found their satisfaction in the adoption of Christianity.

> ## APOLOGISTS
>
> The second century apologists were the first of a new kind of writers, philosophers whose aim was to defend the Faith they had recently embraced. Previously, Christians had suffered persecution without raising a voice in protest; now philosophers used their literary skills in an attempt to remove prejudice and to answer false accusations. But whereas the apostolic Fathers had composed works specifically for the Church, the apologists directed their addresses to the emperor and leading state officials.
>
> Nevertheless, the writings of the apologists were highly valued within the Church, and they did much to strengthen the resolve of believers. Whilst there is no evidence to suggest that heathens were won to the Faith as a result of Justin's *Apology*, it at least made an impression on the emperor. Antoninus Pius commanded that in future no one should be troubled simply because they were Christians, and that their informers should suffer the punishment they had tried to inflict upon their opponents. And in a letter written by him about an earthquake, he acknowledged that the Christians were braver and more confident in times of danger than their heathen countrymen.

Search for Truth

Justin was born at Flavia Neapolis, the ancient Shechem now known as Nablus, a Roman colony founded by the emperor Vespasian. He came from a pagan family, and both his father and grandfather were probably of Roman birth. Early in life, he was educated in the old heathen religion and instructed in the learning and philosophy of the Gentile world.

In a search for truth, Justin set off on his travels to enquire of the various philosophical schools. At first the Stoics, encountered by Paul some eighty years earlier, appeared the most promising, and he joined himself to one of their preceptors. His experience left him no nearer in his quest for a knowledge of God, which his instructor declared to be unnecessary. When he met with the followers of Aristotle, his teacher seemed more concerned about his fee rather than a search for knowledge, and he was dismissed by a celebrated Pythagorean tutor because of his ignorance of the sciences.

Disillusioned, he moved to Ephesus where he became a disciple of the Platonists, and while studying with them felt he would soon arrive at the knowledge of God. 'Such was my foolishness,' he observed, 'I expected presently to see God, for this is the end of Plato's teaching.' Having discovered their philosophy, he felt that he had suddenly become wise and had arrived at a more perfect faith.

One day, wanting to spend time in quiet meditation, he walked by himself in a field near the sea. It was here that he met 'an old man of comely and grave appearance' who engaged him in conversation. In their discussion about the pursuit of truth, Justin asked how, if the ancient philosophers were as ignorant as the stranger made out, was the truth to be learned. The old man pointed him to the Jewish prophets, 'men who lived before Pythagoras and Plato, righteous men and beloved by God who spoke by the divine Spirit and foretold future events'. Before leaving him, the old man encouraged him to 'pray that the gates of light may be opened unto thee, for these things cannot be perceived or understood by all, but only by him to whom God and his Christ have given understanding'.

The meeting stirred Justin's soul. He wrote, 'a love of the prophets and of the friends of Christ took possession of me… I found this philosophy alone to be safe and profitable.' Justin's experience was not that of a Paul on the Damascus road, but rather the sure conviction that in Christianity was the oldest, truest and most divine of philosophies. His decision was further strengthened by the amazing impression made upon him by the martyrs, when he 'heard the Christians reproached and yet saw them rushing fearlessly upon death'.

Following his conversion, which happened about 133, he spent further years travelling around until he settled in Rome where he set up a school to teach enquiring heathens. Though continuing to wear the dress of a Greek philosopher, he constantly reminded his former friends and associates that he had now discovered the true philosophy in Christ. He entered into disputes with his leading opponents and began to write treatises against all the heresies that were plaguing the Church at that time.

A prolific writer, he composed treatises against pagans, Greek philosophers and the Jews. Only three of his works survive, including his *Dialogue With Trypho the Jew*, which gives an illuminating account of an encounter between the two Faiths. Written in Ephesus about 155, the *Dialogue* was based on an actual controversy between Justin and a cultured

Jew, Trypho, and presented the Christian case against Jewish objections to Christianity.

Much of the discussion centred on Jesus as Messiah, with both contestants appealing to the Old Testament and sniping at each other. Justin argued that the Scriptures spoke of the Messiah and that the ceremonial Jewish law had been abrogated by him. Whilst Trypho conceded that the Messiah must suffer, he insisted that it did not prove that Jesus was the messianic person; he went further, by criticising Christians for resting their hopes on one who had been crucified. At one point Justin accused the Jews of killing Christ and his prophets before him, and it was for this reason, he suggested, that their nation had suffered so much.

After two days' debate, neither succeeded in convincing the other; Justin confessed that if they could discuss their views more frequently it would greatly help them in searching the Scriptures. The debate was conducted in a friendly manner and the two contestants finished on good terms, with Justin wishing his adversary that he would come to believe that Jesus is the Son of God.

Defence of Christianity

Justin is chiefly remembered for his defence of the Christian Faith. His *Apology* was written while he was in Rome and was addressed to the emperor, Antoninus Pius (138–161), and his two adopted sons, on behalf of the Christians – 'men of every nation who are unjustly hated and abused'. Later he added a second, shorter defence, addressed to the Senate and the people of Rome. The first treatise, penned somewhere between 150–155, aimed at removing prejudice and misunderstanding about the Christian Faith; it made an appeal to the justice of the emperor and demanded that being a Christian should no longer be made a crime.

He vindicated the Christians against the accusations of atheism, immorality and disloyalty, and argued that they should only be punished if the charges could be substantiated. In order to show the moral superiority of Christianity he contrasted the lifestyle of the believers with that of the heathens. For example, he pointed out that whereas pagans readily abandoned their children to prostitution, the Christians lived chaste lives and shared their goods with people in need.

In his address, Justin struck a new note by adding an explanation of Christian beliefs and describing their rites and practices. His reason for these additions was to allay public distrust, which arose as a result of the secretive nature of Christian meetings. Although his accounts do not give the precise details of a liturgical manual, they do give some insight into church meetings of the second century.

With regard to baptism, Justin emphasised that it was for believers who promised to live according to Christian teaching, who then by the washing with water were born again. Afterwards, the assembly of Christians prayed for the newly baptised, who received their first Eucharist, according to the words of Jesus. Justin went on to describe the weekly worship meeting, which included a briefer account of the Eucharist held each Sunday and gave some reflections on its meaning.

Central to Justin's teaching was the claim that Christianity was the truest of philosophies and that the *logos* ('divine reason') taught by Greek thinkers is the eternal Word of God. He argued that those who lived according to reason, or *logos*, including the Jewish Patriarchs and the Greek philosophers – who claimed to be atheists – were really Christians! (While the term *logos* was common to both Greek and Hebrew thought, they were not used in exactly the same sense; according to the apostle John, the *logos* became incarnate in Christ and was the means by which God revealed himself to the world.)

His second *Apology* was, in fact, a supplement to the first, and was addressed to the Roman Senate and the citizens of Rome. It was an appeal to public opinion, protesting against the summary trial and execution of a number of believers, and replying to various criticisms.

A SUNDAY WORSHIP SERVICE IN ROME.

On the day called Sunday, all who live in cities or in the country gather together in one place, and the memoirs of the apostles or the writings of the prophets are read for so long as time permits. Then, when the reader has ceased, the president instructs us by word of mouth, exhorting us to put these good things into practice. Then we all rise together and pray and, as we have already said, bread, and wine mingled with water, are brought, and the president in like manner offers prayers and thanksgivings according to his ability, and the people assent by saying 'Amen'.

Distribution is then made to each, and they share in that for which thanks has been given, and the deacons take portions to those who are absent. And those who are well-off and are willing to do so give as much as each desires, and the money thus collected is deposited with the president, who takes care of the orphans and widows, and those who are in straits through sickness or any other cause, and those in prison, and our visitors from other parts – in short, he looks after all who are in need.

Justin was writing to pagans who had no idea of what a worship service was like, hence the simplicity of the language.

(From Justin's 'Apology', I.67, quoted by F. F. Bruce, *The Spreading Flame*.)

Martyrdom

Justin met his death during the early years of the reign of Marcus Aurelius (161–180), a time when Christians endured the most severe trials so far experienced. The emperor was an intensely religious man and a disciple of the Stoics, and his aim was to re-establish the ancient reverence for the Roman gods. But he was naturally prejudiced against Christians and condemned the obstinacy with which they met death.

The man responsible for Justin's arrest was a Cynic philosopher called Crescens, a bitter enemy of the Christians. Justin had held a public debate with the man, who became his chief antagonist in Rome and left him with the feeling that one day he would be the cause of his death. His intuition proved correct, for in 165 Justin, together with six other believers, one of them a woman, was brought before Rusticus, the Prefect of the city, on the charge of being a Christian. After enquiring about their beliefs and practices, the Prefect warned the believers, 'Unless you obey (the law) you shall be punished without mercy... Agree together and sacrifice with one accord to the gods.'

Justin replied, 'No one who is right-minded turns from true belief to false... Do what you will; for we are Christians and offer no sacrifice to idols.' His fellow prisoners stood by him, declaring that they also were Christians. At this, the Prefect enquired whether, when he was beheaded, he supposed he would ascend to heaven and there receive a recompense. Justin replied that he did not suppose it, but was fully persuaded of it. At which the Prefect pronounced sentence: 'Let those who have refused to sacrifice to the gods and to obey the command of the emperor, be scourged and led away to suffer the punishment of decapitation, according to the law.' They were beaten and then taken to the place of execution where 'they died glorifying God'. Afterwards their bodies were secretly removed by faithful companions for proper burial.

Indebted

The Church is indebted to Justin and the apologists for the invaluable documents bequeathed us, preserved in the writings of Eusebius of Caesarea, the earliest Church historian. For in these records we have a glimpse of the first attempts to formulate Christian doctrine, though the statements are not always expressed with the exactness of later theologians. We are also provided by Justin with a fascinating account of second century Sunday services and ceremonial rites.

Despite his vigorous defence of the Faith, some of his ideas were anti-Jewish and only served to distance the church from the synagogue. For

Justin was one of a number of Church Fathers who railed against the Jews for being Christ-killers and refusing to accept the Messiah. 'You have slain the Just One and his prophets before him; and now you reject those who hope in him,' he accused Trypho.

The influence of Justin Martyr resounded down through the century as other apologists followed his lead in wielding the pen. And though his theological statements were not always clear, his works made a profound impression on Irenaeus, Bishop of Lyons, whose book *Against Heresies* further developed Justin's attempts to defend the Faith.

When Justin became a Christian he continued to be influenced by his Platonic thinking about mankind and the world. As other Christian thinkers were similarly inclined, the Church absorbed much Greek philosophy. This kind of Greek thinking continued to influence the Church, so that gradually the Jewish foundations of Christianity were eroded away. But today, many Christians have discovered that 'as a mother gives birth to and nourishes a child, so Hebrew culture and language gave birth to and nourished Christianity'.

6

C AD 180 IRENAEUS WRITES *AGAINST HERESIES*

Threat to Orthodox Christianity

The greatest danger to the second century Church was not persecution, but rather the rise of heresy. Its subtle influence was largely a consequence of the relative weakness of the Church's organisation and the lack of an adequate definition of its doctrine. It threatened to overwhelm the historic Faith and cause the gravest crisis experienced by Christianity since Paul's battle for freedom from the law. By the end of the century the challenge had for the most part been met, due to the writings of some of the keenest minds in the Church. Among these was Irenaeus, Bishop of Lyons.

The term heresy, derived from the Greek word *hairesis*, actually means 'choice'. In the New Testament it was originally used to denote a party or sect, such as the Pharisees or the Sadducees; it was also applied to Christians by outsiders (e.g., Acts 24:5, 'the Nazarene sect'). Eventually it came to mean a difference of opinion (1 Cor. 11:19) and later referred to those who had fallen into doctrinal error (e.g., 2 Pet. 2:1).

Gnosticism
During the first two centuries Gnosticism[1] proved to be the most dangerous heresy and opponent of orthodox Christianity, and appealed mainly to intellectual Christians. Arising during the second half of the first century, it infiltrated the Church and reached the height of its influence about 135–160, mainly in Asia Minor and Syria. It was an attempt to blend Christianity with the theosophical philosophy of the age, and included elements drawn from religions of the Orient. Several of the New Testament documents

---

1. A modern term used to cover a variety of second century sects which had certain elements in common.

were written in part to refute false doctrines and to defend the Faith against a tendency towards new ideas.

During the last decade of the first century the apostle John wrote his Gospel in which he is believed to have been deliberately opposing Gnostic teachers who denied the divinity of Christ. Some of them taught that the 'Son of God' had no existence prior to his birth, and others suggested that Christ had not come 'in the flesh' and that his humanity and suffering were apparent rather than real.

The Fourth Gospel was written to set out the truth concerning the deity of Christ. When John penned these words from Ephesus, he opened with his great statement about the Incarnation, which declared that 'the Word became flesh and made his dwelling among us' (John 1:14). He emphasised this truth again in his first Letter, when he testified that Jesus had appeared to the apostles and that they had truly heard, seen and touched him (1 John 1:1-3).

There is also evidence of a similar problem in the church at Colossae. Like John, Paul answered the erroneous teaching by stressing the pre-eminence of Christ and reminding the saints that 'in Christ all the fulness of the Deity lives in bodily form' (Col. 1:15-19; 2:9). He warned the believers against deceptive philosophy, human traditions and the worship of angels, all elements to be found in Gnostic teachings.

Search for Answers

There was a variety of Gnostic sects, all of which had certain features in common. Of first importance was the *gnosis* (Greek, 'knowledge'). This was the supposedly revealed knowledge of God, said to have been handed down by the apostles, by which man could attain to salvation. The Gnostic sects also shared a common quest in their search for the answers to such questions as the origin and nature of evil, and the connection between an infinite spiritual God and a finite material world. The origin of evil was explained by assuming the existence of two absolute and opposing deities in the universe. There was a god of evil and darkness, known as the demiurge, and a god of light and goodness, the supreme God.

Gnostics also taught that everything material was essentially evil, and was opposed to what is purely spiritual and infinite. The supreme God – said to be remote and unknowable – was therefore not the creator of the world; creation was either the work of angels or of the inferior demiurge ('architect'), usually identified with Jehovah of the Old Testament. Nor could this God establish direct contact with the earth, except by intermediaries – angels or aeons (i.e., spiritual beings) – emanating from the Godhead. This multitude of beings formed part of a vast chain of emanations uniting the finite to the infinite.

Since the material world is evil, they argued, there could have been no real Incarnation. They taught that Christ was a phantom, that his apparent birth from a virgin mother was without partaking of material nature. Those who crucified him were deceived and, according to the non-canonical Gospel of Peter, Jesus' cry on the cross was not 'My God, my God...' but rather 'My power, my power, why hast thou forsaken me?'

Like the mystery religions of the day, the Gnostics held to a doctrine of salvation based on a secret knowledge, which was available only to the elite, 'spiritual' men who were able to receive it. Not all Christians possessed this knowledge, as it was a secret teaching that had been imparted by the apostles only to their more intimate disciples.

The most influential Gnostics of the second century were Basilides and Valentinus of Egypt, and Marcion, a wealthy ship-owner from Asia Minor who moved to Rome about 140. Involved in controversy with church leaders in his native land, Marcion was already deeply influenced by Gnostic and Docetic ideas.[2] His chief objection was that Christianity was in bondage to legalism, and so he rejected the law, the Old Testament and its God. He believed that the apostles had corrupted the pure teachings of Jesus, thus he recognised only an edited version of the Gospel of Luke. And as the apostle Paul alone of the New Testament writers understood the contrast between law and grace, he accepted just ten of Paul's letters and rejected the pastoral epistles.

Leading Authority

A considerable body of literature was produced in defence of the Faith during the second century, from writers such as Justin Martyr, Clement of Alexandria and Tertullian. Of the theologians in the West, Irenaeus was the chief opponent of the Gnostics. He had studied their teachings in great detail and became the leading authority on the subject. His monumental five-volume work, The Refutation and Overthrow of Knowledge Falsely So-Called, generally known by its shorter title of *Against Heresies*, provides our main source of knowledge concerning the movement.

Born in Asia Minor, Irenaeus was brought up in Smyrna where he had been a pupil of the martyr Polycarp, who had in turn studied under the

---

2. Docetism (Greek, 'to seem') denied that Jesus actually became man and died, and taught that his humanity and sufferings were more apparent than real.

apostle John. Irenaeus was able to recall John's words concerning what the apostles and the Lord had said and done, and was therefore directly linked to the original Gospel. From Asia Minor he moved to Gaul where he became a presbyter in the church at Lyons. When the great persecution raged at Lyons and Vienne in 177 he was on a mission to Rome, and so evaded arrest. On his return he was chosen bishop in succession to the martyred Pothinus, a position he held until his death about the year 200.

Irenaeus' main controversy was with two of the leading Gnostics, Marcion and Valentinus, and his defence was based on the authority of Scripture and the Faith handed down by the apostles. He asserted that what the apostles preached was to be found in the four Gospels, which alone were accepted in the Church. There were no Gnostic teachings to be found in them, no secret doctrines, otherwise they would have been known in the churches they had founded. These churches, which were to be found throughout the empire, all taught the same doctrine; they had fully preserved the apostolic teaching, and their transmission had been guaranteed by the orderly succession of bishops. 'Go, therefore, to Rome, or Smyrna or Ephesus,' he urged, 'and learn what is taught there; nothing Gnostic will be found.'

Maintaining the unity of the Old and New Testaments, he showed how Adam's disobedience brought about the Fall of Man; but what was lost in Adam was restored in Christ, the incarnate *Logos*, who completed the interrupted work. 'I have shown that the Son of God did not then begin to exist (i.e., at his birth), being with the Father from the beginning; but when he became incarnate and was made a man, he commenced afresh the long line of human beings, and furnished us, in a brief, comprehensive manner, with salvation. So that which we had lost in Adam – namely to be according to the image and likeness of God – that we might recover in Christ Jesus.'

For Irenaeus, simply to describe the Gnostic doctrines was to refute them. But in his disputes with Gnostics he was faced with a frustrating problem, for they did not accept the validity of what we now call the New Testament; they referred to them as 'your Scriptures'. Which caused Ireneaus to retort, 'When they are refuted from the Scriptures, they turn round and accuse these same Scriptures, as if they were not correct or authoritative'.

Unity

By the end of the second century the threat of Gnosticism had been largely overcome and the Church emerged strengthened by the struggle, though not without scars. The Gnostic attacks served rather to draw the churches together; though not united as an organisation, there was a greater degree of fellowship between them. It began to call itself the catholic (i.e., 'universal') Church, a term first used by Ignatius near the beginning of the century. He had reasoned, 'Where Jesus Christ is, there is the catholic Church', a reference to the true Church. Hence the term came to denote those churches that belonged to the apostolic tradition, to distinguish them from the heretical sects springing up in Asia Minor.

Irenaeus' first line of defence against the Gnostics was to formulate a Rule of Faith, a standard of belief by which all innovations could be tested. He drew up a statement of fundamental Christian doctrine based on the three persons of the Godhead, rather similar to the Apostles' Creed. His summary included phrases that were deliberately intended to counter Gnostic teachings, such as the reference to the Church's belief in 'one God the Father Almighty, who made heaven and earth and sea ... and in Christ Jesus, the Son of God, who became incarnate for our salvation...' (terms unacceptable to Marcionites).

This Faith, affirmed Irenaeus, was the same over all the world and was attested by the four Gospels and by the apostolic tradition preserved in the Church. He also realised that it was essential to have a fixed list of authoritative books of approved orthodoxy, and on this point he agreed with Marcion, yet without agreeing to his selection.

RULE OF FAITH

Here is an extract from Irenaeus' statement of the essential faith of the second century Church, though not written in credal form. Compare this with the Nicene Creed incorporated into the Thirty-Nine Articles, dating from the Council of Constantinople (381).

'For the Church, dispersed throughout the whole world, even to the ends of the earth, has received from the apostles and their disciples this faith: in one God, the Father Almighty, who made the heaven and the earth and the seas and all things that are in them; and in one Christ Jesus, the Son of God, who became incarnate for our salvation; and in the Holy Spirit, who proclaimed through the prophets the dispensations and the advents, and the birth from a virgin, and the passion, and the resurrection from the dead...

'As I have already observed, the Church, having received this preaching, and this faith, although scattered throughout the whole world, yet, as if occupying but one house, carefully preserves it. She also believes these points of doctrine just as if she had but one soul, and one and the same heart, and she proclaims them, and teaches them, and hands them down, with perfect harmony...'

The Old Testament, rejected by Gnostic thinkers, was regarded in the catholic Church as divinely authoritative; Irenaeus' contribution was to compile a list of New Testament books which he recognised fulfilled this criterion. He was the first writer to formulate a canon that largely corresponds to the one later accepted as traditional. Gnosticism gave rise to a number of other movements within the Church which also did not commend the true gospel. Some of these groups withdrew into an ascetic lifestyle (cf. 1 Tim. 4:1-5) which in the following century gave birth to monasticism. Others argued that it was possible to disregard the Ten Commandments because they were Jewish – and were led into licentiousness and immorality.

One reaction to this laxity was the formation of the Montanist sect, which tended to the other extreme; it condemned permissiveness and adopted a harsh moral code of living. To check the inroads of Gnosticism the Church had to prohibit freedom: dogma was made rigid, the idea of new revelation was forbidden and ecclesiastical government was inclined to become official and oppressive. Victory was achieved, but at a cost; and the contrast between the early Church and that of the third and fourth centuries shows the measure of the loss sustained.

Gnosticism lingered on into the sixth century, though some of its doctrines have reappeared throughout the history of the Church. As in the second century, the main controversy has continued to focus on the authority of Scripture, the person of Christ and the denial of his resurrection, all issues which have relevance to today's theological debate.

MONTANISM

This was an apocalyptic movement within the Church which began in Asia Minor around the year 156. Its founder, Montanus, claimed to be the Spirit's mouthpiece. Accompanied by two prophetesses, Prisca and Maximilla, he announced that the Second Coming was soon to take place when Christ would establish his thousand year reign upon the earth. People abandoned their homes, families and work, distributed their possessions, and streamed out into the countryside to await the event.

A rigorous system of prohibitions was adopted: the theatre and public amusements were condemned and second marriages were forbidden; any 'deadly' sin committed after baptism could not receive forgiveness on earth, while a martyr's death was considered glorious.

There was a revival of prophecy and the role of the prophet, who was regarded as superior to any bishop or priest. Although their prophecies did not materialise, the movement spread to Rome and into North Africa, where its most notable adherent – for a brief period – was the theologian, Tertullian. In the third century Montanist leaders were excommunicated and the movement discredited, though it survived until finally being crushed by Emperor Justinian (527–565).

7

AD 303 THE GREAT PERSECUTION BEGINS UNDER DIOCLETIAN

Emperor Attempts to Destroy the Church

For the first 300 years the Christian Church in the Roman Empire was subject to violent attacks and persecutions, which reached their climax under emperor Diocletian (284–305). Men, women and children were arraigned before governors and magistrates, and on the simple confession 'I am a Christian' were cruelly put to death. Despite the suffering, the gospel continued to spread, reaching all classes of people and levels of society, even to the emperor's household. As Tertullian exclaimed, 'The more you mow us down, the fuller is the harvest. The blood of Christians is seed!'

In the Roman Empire, the first duty of a citizen was to the state – religious duties were reckoned to be of secondary importance to civil obligations. The state claimed the right to decide which gods might be worshipped, irrespective of a person's private opinions, and no religion was permitted unless proscribed by law.

It was during the reign of Nero (AD54–68) that Christianity first became an illegal religion, though there was no imperial statute constituting it as such. Emperor Trajan (AD98–117) felt that there was not much danger in Christianity, but in a rescript to Pliny, the governor of Bythinia – which was tantamount to an imperial decree – he directed that Christians, if convicted, should be sentenced to death. This was the first formal pronouncement to that effect, and henceforth being a Christian was clearly a crime in itself.

Emperor Hadrian (117–138), like Trajan, discouraged active persecution, but he tended to be more lenient and left a loophole to allow for mercy. For over a hundred years, until the reign of Gallienus (260–280), the Church was in an anomalous position – in theory illegal, yet left undisturbed for considerable periods.

Thus with the exception of the occasional martyrdom and outburst of persecution, the second century was a time of growth and prosperity for the Church. That there was no continuous policy towards the Church was due to the frequent change of emperors and the fact that some of them were military adventurers. Often of foreign birth, they were brought to power by the army and then easily deposed. Those from the eastern part of the empire were inclined to be more tolerant towards any religion of Eastern origin, including Christianity.

Reign of Terror

While in the first two centuries persecution tended to be local and sporadic, the pattern began to change. There arose a different breed of emperor, alarmed at the threat posed by a growing Church and ready to deal harshly with any suspected threat to their position.

The third century witnessed a revival of pagan religion, especially that of the god Mithras, encouraged by Emperor Decius (249–251), whose aim was 'one empire and one religion'. This meant that Christianity had to be rooted out. His violent attack on the Church was the first attempt to systematically destroy the Faith. Many leading Christians were arrested; it was during this period that Origen of Caesarea was put in prison and tortured, and the Bishop of Rome was martyred.

A further reign of terror occurred under Valerian (253–260) who also aimed at totally annihilating the Church. An edict issued in 258, considered to be an important turning-point in the persecution of the early Christians, decreed that all clergy were to be put to death, without offering them opportunity to recant.

By the third century the Church was well organised and strong. Despite persecution, Christianity was spreading rapidly and many believers occupied important positions of state. According to the historian Eusebius, however, peace and progress had produced laxity and sloth among the Christians, and 'the unwonted ease and honour they had enjoyed had robbed them of faith and love'. When the Great Persecution finally fell upon the Church during the reign of Diocletian and his successors, it caught the believers unprepared.

Emperor Diocletian

A man of humble origin, Diocletian adopted the pomp and power of an oriental monarch when he became emperor, and gave the position a dignity it had previously lacked. He insisted that men approach him reverently with a threefold prostration, and was to be addressed as *Dominus* ('lord').

An administrator rather than a military leader, he set about reorganising the empire. He chose Nicomedia (in Asia Minor) as his capital, instead of Rome, and took steps to make the empire more manageable by dividing it into two parts. Each half was ruled by a senior emperor bearing the title of 'Augustus'; two junior rulers were later appointed with the title 'Caesar'. Diocletian assumed charge of the Eastern Empire (i.e., the Balkan peninsula and eastwards), aided by his son-in-law Galerius, while Maximian and Constantius (father of Constantine) took control of the Western Empire.

Diocletion's great palace at Split (Croatia), now divided into apartments and shops.

The Church presented a serious problem to Diocletian, for it was a large organisation within the empire over which he had no control. Moreover, Christians were not disposed to emperor worship or the service of the Roman gods. Although there was no threat of Christians rising up against the state, he may have felt the need to force them into submission.

Attacks on the Church were renewed, largely due to the influence of Diocletian's junior colleague, Galerius, a bitter opponent of Christianity, who persuaded the emperor of the need to move against the supposed threat to his power. Diocletian hesitated, for the Church was well established, and under an edict of Gallienus had virtually been recognised as a *religio licita*. Against his better judgment he finally agreed to action, provided it was done without loss of life.

At dawn on 23 February 303, the Roman festival of Terminalia, the praetorian guards broke down the doors of the main church in Nicomedia, opposite the imperial palace. They were amazed to find that it contained no image of the Deity; but they ransacked the interior, burnt all copies of the Scriptures and then demolished the building. The following day an edict was posted which was aimed at destroying not the members of the Church, but the organisation. It ordered the demolition of all church buildings and the confiscation of church property; all Scriptures and liturgical books were to be surrendered and burnt.

The destruction of sacred books was a new feature of the persecution, for it recognised their importance in preserving the Christian religion; if these were destroyed, it was supposed, then the very life of the Church would be endangered. Whilst this led to the destruction of many valuable manuscripts, lost to the Church forever, others were preserved by being buried or hidden, and were brought out after the trouble had died down.

The renewed persecution was more serious and prolonged than anything the Church had yet faced. It lasted for more than a decade, differing in intensity from region to region, and extended from Britain to Arabia. In some areas it continued far longer than in others. It is possible that the Roman soldier, Alban, was martyred in Britain around this time.

Christians Blamed

The edicts that were to follow struck the Church with increasing severity. In March of that year, just before Easter, a fire broke out in the palace at Nicomedia, for which the Christians were blamed. The fury of the state was unleashed upon them; believers in the imperial household were cruelly tortured, and together with their families were put to death. Others died as a result of scourging, whilst the bishop and two presbyters were executed. Even the emperor's Christian wife and daughter were forced to sacrifice.

A second edict was passed ordering the arrest of all clergy and teachers, probably in an attempt to stop Christians from gathering for worship. When things had quietened down, however, the emperor declared a general amnesty.

In the December, a third edict was issued which allowed clergy to go free on condition they sacrificed. The results were worse than could have been expected, for it led to the most fearful atrocities inflicted on the clergy in an effort to compel them to offer to the state gods. Many were released, either because they recanted or else the goalers assisted their escape. Those who refused remained in prison, some until the end of the persecution. So far Diocletian had resisted using the threat of death, but that was to change when in the spring of 304 he fell seriously ill.

Finally, a fourth edict was passed under the authority of Maximian, the Western emperor, who ordered all citizens of the empire to sacrifice to the gods on penalty of death. Men, women and children were required to attend the temples, where they were closely examined; any who confessed to being Christian were arrested and put to death. The persecutors believed that at last they had triumphed over the Church, and declared, 'The name of the Christians who were seeking to overturn the state has been blotted out. Everywhere the Christian superstition is destroyed and the worship of the gods universally restored.' Yet the persecution continued in several provinces for a further eight years.

Abdication

In 305 Diocletian recovered from his illness and abdicated, forcing Maximian to do the same; Constantius became emperor in the West and Galerius ruled the East. The power inherited by Constantius enabled him more openly to protect the Christians in the Western provinces. In Spain, Gaul and Britain the new Augustus simply pulled down a few churches and left the believers unhurt.

In North Africa and the East, however, where Galerius ruled and Christians were far more numerous, the persecution raged with increasing malevolence; Egypt and Syria (including Palestine) were the worst affected. Although the number of victims is not known, the general impression of 'murderous ferocity' is regarded as substantially true. A common method of execution was by burning, while some were thrown to the wild beasts. A lesser penalty was inflicted on others, who had their left leg disabled and the right eye cut out and seared before being sent to slavery in the mines where further cruelties could be inflicted, and without public knowledge.

As Galerius lay on his deathbed in the spring of 311, he finally admitted defeat. Unable to destroy the Church, the dying emperor issued an edict of toleration and invited the Christians to remember him in their prayers. Although many Christians were freed from prison and Christianity allowed its freedom, a number of local persecutions persisted until the following year when Constantine came to power.

> **THE DONATIST SCHISM**
> The Donatists were a schismatic group in the Church of North Africa. It was their refusal to accept the privately consecrated Caecilian as Bishop of Carthage in 311, because of his conduct during the persecution, that led to the division. This was because during the troubles Caecilian was thought to have handed

over Scriptures to the civil authorities; also his ordination had been received from a traditor (one who had surrendered copies of the Scriptures). The consecration was pronounced invalid and Donatus declared bishop in his place.

An appeal was made to Emperor Constantine. A commission appointed under the Bishop of Rome to investigate the matter came out in favour of Caecilian, causing a furore in Africa; a fresh trial was demanded. The emperor called a church Council which met at Arles (Gaul) in 314, at which Caecilian was again vindicated. Constantine ordered the churches seized by the followers of Donatus at Carthage to be taken from them, to which Donatus retorted, 'What has the emperor to do with the Church?'

In North Africa, the schismatics grew in number until they were a larger body than the catholics. They regarded themselves as alone constituting the true Church.

Witness

Through all the persecutions the Church remained firm, for it was too powerful and widespread to be destroyed. Even pagans were shocked at the terrible penalties inflicted on believers and declared them to be 'vulgar and very much overdone'. But as a result of their courage and fortitude, Christians were regarded with a new respect by the populace, so that many were won to Christ as a result of their witness.

While there is no record of the numbers of Christians martyred during the persecution, the universal reign of terror obviously devastated the Church. The contemporary historian, Eusebius, speaks of 'thousands' being put to death in Egypt alone, where as many as a hundred suffered in a single day, and of 'multitudes' in Asia Minor and Mesopotamia. In 303, one unknown town in Phrygia, entirely Christian, was completely wiped out by Roman soldiers.

During the third century the Church had begun to acquire property; 'great houses for prayer' were erected, catacombs were prepared and houses built for the bishops. Diocletian's first edict had ordered the destruction of churches and houses, and although a later edict restored the property to the Church, many fine buildings and early copies of the Scriptures had meanwhile been destroyed.

One outcome of the persecution was a controversy that resurfaced among the churches of North Africa. It concerned those believers who apparently denied their faith by complying with the state edicts issued against the Church. After the persecution had ended the dispute was brought out into the open, for there were those who maintained that Christians who had sacrificed to idols should not be readmitted to the Church. Opinions were divided, and the ensuing schism continued until the seventh century when the African Church was destroyed by Muslim invaders.

Clearly the persecution was above all a time of testing and sifting for the Church. While it produced an untold number of martyrs, there were those who could not face the challenge to their faith and eagerly rushed to sacrifice. Yet despite the tremendous slaughter there were no reprisals, no cry for revenge; the believers simply 'committed themselves to their faithful Creator'.

Although the Church emerged stronger from its ordeal, it is a matter of regret that the lands where persecution raged the fiercest and most martyrs were made, are for the most part now given over to Islam. These areas today offer strong resistance to the gospel and it is here where the hardest battles are yet to be fought. It is 'a struggle against the powers of this dark world', and victory will be gained only by spiritual weapons.

8

AD 313 THE EDICT OF MILAN

Christians Granted Freedom of Worship

The Edict of Milan is one of the turning-points in the history of the world and marked the beginning of a new era for the Christian Church. Not only did it signal Rome's abandonment of its policy of persecution, but it heralded the decline of paganism and the first step towards the establishment of Christianity as the sole religion of the empire. This dramatic turn of events resulted from the conversion of Constantine, the first ever Roman emperor to publicly embrace Christianity.

In 292, at the age of eighteen and after his father's appointment as Caesar of the Western Empire, Constantine was sent to live at Diocletian's court at Nicomedia, in Asia Minor. There were a number of Christians at court, among them the emperor's wife and daughter, and a thriving Christian presence in the city which suffered terribly during the outbreak of persecution in 303.

When Constantius, now elevated to the rank of Augustus (senior emperor), died at York in 306, the Roman troops immediately hailed his son as Caesar. A power struggle ensued for the succession to the imperial throne, and throughout the empire the next few years were ones of political intrigue and bloodshed. With his position under threat, Constantine gathered an army at Trier (Germany) and in September 312 crossed the Alps and advanced on Rome.

Although brought up a pagan it was nevertheless to the 'Supreme God' he turned as he approached Rome, for he was convinced that he needed greater aid than military force. His prayer was answered, for the day before the crucial battle, as he was praying just before noon, he saw in the sky 'the trophy of a cross of light, above the sun, and bearing the inscription "By this sign conquer"'. The following night Christ appeared to him in a dream and commanded him to have the same sign of the cross – presumably the Chi-Rho symbol – inscribed upon his soldiers' shields. Thus he went into battle, not under the Roman Eagle but under the sign of Christ.

Chi-Rho symbol representing Christ, probably the 'heavenly sign of God' constantine saw in a dream.

Servant of God

At the battle of Milvian Bridge, some miles outside Rome, Constantine defeated his rival and credited his victory to the Christians' God. From then on he regarded himself as a Christian and wrote of himself as 'the servant of God'. Nevertheless, traces of his pagan superstitions continued to surface, especially during the first decade of his reign, raising doubts about the depth of his conversion.

It was in January 313 that the two ruling Augusti, Constantine and Licinius of the Eastern Empire, met for what proved to be a momentous conference. Their high-level talks were held in Milan rather than Rome, away from the interference of the Senate. The immediate occasion, however, was the marriage of Licinius to Constantine's half-sister, which afforded an opportunity for the two emperors to discuss 'all matters that concerned the advantage and benefit of the public'. At the end of the meeting they issued a communique which has become known as the Edict of Milan, though no 'edict' was issued and there is no extant copy of this order.

EDICT OF MILAN

The terms of the agreement were given in a rescript by Licinius to the governor of Bythinia. Here is the main substance of the order:

'Our purpose is to grant both to the Christians and to all others full authority to follow whatever worship each person has desired; whereby whatsoever Divinity dwells in heaven may be benevolent and propitious to us, and to all who are placed under our authority. Therefore we thought it salutary and most proper to establish our purpose that no man whatever should be refused complete toleration, who has given up his mind either to the cult of the Christians, or to the religion he personally feels best suited to himself; ... it is our pleasure to abolish all conditions whatever which were embodied in former orders directed to your office about the Christians ... that every one of those who have a common wish to follow the religion of the Christians may from this moment freely and unconditionally proceed to observe the same...'

(from *A New Eusebius*, edited by J. Stephenson).

The importance of the order was that it recognised the principle of freedom of worship and the right of Roman citizens to choose any religion they preferred. Provision was also made for the restoration of all Christian property seized during the persecution, from churches or individuals, for which compensation could be claimed from the state. Clearly the terms of the edict favoured Christianity, inaugurating three centuries of wide-sweeping changes throughout the empire.

Imperial Favours

Leaving aside the enigma of his lapses into paganism, Constantine's commitment to his new religion was evidenced by the many privileges, lands and revenues he began to shower upon the Church. However, it was not appreciated that a benevolent Christian emperor could be as dangerous as a pagan one, and his patronage was one of mixed blessings.

In an attempt to repair some of the damage caused by persecution, the emperor financed the building of many new churches, particularly in Rome. The most notable ones were erected at the traditional shrines of the apostles Peter and Paul, St Peter's on the Vatican Hill and St Paul's outside the city walls. Other churches were built at sites of special interest in the Holy Land, such as at Bethlehem and Jerusalem, and later at his new capital of Constantinople.

Shortly after the edict was issued the Church was granted permission to receive legacies of money, which over the centuries have enabled it to become rich and powerful. The emperor also assigned a fixed proportion of state revenues to church charitable causes. He ordered fifty copies of the Scriptures from Eusebius of Caesarea, 'prepared on vellum, easy to read and of a portable size', to be produced for church use.

St Peter's Church, Rome, originally built by
Constantine and re-built in the 17th century.

The status of the clergy began to improve as they received imperial favours: they were recognised as civil as well as religious leaders, and were granted immunity from all state taxes and the discharge of civil duties. Bishops were allowed to sit in judgment over secular as well as ecclesiastical affairs.

In 321 Constantine decreed that the first day of the week was to be a day of rest, giving the Lord's Day a recognition it already enjoyed by believers. He called it 'the venerable day of the Sun' (i.e., Sunday). The only occupation exempt under this law was that of farming. Even the military had to parade on this day for Christian prayers.

During the first ten years of his rule the emperor introduced a series of decrees relating to moral issues that were clearly based on Christian teaching. Intended to help the less fortunate members of society, the most significant of these laws were aimed at strengthening family life. Abandoned children were to be supported at the expense of the imperial purse, adultery was outlawed and rape was to be severely punished.

However, not all Constantine's intentions worked for the good of the Church, and in time changes were introduced that began to erode the foundations of the Faith. As a result of imperial favours it became an honour to be a Christian. Many pagans joined the church, for Church members were appointed to the best positions of state. The emperor even went so far as to issue an edict by which he urged the people to become Christians. Church-going became fashionable, while the lives of the 'Christianised pagans' were marked with insincerity and wordliness. And whereas persecution had formerly refined the Church, the influx of nominal converts meant that many of them still clung to their pagan practices.

The position of priest was often filled by men lacking any sense of vocation to the ministry, but who joined the church because of the material benefits it could bring. Services became increasingly formal, and the use of a liturgy made them more a performance than an act of worship. Priests were attired in splendid vestments, candles and incense were used, and the veneration of Mary and praying to the saints were introduced.

Unity of the Faith

Almost from the beginning of his rule Constantine regarded himself as 'Defender of the Church' and gradually assumed the position of head of both State and Church. This was largely the fault of church leaders, who gratefully responded to his benefactions by inviting him to intervene in ecclesiastical affairs, matters that were obviously outside his authority. Anxious to maintain the unity of the one Faith – and of the empire – he took the lead in summoning two great Councils which gave him the opportunity to stamp his authority upon the Church.

The first Council was at Arles (Gaul) in 314, when a group of bishops – including three from Britain – was called to settle a dispute which had arisen at Carthage, North Africa. It concerned a schismatic group known as Donatists, who refused to accept Caecilian as their bishop. The verdict was in favour of Caecilian, and Constantine afterwards ordered the churches of the Donatists to be confiscated.

Church unity was further threatened when a theological controversy regarding the divinity of Christ broke out in Egypt. In June 325 the emperor convened a further meeting of bishops, for what is now recognised as the first ever ecumenical church Council, to deal with the heresy. Some 220 bishops gathered at Nicaea, in north-west Asia Minor. Opened by Constantine dressed in magnificent robes, the Council produced a statement of faith known today as the Nicene Creed, which laid a foundation for Christian belief throughout western Europe and came to be the standard by which orthodoxy was measured. (This creed must not be confused with the longer formula of the same name, found in the Thirty-Nine Articles, drawn up in 381.)

> **THE FIRST COUNCIL OF NICAEA (325)**
>
> The Council met chiefly to deal with the Arian controversy that had arisen at Alexandria (Egypt). A popular presbyter named Arius was teaching that the Father was greater than the Son, and that the Son was greater than the Holy Spirit. He further denied the Trinity by suggesting that Jesus was not fully God, that he was a created being, not eternal, through whom the Father created the universe.
>
> A statement of faith was drawn up that contained a number of anti-Arian phrases intended to safeguard the orthodox position. It included a term which no Arian could accept or explain away: the Son is 'of one substance' (Greek, *homoousios*) with the Father. Some objected on the grounds that the term was not found in Scripture and that it had previously been rejected at an earlier Council. The proposed creed was passed with two abstentions, though many of the members were far from happy about the result. It was sent to the various churches of the East who accepted it as a true statement of the catholic Faith.
>
> Rather than ending the debate about the deity of Jesus, the Council divided the Church. The controversy continued throughout the fourth and succeeding centuries. Today, Jehovah's Witnesses have adopted Arian views, believing that Christ was a created being and not equal to the Father.

State and Church

With the removal of his rival, Licinius, in 323, Constantine became sole ruler of the empire, and his role as head of State and Church was unchallenged. This association between Church and State has continued down the centuries in the Eastern Empire, and is still in evidence today in the West, where a number of countries hold to an 'established' Church. As Christianity expanded, so its organisation became more powerful, by wielding all the scattered Christian communities into one body. Authority became concentrated in the hands of the bishops, especially those who occupied the seats of the great capitals – Rome, Alexandria and Antioch – and they enjoyed power and influence as both religious and political leaders.

In 330 Constantine moved his capital from Rome to Byzantium (renamed Constantinople), situated between Europe and Asia and with a superb defensive position. It left a vacuum in Rome, filled by the chief bishop of that city. Soon the Bishop of Rome was claiming not only political power, but also the highest authority in all the churches, paving the way for him first to become patriarch of Rome, then pope. Before long, however, the Church began to deny to other religious groups the very freedom of conscience for which it had suffered, forgetting the price paid by the martyrs for the liberty to believe. Civil power was used to enforce the Church's position, and in later centuries some countries equated membership of the

State with that of the Church.

Despite his edict of toleration Constantine began to take steps to limit heathen activities. By the end of the century pagan religions and heretical sects alike were outlawed (though it was some time before paganism eventually died out). Emperor Theodosius (379–395) ordered that the catholic (i.e., 'universal') Faith should be accepted by all nations. Henceforth, orthodox Christianity was the only legal religion of the empire.

Death Penalty

Antagonism towards the Jews increased and from the time of Constantine a gradual effort was made to erode their status. Roman citizens were forbidden to convert to Judaism, and those who taught the Torah to Gentiles were threatened with the death penalty. Jews were barred from marrying Christians and from holding public office; even Sabbath observance was forbidden. Imperial pronouncements on Judaism referred to it as the '*secta nefaria*', the 'unspeakable religion'. In this way 'the persecuted became the persecutors', perpetuating one of the most distasteful facets of Church history.

Like Judaism, Christianity was a missionary religion, but it succeeded where Judaism failed. What began as an obscure Jewish sect whose leader was crucified as a common criminal, emerged as the leading religion of the Mediterranean civilisation. Few gains had been made outside the empire – with the notable exception of Armenia and in the Fertile Crescent – and churches were to be found in the major cities and not the countryside. Following the reign of Constantine, however, the Church began a period of expansion. In the succeeding three centuries it spread beyond the bounds of the empire, and whole tribes and nations were won en masse to the Christian Faith.

This same period of expansion also witnessed the collapse of the Roman Empire and the rise of the Byzantium (Eastern) Empire. Despite the fall of Rome, the Church in the West remained to become the Latin Catholic Church under the Pope, while the Orthodox Church took root in the East under the leadership of the Patriarch of Constantinople. With the Church divided, first the barbarians and then the Muslims threatened to overwhelm the Faith. It was not until the tenth century that a renewal took place, brought about by the reforming movement of monasticism.

9

AD 367 ATHANASIUS' THIRTY-NINTH PASCHAL LETTER

The New Testament Canon Defined

In order to counter the rise of false teachings in the early Church it was gradually realised that it was necessary to possess an agreed body of sacred literature by which to judge matters of belief and practice. In which case it was essential to determine which writings were to be admitted as Scripture, in the same way that the Old Testament had been accepted as having divine authority. By about the year 130 the kernel of the New Testament had been generally accepted throughout the Church, though it was not until the fourth century that the present list of twenty-seven books was finally agreed upon. It is Athnasius' 39th Easter Letter that provides the earliest witness to the New Testament canon.

From its beginning the Church used the Jewish Scriptures as the basis of its preaching and teaching, and for eucharistic worship services.[1] But by the end of the first century, alongside these books they began to introduce writings that were specifically Christian though not yet regarded as 'holy Scripture'. By the end of the first century the four Gospels had gained general acceptance. In addition, a collection of Paul's letters, included alongside a group of 'other Scriptures', were used by the early Church (2 Pet. 3:16). His letters were obviously treasured and copies of them passed from one church to another (cf. Col. 4:16).

---

1. When Paul spoke of Scripture being God-breathed (2 Tim. 3:16), he was referring to the Old Testament.

> **OLD TESTAMENT**
> There are frequent references in the New Testament to the scriptures of the Old Testament, which suggests that by the first century AD they were already an established collection of books. In his teaching, Jesus quoted or made allusions to a wide range of them, which he obviously recognised as having divine authority. Paul's letters are also filled with Old Testament references.
>
> The Old Testament consisted of the three sections with which we are familiar, viz the Law (Torah), the Prophets (N'vi'im) and the Writings (K'tuvim). (The initials of these three Hebrew terms make up the word Tanakh, which gives the name of the Hebrew Bible.) It was made up of twenty-four books, equivalent of the thirty-nine today, which were used for study and for reading aloud in synagogue services (e.g., Luke 4:17). The list of books was confirmed at the Jewish synod at Jamnia c AD96, at which point the text of the Hebrew Bible was finally fixed. Excluded by the synod were the books of the Apocrypha; although recognised as suitable for private study and edification, they were not admissible for synagogue worship.

Evidence suggests that by the beginning of the second century many Christian communities possessed a collection of these writings which were accorded the same recognition as the Old Testament. Confirmation of this collection is provided by several writers. The Epistle of Barnabas (c110–130) gives us what is probably the first quotation from a New Testament book, using the authoritative formula 'It is written'. As this phrase is the equivalent of saying 'to quote Scripture', it indicates the progress made in recognising apostolic writings as having a special authority. The writings of early Church Fathers such as Ignatius and Papias also reflect a wide knowledge of Paul's letters, and their language is strongly influenced by his words.

Further recognition is given in the so-called Second Letter of Clement, written around 130–150. In it, the author uses formulas of quotation which imply that the Lord's words now stand permanently in writing. He also makes reference to 'the Books and the Apostles', a phrase which suggests the acceptance of a corpus of writings. Justin Martyr, writing towards the middle of the century, records that 'the memoirs of the apostles', called Gospels, were read at Christian worship, along with Jewish Scriptures.

Heresy
Although the list of New Testament writings was not yet clearly defined, the idea of a Christian canon was taking shape. The problem was brought into focus by the rise of Gnosticism, the heretical religious movement which was a mixture of Christian and pagan thinking. It forced the Church to define the limits of its writings and list those books considered to be authoritative.

Athanasius, Bishop of Alexandria

The most prominent leader of the Gnostic movement was Marcion from Asia Minor, who had settled in Rome in about AD150 and was the first to put forward a list of specifically Christian books. Unable to reconcile Jewish and Christian thought, Marcion drew up a list of books which reflected his ideas. It consisted of Luke's Gospel – without the nativity and the resurrection – plus edited versions of ten letters of Paul, not including the Pastorals (i.e., to Timothy and Titus).

Towards the end of the century a number of works appeared in defence of orthodox Christianity, contributing towards the development of the canon. Irenaeus, Bishop of Lyons, in his five-volume work, *Against Heresies*, quoted from the four Gospels as well as from Acts, the Pauline epistles and the book of Revelation in such a way as to indicate that they were a primary source of doctrine and authority. Thus by the end of this century there emerged a list of writings quite close to our present New Testament canon.

A number of third century writers, particularly Tertullian and Origen, made widespread use of many of the New Testament books which they seemingly regarded as authoritative. Uncertainty about Hebrews, the Catholic Epistles (i.e., James, Peter, John and Jude) and the Revelation of John continued. However, as the century progressed the main issue became not what books should be admitted but rather what should be excluded.

Eusebius of Caesarea, the early Church historian, proved helpful on this matter, for he divided Christian literature into three classes: he distinguished between acknowledged books, disputed books and spurious books. The latter group included deliberate forgeries of Gospels and Acts under the name of apostles, chosen to identify heretical works. These, he argued, should be 'shunned as altogether wicked and impious'.

Defender of the Faith

It was because of his tenacity in defending orthodox Christian belief that Athanasius, Bishop of Alexandria, is mostly remembered. Though not a great theologian, he stood 'like a rock' for his convictions and it was as a result of his struggles that the doctrine of the Trinity was safeguarded. But he was also the first-known Christian leader to recognise the twenty-seven books of the New Testament canon.

Athanasius (c296–373) attended the Council of Nicea in 325 as a deacon of the church at Alexandria, accompanying the bishop as his secretary. The Council was convened by Emperor Constantine to deal with a doctrinal dispute concerning the relationship between God the Father and Jesus the Son. For Arius, a presbyter also from Alexandria, was teaching that there was a real difference in essence between the Deity of the Father and that of the Son, and that Jesus was only a created being – thus denying the atonement. The teaching disturbed not only Alexandria and the whole of Egypt, but it was spreading throughout the Church.

The Council of Nicaea condemned the teaching of Arius and drew up a creed that reflected a more orthodox position; the heretic and his followers were forced into exile. But despite an apparent victory, there followed over half a century of continued controversy in the Eastern Church, opening up rifts between the Greek and Latin Churches. Nicaea was not the end of the controversy, which later widened to include a debate about the relationship of the Holy Spirit to the Godhead.

EASTER CONTROVERSY

There were two divergent practices in second century churches concerning the celebration of Easter. The churches of Asia Minor followed the Jewish Passover tradition, celebrating the festival on a fixed day of the lunar month, viz 14 Nisan (a practice called Quartodeciman, i.e., 'fourteenth'). In the West, the churches commemorated the resurrection on the Sunday after 14 Nisan. In a place such as Rome – where there were Christians from East and West – the practice of two dates was confusing. When Polycarp of Smyrna visited Rome in 154 he discussed the matter with the bishop, but failed to win him over.

A dispute broke out in Asia Minor about 167 as to the nature of the celebration of 14 Nisan. Synods were held in Rome and other places which decided in favour of the Roman practice; the churches of Asia Minor refused to accept the decision.

The issue was resolved at the Council of Nicaea, that Easter should be kept by the whole Church on the same day, viz the Sunday after the full moon which occurs next after 21 March. It was also agreed that the Bishop of Alexandria should each year send a Paschal letter to Rome, declaring the date of the festival. This decision, to separate the celebration of the Passion from the Passover date, seemed another move to cut off the Church from its Jewish origins, though many Gentiles continued to keep the 14 Nisan.

Threatened

With the death of the Bishop of Alexandria in 328, the thirty-two year old Athanasius was elected to succeed him. Before long, his position was being threatened by no less than the emperor, who warned him about his insistence in excluding from the Church anyone who did not submit to the Creed of Nicaea. 'Since you know my will,' Constantine wrote to him, 'grant free admission to all those who wish to enter the church. For if I hear that you have hindered anyone from becoming a member, or have debarred anyone from entrance, I shall immediately send someone to have you deposed at my behest and have you sent into exile.'

Athanasius became the leader of an anti-Arian faction in the Church, and his determined opposition to the heresy earned him many enemies. False accusations were made against him in an effort to have him unseated. Among his many writings were a number of anti-Arian works, his best-known being *The Orations against the Arians* and an apologetic work entitled *The Incarnation of the Word*, written during his exile.

In 331, the Arians were able to persuade the emperor they were ready to conform to the Faith of the Church. Athanasius was directed to readmit Arius to his ecclesiastical office, but he refused. As a result, in 335 he was exiled to Trier where he stayed for four years before being allowed to return. There were five further periods of exile during his fight against the Arians, including one spell of six years in Rome. Each time his flock remained loyal to their bishop and he received a great welcome on his return to Alexandria, much to the envy and alarm of the reigning emperor. His final enforced exile, in 365, was brief and lasted for only one year, and he died in office seven years later.

Festal Letter

During all these absences Athanasius showed himself a true pastor to his flock. Each year, after Epiphany (i.e., 6th January), he wrote a 'Festal Letter' in which he announced the dates of Lent and Easter, helping his people to prepare for the festival. At the same time he took the opportunity to address them about any other issues of importance. In all, Athanasius wrote forty-five such letters, of which thirteen have survived complete in Syriac translation.

The thirty-ninth letter, reconstructed by scholars from fragments of Syriac, Coptic and Greek manuscripts, touches upon the canon of Scripture. After dealing with the customary business, the bishop went on to say, 'It seemed good to me also having been urged by true brethren ... to publish the books which are admitted in the canon, and have been delivered unto us, and are believed to be divine'. There followed a list of books identical with those of our present New Testament.

This letter has come to be regarded as the first authoritative statement on the New Testament canon, a list which was later adopted by the Church in the West. It was intended to put an end to the dispute concerning the apostolic authenticity of Peter's letters and the book of Revelations, as well as to exclude texts such as the Epistle of Barnabas and the Shepherd of Hermas, which in some parts had been regarded as equal to the apostolic letters. Writing of the canon, Athanasius claimed that 'in these alone the teaching of godliness is proclaimed. No one may add to them, and nothing may be taken away from them.'

For the Old Testament he followed the Jewish arrangement which has a list of twenty-two books; Esther was omitted, and Jeremiah had appended to it not only Lamentations but also Baruch and the 'Epistle of Jeremiah' (from the Apocrypha). He commented, 'There are also other books outside this list which are non-canonical, but have been handed down with approval from our fathers to be read to new converts ...the Wisdom of Solomon, the Wisdom of Sirach, Esther, Judith, Tobias.'

Support for Athansius' list is to be found in the *Codex Vaticanus*, a Greek codex (or book) of the Old and New Testaments in the Vatican library. It dates from the fourth century, but as some scholars believe it was written about 350 then it could predate Athansius' list. The codex not only contains the same books as the thirty-ninth Festal Letter, but gives them in the same unusual order.

Approved

Selection of these twenty-seven books seems to have depended upon three criteria. One was that the documents could be traced either to an apostle or to a close disciple of theirs, though there are exceptions to this rule (e.g., Hebrews). Then there was recognition of the writings by the principal churches, by which many apocryphal texts were also rejected. Finally there was the test of sound doctrine, which led to the exclusion of books that were known forgeries or contained heretical teaching.

Following the publication of the canon in the East, the list was adopted in Rome in 383, then approved by the Western Church at the Councils of Hippo (393) and Carthage (397). Even though there was some difference of opinion concerning books such as Hebrews, 2 Peter, and 2 and 3 John, by the end of the fourth century the canon was fixed. Now the Church had a list of God-breathed Scriptures, useful for doctrine and evangelism, and for training in righteousness. At the same time it provided a yardstick by which heresy could be refuted and prevented the later inclusion of any unsound writings.

This did not bring the dispute to an end, and throughout succeeding centuries critics have continued to query the inclusion of some of the books. Martin Luther, for example, referred to James as 'an epistle of straw', because he claimed it had no doctrine. As there had been no further pronouncement on the limits of the canon by an ecumenical Council since Carthage he felt justified in his reservations about a number of other books as well.

Whilst every generation of believers is free to re-examine the acceptance of the biblical canon, it would require overwhelming evidence of some kind of error to challenge its credibility. That the New Testament canon has stood the test of time, with nothing added or taken away, suggests that the Church throughout the centuries has found the Scriptures to be adequate for the task of preaching and evangelism, and for training God's people in right living.

10

AD 405 JEROME COMPLETES TRANSLATION OF THE VULGATE

The First Standard Version of the Whole Bible

In many ways Jerome was the most remarkable of the early Church Fathers. Though he did not have the eloquence of his contemporary Chrysostom (the name means 'golden mouth'), Bishop of Constantinople, or the winsomeness of Ambrose, Bishop of Milan, he had a more powerful pen than either of them and was one of history's most outstanding Bible translators. His Latin translation of the Bible, the Vulgate, remained the Church's source of inspiration for over a thousand years.

During the first centuries there were three 'sacred' languages predominantly used in the Church. Of first importance was Hebrew, the language of the Old Testament and of the synagogue liturgy; it may even have been the language spoken by Jesus, rather than Aramaic, though a matter of some dispute.

Following the introduction of Hellenism – Greek culture and language – into the lands of the Middle East during the fourth century BC, Greek became the common language of the Mediterranean world. Not only educated people, but traders and even ordinary citizens acquired a knowledge of the language, and it was in use in Judea at the time of Jesus. During the third and second centuries BC a large Jewish population resided at Alexandria (Egypt), so that it became necessary to provide them with a Greek version of the Old Testament. It was known as the Septuagint (or LXX), from the seventy scholars said to have worked on it.

For the first two centuries the language of the Church was Greek, even in Rome. The Septuagint was read in worship services alongside Christian writings such as Paul's letters, also in a simple Greek (known as the *koine* or 'common' dialect). Greek words such as Christ, eucharist, apostle, evangelist and bishop, were incorporated into the Church's vocabulary. Anyone who knew Greek, therefore, had access to the whole of the Bible.

Latin

It was not until the third century that Latin, the third sacred language, began to take hold in the Church. The theologian, Tertullian, was first to write in Latin, around the year 200 in North Africa. By about 240 it was beginning to be used by Christians in Rome, as witnessed by catacomb inscriptions, where there was continued competition between Greek and Latin. Before the end of the century Latin had ousted Greek and established itself as the standard language of the Western Church.

The increasing use of Latin made it essential to have a Latin version of the Scriptures. The earliest Latin translation was from North Africa, though it did not include all the books we have in the Bible today. Others were made, based on the Septuagint, but the translators did not always have a good command of Greek nor a regard for accuracy. Hence many of these 'Old Latin' translations were generally poor and sometimes unintelligible.

Concerning this situation, Jerome was prompted to write in 382 to Bishop Damasus of Rome, 'If we are to rely on the Latin versions, then let us be told which of these we are to rely on, for there are almost as many distinct versions as there are copies of the Scriptures.' Damasus, who wanted to establish Latin as the language of the Western Church, wanted an accurate Latin Bible. In response to Jerome's letter, he invited the scholar to make an accurate Latin translation according to the 'the true Greek text'.

Commitment

Little is known of Jerome's early years. He was born into a wealthy family who professed Christianity, and lived in Stridon, a small town in Dalmatia, close to the border of Italy. Instructed at first by his father, he was later sent to Rome to complete his education where he studied the two foremost classical disciplines of the day, grammar and rhetoric.

In Rome he seems to have been taken up by the usual wordly pleasures and attractions of the capital, but soon found himself on the 'slippery path' of youth. Fortunately he recognised the folly of his ways and around the age of twenty made a Christian commitment. After he was baptised, Jerome joined other Christian young men on the Lord's Day in visiting the catacombs beneath the city. Their purpose was to discover the tombs of famous martyrs buried there and to note the inscriptions on their crypts.

Following what was becoming a popular ascetic practice of the time, Jerome determined to break with the world in order to keep himself 'free for God and Christ'. Leaving Rome, he set out with the aim of pursuing knowledge whereby he could better serve God. His travels took him first to France and Germany where he settled in the town of Trier, on the Moselle, and spent time copying the texts of sacred books.

His desire to follow a more devout life, however, led him next to Aquileia, a city in north-east Italy not far from his native home. Here he joined a community of like-minded young men who were similarly intent on leading an ascetic life. Despite his pleasure in the fellowship, however, his fiery temperament caused trouble and he felt it wiser to withdraw.

MONASTICISM

The rise of Christian monasticism owes much to the practice of asceticism, which taught that the material order – and especially the body – was inherently evil. Hence the ascetic was one who denied himself the natural pleasures of human life in order to subdue the flesh and set the spirit free. Some Christians attached great honour to the ascetic life, renouncing marriage and giving themselves to the simplest form of existence. Among them were Athanasius and Jerome.

In Christianity, asceticism was usually expressed in monasticism. The founder of the movement is generally recognised as Antony (251–356), from a Christian family of Upper Egypt, who towards the end of the third century gave away his wealth and retired to the desert to live a solitary life. His example attracted others to join him, and a colony of over 5,000 ascetics was established, living in separate cells but meeting for worship.

By the end of the following century monasticism had spread through Palestine, Syria and Asia Minor. It was introduced to the West by Athansius during his exile to Rome. Jerome spent over two years in Syria as a hermit; he popularised the movement in Rome, and later retired to live in a cell at Bethlehem for the rest of his life.

Still eager to further his studies, in 374 he moved with some of his friends – and his library of books – to Antioch, the capital of Syria, another leading centre of Christianity. Even here his spirit was restless, but it was while in this frame of mind that he reached a turning-point in his Christian life.

One night, ill with a fever, he had a remarkable dream. In it, he saw himself before the judgment throne of God, who accused him of devoting more time to secular than to Christian writings. Asked who and what he was, Jerome replied, 'I am a Christian.' 'You lie', was the response. 'You are a disciple of Cicero and not of Christ. For where your treasure is, there is your heart also.' When ordered to be flogged for his worldliness, he pleaded for mercy and promised never to read secular books again. 'Lord, if I ever again possess worldy books or read them, I have denied you.'

The effect on Jerome was startling, for he began more earnestly to study Christian books. From Antioch, he retired into the deserts of Syria where he joined a colony of hermits living the solitary life in a cave. This period of isolation proved most fruitful, for it was here that he took the opportunity to perfect his mastery of Hebrew and to add a knowledge of Greek.

Rome

The solitude of this kind of living did not appeal to Jerome, and he quit the desert. Following his ordination around the year 379, he moved to Constantinople and thence to Rome. In 382 he was invited by Damasus, Bishop of Rome, to assist him in the work of a Council being held to discuss divisions that had arisen in the church at Antioch. It was at this point that the Bishop asked him to make an accurate translation of the Bible. It was felt necessary to replace the variety of Old Latin versions that were full of mistakes and 'the blundering alterations of confident but ignorant critics, and, further, all that has been inserted or changed by copyists more asleep than awake'.

Jerome was reluctant to attempt the task. He was aware that there would be many who would be greatly incensed by having their favourite texts changed, even in the cause of accuracy.[1] Nevertheless, he began with the Gospels as they had fared worst with numerous false insertions, and only made changes where sense demanded it. He often left passages untouched which he might otherwise have corrected, in order to preserve the familiar form. They were finished early in 384, and the rest of the New Testament – which he only revised slightly – was published in 391.

While in Rome Jerome became spiritual adviser to a group of aristocratic ladies. He formed a special friendship with one, Paula, and her three daughters, whom he encouraged in the practice of ascetic living. When one of the ladies died due to the rigors of fasting, accusations quickly mounted against him. Added to which, his failure to become bishop following the death of Damasus upset him, and in 385 he decided to quit Rome. His journey took him to Antioch and Egypt before finally settling down to a monastic life in Bethlehem.

---

1. Augustine, Bishop of Hippo (North Africa), was among his critics, who considered it unwise for him to alter the words of Scripture to which people had become accustomed.

Bethlehem

For the next thirty-five years Jerome remained in the Holy Land, devoting himself to translation work and writing commentaries on the Scriptures. His monastery became a centre for Bible teaching and for receiving pilgrims, while other activities included preaching in the Church of the Nativity and engaging in theological controversy. A number of Roman ladies – including his friend Paula – followed him to Bethlehem, where they built a convent and continued in their celibate life.

The 4th century Church of the Nativity, Bethlehem, where Jerome preached and taught - it was rebuilt in the sixth century.

Jerome had already made a start in Rome on revising the Old Testament, working from the Old Latin versions. Following a request from the church there, he had begun with the Psalter, but his first attempt was neither successful nor complete. When he reached Bethlehem he began another, more thorough revision, this time with the help of the Greek text, while at the same time endeavouring to represent the real rendering of the Hebrew. The translation was successful, and was followed by a revision of other Old Testament books along the same lines.

Even so, Jerome found working from the Greek version a hopeless task; persuaded by some of his friends, he set this work aside in favour of a translation directly from the original Hebrew – to 'give my Latin readers the hidden treasures of Hebrew erudition', he remarked. He even went so far as to consult Jewish rabbis concerning the text.

The first books made available were Samuel and Kings (around 391);

the sixteen prophets were in circulation by 393, followed by Job, Ezra and Nehemiah (394), Chronicles (395), the three books of Solomon (398), plus the Pentateuch, Joshua, Judges, Ruth, and Esther (after 400). The remaining books were completed by around 405.

It should be noted that the Greek Old Testament differed from the Hebrew Bible in that it contained the books of the Apocrypha, books not recognised as canonical by the Jews. Neither did Jerome accept them as God-inspired, but was nevertheless compelled by the Church to include them in the Vulgate. (In his opinion, they were helpful only for edification. Later, Protestants followed his example by similarly rejecting them.)

This great piece of work was accomplished after twenty-three years of labour, while at the same time continuing his many other activities. As expected, his translation received a hostile reception, and those familiar with the Old Latin versions did not easily take to the new one. It was not received by the Church as the 'official' version until well into the eighth century, but from then onwards it remained the Bible of the Western Church until the end of the Middle Ages. It was not called the 'Vulgate' (meaning 'common' language) until the 1530s and was only recognised by the Roman Catholic Church at the Council of Trent in 1546.

Standard Version

By the end of the fifth century there existed for the first time a standard version of the whole Bible, which brought order into the confusion of the variety of Old Latin texts. The complete Bible of sixty-six books – which Jerome rightly called 'the Divine Library' – involved a tremendous amount of work for copyists. It was rare to have all the books within one cover, partly because they were expensive and only the rich could afford such a luxury. Added to which a handwritten Bible was bulky, hence they were often produced either as individual books or in sections.

The use of Latin by the Western Church continued through the Middle Ages, both in its services and for missionary outreach in northern Europe. It was understood by educated men from one end of the continent to the other, as well as by the clergy, and was a means by which the Church was linked to culture and learning. For a thousand years translators used this version for their work, before finally once again making use of the Greek New Testament. But whereas Jerome had intended to make the Bible a more readable book, over the centuries the practice of using Latin in church services – rather than the vernacular – eventually made it impossible for lay people to understand the words.

Greek, meanwhile, continued to be used in the Eastern Church. But as Christianity spread other translations of the Scriptures were made available. From around the third century Syriac, Coptic (Egypt), Armenian, Georgian, Ethiopic and Persian versions of the Bible appeared, which gives some idea of the expansion of the Church.

In time certain guiding principles for Bible translation seem to have emerged. One was that it was essential for the Scriptures to be available for new converts and for each tribe or nation in their own language. Then it was recognised as important to return to the best available manuscripts of the original Hebrew or Greek texts for purposes of translation.

It was not until the sixteenth century that there existed in England a translation in the common language, made by William Tyndale. Two years after Tyndale's martyrdom, in 1538, Henry VIII ordered a copy of the Great Bible to be placed in every parish church so that lay people might have access to it. With the onset of the Reformation there was a new desire to recover the original Greek and Hebrew texts of the Bible, which led increasingly to translations of the Bible in the 'common tongue'.

11

AD 440 LEO THE GREAT CONSECRATED BISHOP OF ROME

The First Officially Recognised Pope

In Leo 1 (440–461) Rome had one of the greatest men of the age, who more than any other bishop was responsible for establishing the might of the Roman Church. Rome's claim to be the authoritative centre of Christianity dates from the second century, and although widely acknowledged as a church 'worthy of honour', attempts to exert its authority over other churches failed. It was not until the sixth century that Rome achieved supremacy, when the Bishop of Rome was for the first time accorded the title of pope.

In New Testament churches the usual form of government was the collective rule of elders and deacons. By the beginning of the second century, however, the custom of one ruling elder (or bishop, meaning 'overseer') was becoming the normal practice. At Rome the first man to be clearly acknowledged in this capacity was Anicetus (c154–166), although Hegisippus (c175) puts forward a list of the names of men who it is claimed were bishops of Rome from the beginning of the church there, and tracing the line of succession back to the apostle Peter.

Before the end of the second century a deeper sense of unity among the churches opened the way for them to begin consulting each other on questions of faith and practice. Bishops, especially of Gaul and the western provinces, looked to Rome for an opinion, for the church there was held in high regard. There were several reasons for this mark of esteem.

Martyred

In the first place, the apostles Paul and Peter had been martyred in the imperial capital and their shrines erected there. It had endured much suffering from persecution, and yet remained true to the faith – a testimony that aroused the admiration of other churches. As the capital of the empire all roads led to Rome, and it consequently attracted prominent Christians – and heretics – from all parts of the Church. Rome, moreover, was the only Western church to have received a letter from the apostle Paul. And following the destruction of Jerusalem in AD70 the focus of Christendom moved westwards, towards Rome.

While churches regarded Rome with great respect, they did not necessarily submit to its authority. Advice given by Rome was not always followed, for each church felt free under the Holy Spirit to arrive at its own decisions. In 190 Victor, Bishop of Rome, presumed to excommunicate the churches of Asia Minor for refusing to follow the Roman dating for Easter. But the Asian bishops, together with Irenaeus of Lyons, rejected this attempt to establish the rule of Rome, and the move failed. Cyprian (c248–258), a leading bishop of North Africa, also took the view that despite Rome's pre-eminent position it could not assert any authority over other bishops.

Throughout the third century the Bishop of Rome's authority gradually extended over the Christian communities of the surrounding district; no decisions of importance could be taken without first informing him. In the fourth century, the standing of the church of Rome was greatly enhanced under the Christian emperor, Constantine. It acquired numerous properties and estates; new churches were built, including a basilica on the Vatican Hill over the shrine of Peter and another on the Ostian Way, the place of Paul's martyrdom. The Empress Fausta gave her Lateran Palace to the bishop as his residence, adding considerably to his prestige.

Developments

Over the next three centuries momentous developments took place throughout the Western Church which ultimately gave birth to Roman supremacy. Constantine left Rome in 330 and re-established his capital at 'New Rome' – Constantinople (previously called Byzantium). This move increased the power of the Roman bishop, who became the city's leading citizen and supreme authority. His position was reinforced by the Councils of Nicaea (325) and Constantinople (381), which recognised Rome as the leading city of the empire, but for geographical rather than theological reasons. These moves culminated in the adoption of Christianity in 392 as the sole religion of the Roman Empire; paganism and other heresies were outlawed by imperial decree. Rome became not simply the leading city of the empire, but the ecclesiastical capital of Christendom.

By this time the Bishop of Rome's power was such that the emperor was no longer able to dominate the Church; rather the reverse, for now the emperor was reckoned to be 'in the Church and not above it'. Following the death of Constantine a number of able bishops were appointed to the see of Rome who step by step secured additional rights for their office. Each of them assumed the role of supreme bishop and worked to boost their claim to primacy.

Damasus (366–384) was given imperial authority to hear appeals by bishops over the head of their metropolitan bishops. He began to issue decretals (i.e., instructions, rather like an imperial decree) and addressed other bishops as 'sons' rather than 'brothers'. Siricius (384–399), a tough administrator, distinguished himself not only by his zeal against heresy, but also by his firm belief in the prerogative of the Roman see. Innocent I(401–417) ordered that nothing done in the provinces could be concluded until first submitted to him.

Claim to Primacy

Rome's claim to primacy was based on theological rather than geographical grounds, on the words of Jesus to Peter: 'I tell you that you are Peter, and on this rock I will build my church...' (Matt. 16:18ff).[1] It was held that the Lord had singled out Peter to be head of the Church, with responsibility for teaching and caring for the whole body of Christ (cf. John 21:15ff). Later he was claimed to have been the founding bishop of Rome, and that consequently all his successors inherited the authority invested in Peter. The bishop of Rome was therefore the leader of the Church, with the power to rule over Christendom and to speak on the behalf of Peter.

It was Leo the Great who, more than any other, advanced and consolidated the influence of the Roman see and steered Rome towards papal supremacy. He was the most able Roman bishop of the fifth century and the first to be granted the title of pope. He came to office at a time when barbarian hordes were again threatening the empire, and proved himself to be the dominating figure in both Church and State. His influence was felt not only in Italy, but in Constantinople, Antioch, Egypt and Spain.

---

1. It was not until Damasus (in 382) that this text was first seriously taken as a claim to primacy.

'YOU ARE PETER...' (Matt. 16:18ff)

This text focuses attention on the major point of disagreement between Protestant and Roman Catholic Churches, and is used by Catholics to defend the supremacy of Rome and the position of the pope. Like many other passages in the Gospels, a knowledge of the Hebrew background gives new insight into the words. In Matthew 16:18, 'I tell you that you are Peter (Greek, "*petros*"), and on this rock ("*petra*") I will build my church...' All scholars agree that here is a play on words using Simon's nickname, Petros.

In a rabbinic commentary on Numbers 23:9, written in Hebrew, the interpreter uses an allegory describing God's dilemma when he wished to create the world. He speaks of a king searching for rock on which to build a palace. Though he dug on several sites, he found only mire. But when he struck solid rock (petra), he said, 'Here I will build'. Thus when the Holy One saw Abraham, he said, 'Here I have found solid rock (petra) on which I can build and upon which I can lay the world's foundations'. It seems as though Jesus may have been alluding to a tradition that God built the world on the sure foundation of the 'rock' of Abraham's faith and obedience (cf. Isa. 51:1ff).

The words 'I will give you the keys of the kingdom of heaven' (Matt. 16:19a) are to be recognised as an allusion to Isaiah 22:22 and 1 Chronicles 9:26ff. As often in the Gospels, Jesus alluded in his teaching to Old Testament texts, and here is an example of ancient Jewish exegesis. Behind these verses is the idea of stewardship, that the keys of the kingdom of heaven are entrusted only to faithful individuals, though for what purpose is not clear.

(For a more detailed treatment of the subject, see articles by David Bivin and Joseph Frankovic in Jerusalem Perspective, No's 46/47 and 50.)

Emperor Valentinian III, in dire need of support at a time when civil rule was breaking down, made overtures to Leo. In 445 he issued an edict by which nothing was to be attempted 'contrary to ancient custom... without the authority of the venerable man, the pope of the eternal city...' Thus by law the Bishop of Rome was declared supreme head of the Western Church, and resistance to his authority constituted a state offence. The emperor further recognised the bishop's claim by honouring him with the title 'chief wearer of the episcopal crown'.

When Attila the Hun invaded Italy in 451 the people looked to their bishop rather than their emperor for leadership. Leo went out to meet the Hun at the head of an embassy of leading Romans; his majestic figure, it is said, so impressed the barbarian that he consented to be bought off and retire. Four years later, when the Vandal chieftain Gaiseric attacked Rome, it was Leo who once again intervened.

Successor of Peter

There is no doubt that Leo regarded himself as the successor of Peter. He claimed that as Peter was above all the apostles, so the Bishop of Rome was above all other bishops. Thus when he preached or wrote a letter, he contended that those who heard or received his words should receive them as if they were from St Peter himself. In which case, his words were to be obeyed.

One bishop, for example, was warned not to assume equality with Rome and was instructed to send a confession of his faith so that it might be judged whether or not his standing might be acknowledged. And a metropolitan bishop was rebuked for having taken action without first having consulted Rome. Even the renowned Hilary, Bishop of Arles, was disciplined by Leo for exceeding his rights in deposing a bishop.

Leo's intention was to establish Rome as the one apostolic see, and he always availed himself of opportunities to further this cause. He played a full part in the on-going doctrinal controversies of the fifth century regarding the true nature of Christ, a dispute that had been simmering in the East for years. In response to the heresy of Eutyches, the head of a monastery in Constantinople, Leo wrote a Tome (or theological treatise) addressed to the Patriarch of Constantinople in which he set out the doctrine of the Latin Church.

St Peter's Church, Rome, originally built by
Constantine and re-built in the 17th century.

Rejected by a council at Ephesus (449), the Tome was resubmitted to the Council of Chalcedon (451), and following imperial pressure was read and ratified by the bishops. Known as the Chalcedon Definition, it has since been accepted as a statement of faith by mainstream Christian traditions. The document was yet another attempt to define the doctrine concerning Jesus, and was aimed at countering the heresies then disturbing the Church.

The same Council drew up a canon which reaffirmed an agreement reached at Constantinople (381) concerning the position of Rome. Again, Rome's petrine basis for papal supremacy was rejected, but it was accorded the primacy because it was an imperial city. At the same time, equal honour was granted Constantinople because it was the seat of the Eastern Empire and the senate.

The Roman delegates refused to sign the final document and Leo's protest was made in vain. Nevertheless, his success in the theological controversy was complete, and the Council's statement of faith was the result of his efforts. Leo afterwards regarded with horror any attempt to reopen the issue, even though it made permanent the divisions within the Eastern Church – the Coptic churches of Egypt and Ethiopia, for example, refused to accept the Definition.

The Papal Office

More than any other before him, in both practice and theory Leo upheld the supremacy of Peter as the founder of the papal office and as the ruler of the Church through his successors at Rome. He reckoned that it was not the secular greatness of Rome that determined the issue, but that it was confirmed by the Council of Nicaea (325) which asserted that the Bishop of Rome had authority over all other bishops. (In fact, Nicaea had only stated that the bishop of Rome was 'the first among equals', nothing more.)

It was under Bishop Gelasius (492–496) that the theory of Roman primacy was finally settled. When the Byzantine emperor attempted to interfere in ecclesiastical affairs, Gelasius reminded him that his powers had been conferred upon him by divine disposition; in which case he had to 'bow the neck' to those in charge of things divine. Nobody, he informed the emperor, could set himself above 'the office of the pope, who by Christ's order was set above all and everyone'.

Not only was the Roman primacy established, but the title of pope (*papas*, 'father') was now applied to the Roman bishop. At first the title had been used in the West to denote the relationship between the spiritual teacher and the convert. Later it was accorded to all bishops, then exclusively to Rome, though the title was not officially confirmed until 1076.

Imperial Titles

Although the Western Empire was finally overthrown in the sixth century by barbarian invaders, the papacy survived. With no emperor in authority, the pope began to annex imperial titles and claims, including that of *pontifex maximus* (originally a pagan title for the chief priest of Rome). Despite the wars, the Latin Church continued to expand, making further gains in the Iberian peninusla, France and northern Europe.

The Greek-speaking eastern half of the empire, which rejected Leo's claim to supremacy, weathered the disasters and became the Byzantine Empire. It enjoyed a revival of power and enlarged its borders to include the Holy Land and Syria among its conquests. Under the Patriarch of Constantinople, what is now known as the Eastern Orthodox Church continued to exist alongside the Catholic Church of the West, but differences began to emerge and the two gradually drifted apart.

It was during this period that the new religion of Islam challenged the Christian world, making considerable gains around the Mediterranean at Christendom's expense. Large numbers of Christians became Muslims, while others emigrated to the West.

Yet the two Churches survived, and Rome went on to play an increasingly dominant role in the civilisation that gradually emerged in a new Europe. Papal power was once again asserted when on Christmas Day, 800, Pope Leo III crowned Charlemagne as emperor of the Holy Roman Empire. Though imperial power and papal authority were seen as 'two sides of the same shield', it raised issues that persisted throughout the Middle Ages. By the thirteenth century the pope once again held sway over both Church and State, though before long this power was wrested from him.

THE CATHOLIC CHURCH

The term 'catholic' was first used with reference to the Church by Ignatius of Antioch at the beginning of the second century when he wrote, 'where Jesus Christ is, there is the catholic Church'. That is, wherever a congregation met together in the name of Jesus, there was the local expression of the universal Church.

Before long the term was more widely used to describe the true Church, to combat heresy by identifying as 'catholic' those churches which held to the orthodox faith. By the end of the second century the previously independent congregations were beginning to act in union, with a Rule of Faith and the makings of an agreed list of Scriptures.

But any who wished to belong to the catholic Church had to abide by its orthodoxy. Around 251, a group in Rome, called *Katharoi*, or 'Pure Ones', organised breakaway churches. Despite their orthodox doctrine they were put out of communion with the catholic Church, for – according to Cyprian – there was no salvation outside the catholic Church.

In the fourth century, after the reign of the emperor Constantine, the former loose federation of congregations gradually became an organised Church. Based on the Roman imperial system of civil administration, a hierarchy was established whereby each city had a bishop and each province an archbishop. Over them were five patriarchs – of Rome, Constantinople, Antioch, Alexandria and Jerusalem. The Bishop of Rome, who assumed supreme authority over the catholic Church, was eventually accorded the title of 'pope'. Following the sixteenth century Reformation, the former Latin Church became known as the Roman Catholic Church.

12

597 AUGUSTINE'S MISSION TO ENGLAND

Celtic Christianity Submits to Rome

Towards the end of the sixth century a band of forty-one monks landed on the coast of Kent. Headed by Augustine,[1] prior of a monastery in Rome, they had been sent by Pope Gregory on a mission to convert the Angles and Saxons, and to bring the remnants of the Church in Britain under papal authority. But Gregory underestimated the strength of British Christianity, which vigorously resisted the advances of Rome before finally yielding to the whim of an Anglian king.

For nearly four hundred years the Romans occupied much of Britain, establishing a period of peace and civilisation. It would seem that Christianity probably entered Britain early on during the Roman occupation, certainly by the second century. By the fourth century a thriving Church had emerged, with an organisation headed by bishops some of whom were present at the Council of Arles (Gaul) in 314.

When hordes of barbarian tribesmen began to press upon the northern frontier of the empire, however, Rome was forced to withdraw its troops from Britain to defend the capital, leaving Britain open to attack by sea-raiders from the Continent. The British were easily defeated by the pagan Anglo-Saxon invaders, who settled along the eastern side of the country before penetrating inland by sailing up the Thames, Trent, Humber and other rivers.

Many Britons escaped westwards and made their homes in Devon and Cornwall, Brittany (in France, which had its name from British settlers), Wales, Strathclyde and Cumbria. Although now cut off from the Church

---

1. Not to be confused with Augustine, Bishop of Hippo (395–430), from North Africa.

on the Continent, Christianity continued to flourish in these western areas, some of which became centres for evangelism. Small communities of Christians continued to live in the Anglo-Saxon kingdoms, though increasingly without organisation or pastoral ministry.

By around the year 600 a number of Anglo-Saxon kingdoms had been set up by the settlers. While the Jutes controlled Kent, the Saxons occupied the remainder of the south as far as Cornwall (to form the kingdoms of Essex, Sussex and Wessex). The Angles claimed the east of the country (East Anglia), the land as far north as the Firth of Forth (Northumbria) and the Midlands (Mercia). Despite this considerable incursion, British survivors in the west remained firm.

EARLY CHRISTIANITY IN BRITAIN

Christianity may have been introduced into Britain by the Roman occupying forces, though recent scholarship suggests it may also have been carried to these shores by traders, merchants and immigrants, including skilled workers, physicians and schoolmasters. The earliest indication of a Christian presence in Britain is given by the apologist Tertullian. Writing about 206, he lists the places where people believed in Christ, mentioning 'places in Britain which, though inaccessible to the Romans, have become subject to Christ'. In which case there would have been an embryo church in Britain by the latter part of the second century.

The earliest known names of British Christians are those of three martyrs – Alban of Verulam (St Albans), and Julius and Aaron of Caerleon, who probably suffered during the reign of either emperor Decius (250) or Valerian (257). The Church nevertheless survived, and in 314 we read of three bishops, a presbyter and a deacon in attendance at the Council at Arles (Gaul). The British Church was obviously orthodox in its beliefs, but in the fifth century it was troubled by the Pelagian heresy. Bishop Germanus of Auxerre (Gaul) was dispatched in 429 (and again in 447) to deal with the problem. The Church was further weakened in the fifth and sixth centuries by the pagan Anglo-Saxon invaders, but it survived in the West, even though fragmented.

Revival

In Wales, the saints Illtyd and David were associated with a work of revival. Illtyd (c470–535), from Brittany, founded a monastery at Llantwit Major, South Glamorgan, which was a centre of missionary activity in Wales. The Welsh-born David (c520–588 or 601), the patron saint of Wales, was also an evangelist and founder of monasteries, including one at Glyn Rhosyn, Dyfed, the present-day site of St David's Cathedral.

Christianity was already established in Ireland, introduced under the leadership of Patrick (390–461) who as a child had been carried away from

Britain to Ireland by slave raiders. Consecrated as a bishop for work in Ireland in 432, he spent the next thirty years in evangelism and building up the Church. Patrick centred his work on the monastery rather than the cathedral, and dioceses were ruled over by an abbot rather than a bishop.

There were two other major centres of evangelism during this period. One was at Whithorn, Galloway, where the monk Ninian (c360–c432) founded a church and monastery known as the White House, or Candida Casa, in 397. Ninian was the son of a Christian king in Cumbria and had studied in France under Martin of Tours. His monastery became the base from which he and his monks took the gospel to the Picts along the Roman Wall, as far as the east coast of Scotland, and into Ireland.

The other centre was the island now known as Iona, from where the gospel radiated out not only to Scotland, but the following century also to England and parts of Europe. The driving force behind this mission was Columba (c521–597), an Irish monk of royal descent, who left Ireland to settle on Iona in 563. He made missionary journeys to the northern Picts, travelling as far as Inverness and even the Orkneys. According to Bede, the Church historian, he 'turned the nation to faith in Christ by word and by example'. Meanwhile, missionaries from Scotland and Britain ventured abroad to plant the gospel in the Low Countries and central Europe, though they failed to evangelise the pagan Anglo-Saxons who were their more immediate neighbours.

Heathens

Augustine had been sent by Pope Gregory the Great (590–604), who was anxious to bring the Anglo-Saxon heathens into the fold of Rome. He told Augustine, 'all the bishops of Britain we commit to thy fraternal care, so that the unlearned may be taught, the weak strengthened by persuasion, the perverse corrected by authority'. It was obviously not a mission solely to convert the British, but rather to bring the Church there under the arm of Rome. Kent may have been chosen for the mission partly because of its nearness to the Continent, but also because the heathen king Ethelbert had a Frankish wife who was a Christian and had already appealed for someone to give instruction in the Faith.

Within a short time Ethelbert had embraced Christianity and his capital at Canterbury became the centre of a Christian community. The king gave Augustine an old church, 'built long ago by Roman Christians', which was to become the cathedral. The following year the monk founded the church of Saint Peter and Paul, later known as St Augustine's Abbey. The mission

The 6th Century St Martin's Church, Canterbury, given
by King Ethelbert to his Christian wife, Berthat, in 562

was initially successful and Augustine was able to report that on his first Christmas Day 10,000 pagans had been baptised. In order to be able to minister to the new Christians he was consecrated Bishop of the English. Later, the pope appointed him Archbishop of Canterbury. From Kent, the Faith was introduced into Essex and East Anglia.

Ethelbert at that time was recognised as Bretwalda (the king accepted by the other kings as 'ruler of Britain'). It followed that the religion which the Bretwalda held was favoured by those kings who recognised his leadership, hence the conversion of a Bretwalda to Christianity was a contributing factor to the spread of the Faith among the Anglo-Saxon peoples. The decision to follow the Bretwalda had a serious weakness, however, in that it lent itself to external conformity without inner conviction. And should a pagan king succeed a Christian, there was always the chance that the kingdom could revert to paganism.

Relapse

This was the case with Redwald, king of the East Angles, who received Christian baptism during a visit to the court of Ethelbert. But he relapsed into paganism, though in his temple he kept both a pagan and a Christian altar. It was not until 628, when his successor was baptised, that East Anglia accepted Christianity. Similarly in Essex when the king, Ethelbert's nephew, accepted the new religion, his people followed him and a Bishop of London was consecrated, in 604. But there was a temporary reversion to heathenism when the king died and his pagan sons expelled the bishop. It was some while before the lost ground was recovered.

In the areas under Augustine's control the customs and practices of the Roman Church prevailed, but it was the pope's intention that Augustine should also bring the British churches under the authority of Rome. Twice, attempts to negotiate with the British bishops failed, for the Britons could not submit 'to the haughtiness of the Romans or the tyranny of the Saxons', or accept their practices.

Yet fearful that they might be rejecting God, the British sought the counsel of an aged hermit. Should they accept Augustine or refuse him? 'If he is a man of God, then follow him,' the hermit advised them. 'But how shall we know he is a man of God?' they asked. 'When you come to the place of meeting, if he rises to greet you, you will know that he is a servant of Christ.'

Led by Dionoth, the abbot of the great monastery at Bangor-Iscoed, south of Chester, the bishops again met Augustine in conference, under an oak at Dyrham, near the River Severn. When the British delegation approached Augustine, the Roman bishop kept his seat, perhaps in an attempt to affirm his superior position. When the British bishops refused to listen any further, Augustine warned them, 'If you will not receive brethren who bring you peace, you shall receive enemies who bring you war. If you will not unite with us in showing the Saxons the Way of Life, you shall receive from them the stroke of death.'

Foothold

Augustine died in 604, by which time he had established a foothold in Kent, though his overtures to the Celtic Church had failed. During the seventh century the struggle to convert the Anglo-Saxon peoples continued from both Iona and Canterbury. Northumbria, which consisted of the lesser kingdoms of Bernicia and Deira, was next to receive Christianity. It came about through the marriage of King Edwin to Ethelberga, daughter of Ethelbert of Kent (in 625). She was accompanied by a Roman monk called Paulinus, who had been consecrated bishop in order to accompany the princess. After much hesitation, Edwin, Coifi (his chief priest) and many of the leading men accepted the Faith and submitted to baptism (Easter 627), in a wooden church erected at York for this purpose.

When Edwin was killed in battle at Hatfield (near Doncaster) in 633, he was succeeded by Oswald, who had lived among the monks on Iona, and from whom he had learned of Christ. Northumbria had in part reverted to paganism, so Oswald sent to Iona (and not Canterbury) for a bishop to come and teach the Faith to his subjects.

In 635, Aidan (who died in 651) was sent as bishop and given the island of Lindisfarne as his episcopal see. His love of peace and humble piety made him an admirable choice and people flocked to hear him preach. Converts were made, churches built and Christianity firmly established throughout Northumbria. He sent for other monks to assist him, so that Lindisfarne became a second Iona.

Wessex and Mercia

It was about this time (634) that Pope Honorius sent Birinus as a missionary-bishop to 'sow the seeds of the holy Faith' in the hearts of the people of Wessex. The king and his people accepted the Faith; when the king was baptised, he was sponsored by King Oswald of Northumbria, who was then the Bretwalda. Birinus was given Dorchester-on-Thames (Oxfordshire) as his episcopal see, later changed to Winchester.

The kingdom of Mercia was ruled by King Penda, a pagan, though he had no objection to any of his family becoming Christian. In 641 Penda attacked and conquered Northumbria, killing Oswald and dividing the kingdom in two. It was not long before King Oswy, of Bernicia, defeated Penda and reunited the kingdom. Though his wife was of the Roman communion, Oswy was brought up under the influence of Iona, but used his religion for his own political ends.

In 654, the year Penda died, a party of four monks from Lindisfarne gained an entrance into Mercia to preach; the kingdom was eventually claimed for Christ and a see established at Lichfield in 669. The last pagan stronghold to receive the gospel in England was Sussex, evangelised by Wilfrid of Ripon (681–685).

Up to this point the Roman and Irish missions had worked independently from Canterbury and Northumbria to spread Christianity through England. But as the two movements merged, it was inevitable that their differences should come to the fore. One concern was the introduction of foot-washing at baptism, and another was to do with the style of tonsure (the monastic custom of shaving part of the head).

Dissension

But the real cause of dissension was that of fixing the date of Easter, for there could be some weeks difference between the celebrations of the two Churches. Though the question had been settled at the Council of Nicaea (325), the Irish and Celtic Churches had persisted with their own methods of reckoning.

Matters came to a head in Northumbria in 663, and King Oswy was persuaded to have a public disputation in order to resolve the question. What was at stake, however, was not so much the date of Easter, but rather the future direction of the Church in England – would it come under the authority of Iona or Rome? It was at the monastery at Whitby, founded by the abbess Hilda in 657, where one of the most momentous synods in English Church history took place.

The Irish Church was headed by Colman, a successor to Aidan at Lindisfarne, while the party of Rome had Wilfrid, abbot of Ripon (who had lived in Rome), as their spokesman. King Oswy opened the debate by urging that there should be an end to division and that the two Churches should follow 'the same rule of life'. For the Irish, Colman spoke first, pleading with the synod not to despise the teaching of Columba (of Iona), whose claim for their practice was based on that of the apostle John. For the opposition, Wilfrid declared that their custom was that of Rome, where the apostles Peter and Paul had taught, adding that it was to Peter that Jesus had said he would give the keys of the kingdom of heaven.

Oswy was taken back by this assertion. He asked Colman whether these words were true and whether Columba had been given similar authority. When the bishop admitted they were true and that Columba had no such power, Oswy yielded to the Roman tradition. 'Well, I am in no mind to go against this doorkeeper ... otherwise when I come to the doors of the kingdom of heaven, I may find none to open to me'. Despite having been brought up to follow the Irish practice, his fear of being refused entrance to heaven determined him to follow Rome. With these words, the delegates accepted his decision and agreed to implement the Roman practices.

After this, the Church in England came increasingly under the authority of Rome, though in Scotland and northern Ireland the older practices continued until the Norman period. By the following century, however, the papacy had achieved virtual supremacy in England. It was to be over 800 years before the Reformation released the Church in England from Rome.

13

622 THE BIRTH OF ISLAM

The Greatest Threat to the Gospel

One of the most remarkable religious phenomenon of modern history has been the rise of Islam. Following the death of its founder, Muhammad (570–632), it spread rapidly from Arabia, and within a century boasted an empire that stretched from Spain in the West to the borders of China in the East. Now with over one billion adherents and an avowed aim of 'One Prophet, one Faith for all the world', its advance continues to pose a serious threat to the gospel.

At the beginning of the seventh century the Arabs were still a polytheistic people. But spread around the Arabian peninsula were a number of Christian communities, together with a scattering of itinerant hermits of the Byzantine Church. There was also a strong Jewish presence in the south of the country, particularly in the town of Medina, some 200 miles north of Mecca. None of these groups attempted to evangelise their Arab neighbours and the country remained overwhelmingly pagan.

Little for certain can be said of Muhammad's early years. It is known that he was descended from the family of Hashim and the tribe of Quraysh. Orphaned at the age of six, he was afterwards brought up first by his grandfather and then by his uncle, Abu Talib. From childhood he appears to have suffered from epilepsy, which may have influenced the course of his life. From the age of twelve he accompanied his uncle on visits to Syria, during which time he came into contact with Jews and Christians. Though he learned something of their religions and had some awareness of biblical stories, his knowledge was confused, often inaccurate. This was probably because his knowledge was based on hearsay rather than on knowledge of the biblical text.

For the first forty years of his life Muhammad lived in Mecca, which was an important trading centre for western Arabia and on a caravan route between India and Africa. Mecca was a pagan city, famous for its shrine, the *Ka'ba* ('cube'), surrounded by sacred stones and containing the black meteorite which was said to have come down from heaven. Some 360 deities were worshipped at the Ka'ba, which attracted large numbers of pilgrims to the city and provided a lucrative source of revenue for the keepers, who were members of the Quraysh tribe.

As a young man he worked as a tradesman, but was later employed by a wealthy widow, Kadijah, as leader of her caravans. When he was twenty-five the two of them were married, though she was fourteen years older than himself; they had several sons and daughters, of whom only one daughter, Fatima, survived.

One True God

Increasingly dissatisfied with the polytheism of his native Mecca, Muhammad's thoughts turned towards the one true God, a knowledge he must have gained on his journeys to Syria. But he may also have been influenced by another religious movement in Arabia, a group of men known as Banifs. Though paganism in Arabia was on the wane, these men had been impressed by Jewish and Christian monotheism and, rejecting idolatry, had branched out into asceticism.

At the age of forty he began to practise fasting, and spent time in seclusion and meditation. He retired to a mountain cave some three miles from Mecca where over a period of years he was said to have experienced visions and dreams, and received revelations from heaven. These occasional messages were later written down and collected to form what is now called the Koran ('to read' or 'to recite'). They were said to have been given him by the angel Gabriel and were passed on orally to his followers. Told that he was the 'Apostle of God', Muhammad took upon himself the mantle of a prophet; he urged the people of the need to repent and reform their ways, for the Day of Judgment was at hand.

For three years Muhammad made known the message among his family and friends. His wife and some of his relatives believed in his mission, but others of the Quraysh tribe were more concerned to retain the economic advantages they enjoyed as keepers of the Ka'ba. When he publicly began to attack the idolatry of Mecca he was met with resentment and hostility; his message of repentance and his warning of the judgment to come were greeted with ridicule. Soon the tone of his revelations changed, and he began to recount the histories of (mostly) biblical prophets telling how they too had been mocked and had come under judgment.

Turning-point

Disappointed by the response to his message in Mecca, in 622 Muhammad withdrew with his followers to the city of Medina, 200 miles north of Mecca, invited there by a group of men who had accepted his message. This withdrawal from Mecca, known as the Hegira, was first celebrated on 16 July 622. It is regarded as the beginning of the Muslim era and the time from which the dates on the Muslim calendar are reckoned.[1] But it also marked a new phase in Muhammad's mission and from then on he began to enjoy an increasing success.

During his eight years at Medina he established a small theocratic community. Declaring himself to be the spokesman of Allah,[2] he set himself up as head of state, law-giver and judge, and assumed the role of both a religious and political leader, a step which was to determine the future direction of his movement. At first Muhammad favoured both Jews and Christians, for they were People of the Book; he even regarded the biblical prophets – including Jesus – with honour. He believed that his religion was that of Abraham, the patriarchs and the prophets (though a somewhat corrupted version) and he even adopted a number of Jewish practices.

Opposed by neighbouring tribes of Arabs and ridiculed by the Jews because of his inaccurate biblical accounts, Muhammad changed his tactic. Whereas initially he had worked peaceably to spread his message, the rejection he had experienced convinced him of the need to use force to fulfil his mission. This meant the use of military action to achieve his aims, which has continued as an element of Koranic teaching to this day. Announcing that he had had a revelation of the solemn duty of *jihad* ('holy war' or 'struggle'),[3] he raised an army and marched against his enemies. Idol worshippers had either to accept Islam or be put to the sword; monotheists were given a choice: convert, or submit and pay tribute.

Submit!

Many Christian communities converted to Islam, but the Jews of Medina refused to submit to his new religion; they repudiated his claims and plotted

---

1. All dates are preceded by the initials AH, meaning Anno Hegira, i.e., from the year of the flight to Medina.
2. Allah was the name of the supreme Semitic god.
3. Jihad is a religious duty for Muslims when their religion is under threat.

against him. He proceeded to destroy the community; many of them were beheaded while others were sold into slavery. A number of Arabian tribes were won over to the new religion, and in 630 at the head of an army of 10,000 Muhammad finally returned to Mecca in triumph. Once in control of the city, he destroyed the idols which surrounded the Ka'ba and made it the central place of pilgrimage for the worship of Allah. His followers declared, 'There is but one God, Allah, and Muhammad is his prophet.'

From this point Muhammad no longer enjoined his followers to turn to Jerusalem when they prayed, but rather to Mecca. He named the new movement Islam, meaning 'submission' (i.e., to Allah), and an adherent was a Muslim, meaning 'a surrendered man'. The sayings of Muhammad were memorised by his followers and after the prophet's death a start was made on compiling them before they were lost. A little larger than the length of the New Testament, the Koran was composed in rhyming prose and has been described as 'the greatest masterpiece of Arab literature'.

Conquests

Determined to establish an independent state based on Islam, Muhammad successfully led his army throughout the Arabian peninsula. By the time of his death he had conquered virtually the whole of the land. Under the leadership of the Caliphs ('successors'), Islam pursued a policy of bringing other nations to submission. Inspired by tremendous religious enthusiasm and the promise of immediate entry to Paradise for those killed in battle, Arab armies marched north. Between 635 and 651 they swarmed through the Middle East, conquering the Persian empire and Mesopotamia, and then advanced on Christendom.

The Byzantine Church was divided and ill-prepared for the challenge, and though attacks on the capital, Constantinople, were repulsed, Egypt, Palestine and Syria fell to Islam during this period. Large numbers of Christians embraced the new religion rather than face the consequences. By the turn of the century all of North Africa had been conquered, and where once there had been many flourishing Christian communities – where Augustine and Cyprian had laboured – only a few remained. Over 3,200 churches were either converted into mosques or razed to the ground. In Alexandria the greatest Christian library of the day was destroyed, whilst in Jerusalem a Muslim shrine, the Dome of the Rock,[4] was built on Temple Mount.

---

4. It is supposed to have been built over the rock on which Abraham prepared to offer his son Isaac.

The Dome of the Rock, erected on the Temple Mount in 691 by Muslim conquerors, said to be over the rock where Abraham offered Isaac.

In 711 the Muslims crossed the Straits of Gibralter into Spain (where they were known as Moors) and overran nearly all of the Iberian peninsula. They continued to advance on Christian Europe, but in 732 were halted at Poitiers, in France, by a powerful Frankish army, some 125 miles short of Paris. They were driven back into Spain, from where they were not finally banished until 1492. The Western Church was meanwhile saved from being subject to Islam.

Although lacking in political experience and aptitude, Islam became an established political power. During the eighth century the Muslims gradually developed their own style of government, based on Islamic legislation known as the *Shar'iah* ('The Clear Path'). Still practised today, this medieval body of law deals with all aspects of life and prescribes everything a Muslim should – and should not – do.

Some of the reforms in the Koran were good. It condemned idolatry, forbade the burial of baby girls while yet alive and commended the care of orphans. But it also laid down harsh forms of punishment, such as stoning an adulterer to death or amputating the hand of an habitual thief, practices still enforced by some Muslim governments today.

JIHAD
The terrorist attacks of 11 September 2001 on targets in America brought to public attention as never before the threat of Islamic jihad. It has given rise to cries of shock and disbelief, that any religion – in the name of God – should feel able to commit such atrocities. For a long period this particular teaching of

Islam has gone unnoticed, though since the seventh century it has been embodied in the Koran.

Today, Muslims are not agreed about Jihad, whether it should be a spiritual struggle or military warfare. Some suggest that it is simply a struggle to lead a pure life and to obey the teachings of Muhammad. Others see it literally as warfare, for it follows the teaching of the Koran, as well as the example of the prophet when his army put the Jews to the sword and subdued Arabia.

While Muhammad urged his followers to oppress or kill non-Muslims, there was always an escape route for Christians and Jews, if they were prepared to accept *dhimmi status*. *Dhimmis* were to be completely submitted to Islam and were to feel themselves subdued. Treated as second-class citizens, they could continue their religion on payment of a special tax called *jizya*, but had to wear special clothing and were denied the right of participation in political power.

Muslim teaching divides the world into two opposing camps: *Dar es Islam* – The House of Islam – which is composed of those areas of the world where Islam rules; and *Dar el Harb* – The House of War – which refers to those lands occupied by non-Muslims. The belief is that these two factions will be at war until Islam is finally established throughout the world. Whilst many Muslims today are content to live at peace with their neighbours, there has emerged a fundamentalist element which is restoring the ancient Muslim belief of Jihad.

Developments

The Arab conquests led to the foundation of a civilisation from which flowed impressive cultural and scientific developments, and learning spread throughout the whole of the Arab world. Beautiful and distinctive art forms were created during this period, which stamped the imprint of Islam throughout the empire, and many fine mosques were built.

Great advances were made in mathematical, medical and physical science, and the very names algebra and chemistry are Arabic. Their alchemists made new discoveries such as alloys, dyes, distilling and optical glass. The use of Roman numerals was ousted by the Arabic figures we use to this day, and the zero sign was first adopted by them. In the eighth century they learned the manufacture of paper from the Chinese, and Baghdad, Damascus and Valencia became important centres of paper manufacture.

Some of the credit for these developments, however, must be given to Christians, for many who converted to Islam were more cultured than their masters. They instructed the Arabs in Greek philosophy, medicine and science, and many of their ideas were taken over by Muslim scholars. Christian artists and architects were also used to develop the art forms associated with Arabs. These advances stopped, however, around the end of the eleventh century and since then there has been no similar period of achievements.

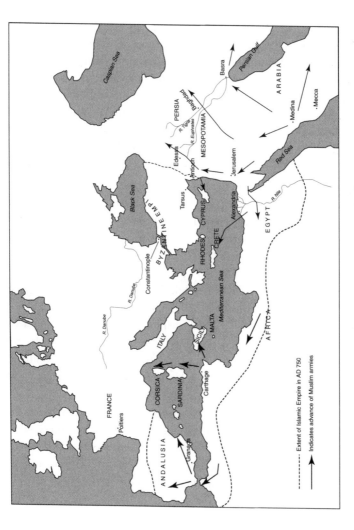

THE ISLAMIC EMPIRE IN AD 750

----- Extent of Islamic Empire in AD 750
→ Indicates advance of Muslim armies

In the realm of religion Islam is largely indebted to both Judaism and Christianity, though Muhammad's teachings often contradict those of the Bible. It would appear that the prophet had not read the Scriptures for himself and had obviously heard much that was in error. Even so, he exhorted both Jews and Christians to obey the law and the gospel, and commended their teachings to Muslims. Yet there is another side to Islam (and to Muhammad) which is inconsistent, for in a number of places in the Koran Muslims are urged to kill infidels and unbelievers who refuse to submit to Islam, and it also commends breaking oaths or treaties, if they are to the Muslim's advantage.

Despite holding to the same biblical foundational principle, that of monotheism, there is still much in the Koran that conflicts with the beliefs of the Bible. The Koran, for example, denies the deity of Jesus[5] alleging that he was simply a great prophet who had been deified by his followers. It explains away his death on the cross by suggesting that another had been mistakenly crucified in his stead, which invalidates the efficacy of the atonement. It further claims that the Trinity was composed of the Father, the Virgin Mary and their child.

Spiritual Force

For the first six centuries the Church had made steady gains throughout the Western world and spread beyond the bounds of the Roman Empire. But the sudden emergence of the Arabian invaders overwhelmed large areas of Christendom. What were once traditional strongholds and highly civilised centres of Christianity were lost to Islam. Over a period of five centuries the two powers were often locked in battle and gains were made on both sides. In the eleventh century the Seljuk Turks, recent converts to Islam, overran much of Asia Minor, Syria and Palestine. It was partly for this reason that the Crusades were launched in 1095, when for a while Christianity appeared to have halted the Muslim advance.

In the fourteenth century fresh Muslim invaders, the Ottoman Turks, crossed into Europe, conquering Bulgaria, Serbia and Macedonia. The Byzantine capital, Constantinople, was finally captured in 1453 and the Byzantine empire – the bulwark of Christianity against Islam – came to an end. Islam rather than Christianity became the state religion of the Eastern Church, and the head of the Greek Orthodox Church became subject to

---

5. Written on the outside of the Dome of the Rock in Jerusalem is a statement in Arabic script which reads 'Do not say that God has a son'.

the sultan. Further advances were made the following century, when Suleiman the Magnificent reached the gates of Vienna in 1529, but was eventually driven back. With the exception of the Balkans, European civilisation and Christianity were once again saved from Muslim armies.

Growth

Throughout the conquered lands thousands of Christian communities converted to Islam; one estimate puts the figure at 90 per cent of the Church. With some, it was for economic or social advantage; for others it was preferable to being labelled *dhimmis* (i.e., non-Muslims, treated as second-class citizens). In many cases conversion was a result of compulsion. Either way, under Muslim rule the Christian churches declined in number as well as vitality.

Although the youngest of the world's major religions, Islam is today experiencing renewed growth. There is a powerful fundamentalist Islamic revival taking place and already there are several countries where fundamentalist governments are in control and the Shari'ah code of law is enforced. In other countries Islam is the state religion; the practice of Christianity is forbidden – even in private – and conversion can warrant the death sentence. All this is in sharp contrast to the liberty Muslims enjoy under Western (Christian) governments.

Behind Islam is an 'other world force', and Christians engaged in taking the gospel to Muslims have to do battle with spiritual powers of darkness in a way not often experienced. Throughout the Muslim world and beyond, attempts are being made to eliminate the Church and the influence of Christianity. In a number of countries where militant Islam prevails, churches are being looted and burnt down, while believers are either forced to convert to Islam or – in some instances – are killed.

Islam is rapidly gaining ground in America, Europe and Britain, not so much by conversion as by immigration. The Church – and governments of the West – needs to be aware of the threat. As one former missionary to Muslims has warned, 'Islam is an outward-looking, evangelistic, aggressive, militant philosophy and religion... (it is) a spiritual force, and the fanaticism of that force is not discerned by the unspiritual man.' The Muslim hope of world domination is still on course.

ISLAM TODAY
Islam is the fastest-growing, non-Christian religion in the world with nearly two 1,200 million adherents, a fact that in some areas is due more to a higher birth rate than to conversions. More nations are accepting Islam as their state religion,

including Afghanistan, Algeria, Bangladesh, Egypt, Malaysia, Morocco and Pakistan. And more Islamic nations are coming under the control of fundamentalist Muslim governments, the most notable being Iran, Libya, the Sudan and parts of Nigeria. Increasingly, Islamic law is being implemented. This means that proselytism is not allowed, and anyone allegedly blaspheming the prophet Muhammad will face the death penalty, as will anyone who converts to another religion.

The largest Muslim nation in the world is Indonesia, and of its 180 million citizens 87 per cent is said to belong to Islam. The nation is in the process of becoming an Islamic state and government policies are weighted in favour of Muslims. Restrictions are placed on Christian meetings and outreach, and in recent years the Christian minority has suffered terrible persecution. Yet the Church is growing stronger as the number of new believers continues to rise, a result of Christian witness under the pressure of persecution.

In recent years the number of refugees fleeing Muslim countries for the Christian West (rather than to affluent Islamic countries) has been on the increase. France now has a Muslim population of over five million, while the UK has two million (2001 census), many of them coming from Third World countries formerly ruled by Britain, but also from Iraq, Afghanistan, Iran and Pakistan. At the same time, an increasing number of ethnic Britons have converted to Islam in recent years. (The current figure stands at about 20,000.) In the UK there are now more than 1,800 mosques and prayer houses, and 3,000 Koranic schools in the UK.

14

988 THE CHRISTIANISATION OF 'RUSSIA'

The Quest For a New Religion

Can a nation be 'Christianised' in a day? To the Protestant mind, where conversion is thought of in terms of an individual act of dedication, the idea of a whole people turning to Christ at the command of a ruler seems inconceivable. Yet in 988 Prince Vladimir of Kiev, in the Ukraine, ordered his subjects to gather at the River Dnieper to receive the rite of baptism, thereby establishing Christianity as the religion of Kievan Russia.

The cradle of Christianity was the southern city of Kiev, in the state of Rus, which came to prominence towards the end of the ninth century. Its rulers were Varangians (or Russes) who had been invited by the quarelling Slavic tribes to enter the region and restore order. In 882 they occupied the city of Kiev and brought the Slavic tribes under their control. Although a pagan people, there may have been a Christian presence in the land for several centuries. Legend has it that between AD50–60 the apostle Andrew visited the region, then known as Scythia, and made converts.[1] Then, as the state of Kiev bordered on the ancient world of Greece, Rome and Byzantium, several bishoprics were established in the fourth century among the Greek colonies along the Black Sea. Nevertheless, the Faith did not take root, and it was not until the ninth century that more favourable conditions existed for the gospel.

It was quite likely that Christianity was reintroduced into the region following the evangelisation of the Slavic tribes by the missionaries Cyril and Methodius (c860). There may have been a diocese of the Byzantine Church at Kiev as early as 867; and there was at least one church in the city

---

1. The region is mentioned by Paul in Colossians 3:11.

early the following century. There were known converts among the Kievan merchants, knights and soldiers, and it appears there was even a number of believers at court. It was possibly from them that the Princess Olga learned of the Faith, though she did not declare her belief until some years after her husband's death.

Princess Olga

Olga was the wife of the ruling prince, Igor (913–945), and ruled Kiev after her husband was killed in battle. In c955, at the age of sixty-seven, she journeyed to Constantinople to visit the Byzantine emperor, Constantine VII, where she was taught the doctrines of the Orthodox Church; she was baptised, and declared her new Faith. On her return journey she preached the gospel in towns and villages when, it was said, 'she shone like the moon by night, and was radiant among the infidels like a pearl in the mire.'

Though Olga's son, Prince Svyatoslav, refused to accept Christianity, her grandson, Prince Vladimir (973–1015), eventually adopted the Faith, a decision partly motivated by political considerations. Vladimir was a ruthless leader; he strengthened the authority of the Kievan state, extended its boundaries and subdued neighbouring warlike tribes. During the early years of his reign he built a number of pagan temples, which led to a strong pagan revival in Kiev.

Religious Quest

The story of his quest for a new religion is part legend,[2] but was actuated by the visit to his court (c986) of a delegation of Bulgars (from the region of Bulgaria) who were Muslims. 'Though you are a wise and prudent prince, you have no religion. Adopt our Faith and revere Muhammad,' they implored him. When Vladimir enquired the nature of their religion, they spoke of their belief in God and mentioned some of the practices demanded of them as followers, including that of abstaining from alcohol. Vladimir listened, but was not attracted by what he heard, for 'drink is the joy of Russians'.

This visit was followed by representatives from other religious groups, each one intent on persuading the prince to adopt their Faith. A group of Germans came as emissaries of the (Western) Catholic Church, but he had little patience for their idea of fasting. These were followed by Jews of the Khazar tribe. When he learned that their race had been defeated and they were without a state, the prince demanded, 'How can you hope to teach

---

2. The story is told in the *Primary Chronicles*, a document written about the year 1100.

others while you yourselves are cast out and scattered abroad by the hand of God? If God loved you and your Faith, you would not be thus dispersed... Do you expect us to accept that fate also?'

Finally there came a scholar from Greece who was of the Eastern Orthodox Church. The Greek spoke of Jesus as God incarnate, who was crucified, rose again and ascended to heaven. The news that God should have descended to earth and endured such pain aroused the prince's interest and he agreed to hear the Bible story. Even so, Vladimir remained uncommitted. 'I shall wait yet a little longer', he concluded, for he wished to enquire further about all the Faiths. On the advice of his leading nobles and city elders he chose ten 'good and wise men' to conduct an investigation. 'If you desire to make certain,' they said, 'you have servants at your disposal. Send them to inquire about the ritual of each and how each one worships God.'

The emissaries set off, first to observe the Bulgars, then to view the German's ceremonies, and finally to examine the Orthodox Faith. (There is no mention of a visit to a Jewish synagogue.) At Constantinople, when the Byzantine emperor discovered the nature of their visit, he felt honoured. He ordered the patriarch to prepare the church and the clergy, and to array himself in his sacerdotal robes, so that the Russes might behold the glory of the God of the Greeks.

The 6th century Church of St Sophia, Constantinople (Istanbul), visited by Vladimir's emissaries. It is now a museum.

EASTERN ORTHODOXY

The Eastern Orthodox Church embraces both the Greek and the Russian Orthodox Churches. The term 'Eastern' connects with the division of the eastern half of the Roman Empire; 'Orthodox' is associated with correct doctrine, but also includes 'correct worship'. In fact, the name of the religion in Slavonic, *Pravoslavie*, means 'true worship' or 'right glory', which emphasises the centrality of the liturgy. The full title implies it is the true Church of Christ and points to the Church as the heir of the ancient traditional Faith.

The Eastern Orthodox consists of a family of Churches, mostly in Eastern Europe. Whilst each one is independent in its internal administration, all share the same faith and acknowledge the primacy of the Patriarch of Constantinople. From the ninth century onwards there was an increasing tension between Constantinople and Rome. Though the final breach with the Roman Church is usually dated as 1054, it was not until the fifteenth century that the two Churches went their different ways.

It is for this reason that an orthodox service is said to reflect 'true worship': the priest is arrayed in royal vestments (to represent the royal presence of the Lord Jesus) and incense is used (representing the presence of the Holy Spirit). The liturgy contains a synopsis of Christ's life, and all the major events are recalled through symbolic actions. The church building is adorned with icons – said to be 'windows of heaven' – which are intended to help worshippers focus on the invisible God, as well as to serve for didactic purposes.

Splendour and Beauty

The emperor accompanied the visitors to the church, calling their attention to the beauty of the building, the chanting and the services, and explained the worship of his God. The Russians returned to their own country full of praise for the Greek ceremonies, saying, 'We know not whether we were in heaven or on earth. For on earth there is no such splendour or such beauty, and we are at a loss how to describe it. We only know that God dwells there among men, and their service is fairer than the ceremonies of other nations.'

Vladimir's nobles responded, 'If the Greek Faith were evil, it would not have been adopted by your grandmother Olga, who was wiser than all men.' Despite the favourable report, the prince delayed his decision, intending to resume his religious quest after carrying out a siege of the Byzantine city of Kherson. Yet he was obviously impressed with the Christians' God, for he told the Almighty that should he end up capturing the city, he would be baptised in gratitude for his help.

When the city fell to his army, Vladimir made a bid for the hand of the emperor's sister, Anna. His hope was that by such a marriage he would cement his possession of the city and ensure a peaceful co-existence with the Byzantine empire. At the time, the prince was suffering from an eye disease which seriously impaired his vision. Anna told him that if he desired to be healed, then he should be baptised, otherwise he would not be cured. 'If this proves true,' he declared, 'then of a surety is the God of the Christians great.' Vladimir submitted to baptism, and as the bishop laid hands on him he straight received his sight. Upon experiencing this miracle, the prince glorified God – 'I have now perceived the one true God.'

Mass Baptism

Back in Kiev, he ordered that all idols should be destroyed. Heralds were despatched throughout the whole city to announce that all inhabitants had to present themselves at the River Dnieper for baptism, or risk the prince's displeasure. When the people heard of it, they exclaimed, 'If this were not good, the prince and his nobles would not have accepted it.'

On the following day, a large number of people gathered at the river for the occasion, together with the prince and the priests of the princess. The people went into the water; some waded out, up to their necks, while others with children in their arms stayed nearer the bank. The priests stood by and offered prayers. It was said that 'there was joy in heaven and upon earth to see so many souls saved', while the Devil lamented, 'Woe is me ... my reign in these regions is at an end.'

Not everyone presented themselves for baptism, and it is admitted that there was some use of coercion and some rebelled. But for the most part, the conversion to Christianity came quickly and painlessly, though initially it may have only gained a superficial hold upon the people. Nevertheless, the mass baptism in the Dnieper signalled the beginning of the Orthodox Faith as the state religion of Kiev and, ultimately, of Russia.

Under Vladimir, Christianity spread to other towns; just as previously he had strengthened the pagan religion, so now he devoted his efforts to building up the Byzantine religion. The preaching was especially helped by the fact that the message was delivered in a Slavic tongue akin to the people's own. Churches were built; schools were established throughout the realm, so that people could learn to read the Scriptures; welfare institutions were opened for care of the needy; and the death penalty was abolished.

Eastern Christianity

It is important to be aware that Russia adopted Eastern rather than Western Christianity, that its spiritual and cultural inspiration came from Constantinople rather than Rome. The result was Russia's relative isolation from the West and the development of a Christianity that took Byzantium as its model. The use of local languages rather than Latin understandably made the new religion more inviting and gave a powerful impetus towards the creation of a national culture. Ultimately, the establishment of a state religion contributed towards the unification of the tribes and was the basis for the founding of modern Russia.

There gradually emerged a distinctive church architecture and art, with the pervasive presence of icons,[3] and with priests and bishops arrayed in vestments more reminiscent of royalty. Monasticism made its appearance in the eleventh century, stressing the social ideal of service and promoting education, while the Church obtained vast holdings of land. A written Russian language emerged which gave birth to the development of both religious and secular literature. When the Kievan period came to a close in 1240 (when the city was destroyed by the Mongols), it left behind a rich legacy of religion, culture, and political and social institutions.

Following Vladimir's baptism, the Kievan Church was established as a special see with a metropolitan. His son and successor (1019–1054) built a cathedral, dedicated to St Sophia and named after the one in Constantinople. The see formed part of the patriarchate of Constantinople and was consequently subject to its authority. The metropolitans were Greeks, chosen by Constantinople.

When a breach occurred in 1054 between the Byzantium Church and the Latin (Western) Church, the Russian Church took the side of the East. It was not until the fifteenth century that the Russian Church broke free of Byzantium and elected its own metropolitans. Complete freedom was finally achieved in 1453, when the Turks captured Constantinople; Moscow emerged as the world's leading Orthodox city and became known as 'the third Rome'.

THE EAST-WEST SPLIT

Following the collapse of the Roman Empire in the early Middle Ages, there were two main centres of Christianity: Rome under the pope and Constantinople under the patriarch. A growing hostility developed between the two groups which finally led to a complete separation between the Eastern (Orthodox) and Western (Latin) Churches.

One disagreement arose in the eighth century over the use by the Eastern Church of icons (sacred pictures of Christ, the Virgin Mother and the Saints), often treated with veneration because they were believed that through them the

---

3. Icons are stylised religious portraits, either painted or carved, usually of Christ, the apostles or saints.

saints could exercise beneficient powers. A further strain on relations arose on a matter of doctrine, when the West amended the Nicene Creed (325) to state that the Holy Spirit proceeded from both the Father and the Son, while the Eastern Church spoke of the Spirit as proceeding from the Father **through** the Son.

Other differences were seemingly ordinary concerns: Latin was the language of the Roman Church and Greek in the East; there were also differences in forms of worship, and for the Eucharist the Westerns used unleavened bread against the Eastern use of leavened bread. In the East the clergy were allowed to marry, whereas in the West they were compelled (theoretically at least) to be celibate.

In the eleventh century there was a renewed call from the West for papal authority over the whole of Christianity, based on the belief that the pope was the successor of the apostle Peter, a claim rejected by the East. An attempt by the papacy (in 1054) to excommunicate the Patriarch of Constantinople failed (an event which in later years was supposed to have marked the division between the two Churches), and tensions continued to increase. The split finally came in 1453 when Muslim Turks overran the Byzantine empire and captured Constantinople.

In 1721 Tsar Peter the Great, anxious to subjugate the Church to his authority, abolished the office of patriarch. He replaced it with a Holy Synod, set up to supervise the Church, with members chosen by himself. When the patriarchate was restored in 1917, following the tsar's abdication, the Russian Orthodox Church seemed about to enter a new era when its former glory would be restored.

But the Bolshevik revolution later that same year put an end to this hope, as the new government was determined to destroy the Church and abolish religion. With the exception of a lull during the Second World War, there followed a period of seventy years of persecution. Thousands of Orthodox churches were either destroyed or secularised, many religious activities were outlawed, bishops and priests were killed, and thousands of ordinary Christians martyred.

With the approach of the Church's millennium in 1988, however, the government's attitude moderated. Under the banner of *glasnost* ('openness'), Secretary Gorbachev supported the planned celebrations: a few Orthodox churches were reopened, Bibles were allowed to be imported, believers were released from labour camps and the voices of Christian spokesmen were heard in the media.

The collapse of Communism in 1991 brought an end to the persecution, and freedom of religion – already written into the Constitution – became a reality. Citizens could openly practise their religion, evangelism was allowed once more, and Jewish people were permitted to emigrate to Israel. But already there are signs this situation could worsen:[4] the Orthodox Church is endeavouring to have evangelism outlawed[5] and emigration to Israel is under threat. The Iron Curtain could easily fall again.

---

4. Legislation passed in 1997 made illegal any free church formed in the previous fifteen years. This left only the Russian Orthodox Church, together with Buddhism, Hinduism and Judaism free to operate within the law.
5. Local authorities are to decide whether or not to implement the law, and there is little evdence so far to indicate how the law is being enforced.

15

1095 POPE URBAN II LAUNCHES THE FIRST CRUSADE

Battle For the Holy Land

A new force appeared in the Middle East in the eleventh century. The Seljuk Turks, a nomadic tribe from the steppes of central Asia, recently converted to Sunni Islam, swept through Afghanistan, Iran and Mesopotamia. They heavily defeated the Byzantian army at Manzikert in 1071 and came within striking distance of the capital, Constantinople. By 1092 they had added Syria – including much of the Holy Land – to their conquests, so that within a space of fifty years they had carved out a formidable empire. Reports that the holy places had been plundered aroused the wrath of Christian Europe, and Pope Urban II's call for a crusade against the Muslims was greeted with enthusiasm.

Since the rise of Islam in the seventh century, when Muslim forces conquered many of the Christian lands around the Mediterranean, pilgrimages to the Holy Land had become an increasingly hazardous undertaking. By the tenth century the situation was more settled and travel overland was easier, attracting a greater number of pilgrims to Jerusalem. But the Seljuks desecrated the holy places and prevented pilgrims from reaching Jerusalem, causing considerable alarm in the Western Church.

In the Middle Ages pilgrimages formed an essential feature of Christianity. Jerusalem had begun to assume a greater significance in the thinking of many pious Christians, especially as it was expected that Jesus would return 1,000 years after his death and resurrection, and that the Day of Judgment would take place in Jerusalem. Thus pilgrimages to the Holy City acquired an even greater importance.

The Byzantine emperor, who had so far endeavoured to protect the pilgrims travelling to the Holy Land, was powerless to act against the Turks. With his treasury bankrupt and unable to halt the Seljuk advance, Emperor Alexius I sent an envoy to Pope Urban II in March 1095, pleading for help to repel the invaders.

Deus Vult!

It was not until the following November, at the Council of Clermont (France), that the pope finally made his response. Standing outside the eastern gate of the city he preached a momentous sermon that was to launch the first crusade. 'From the confines of Jerusalem and from the city of Constantinople a horrible tale has gone forth,' he declared. 'An accursed race utterly alienated from God ... has invaded lands of the Christians and depopulated them by the sword, plundering and fire... Start upon the road to the Holy Sepulchre, to tear that land from the wicked race and subject it to yourselves!' The appeal stirred the people and was received with cries of '*Deus vult! Deus Vult!*' ('God wills it!'), a response which Urban made the crusaders' battle cry.

The pope's call to Western knights to recover Jerusalem and liberate the Eastern Church was backed by a plenary indulgence to all those who enlisted. It included remission of all sins, plus direct entry into heaven or reduced time in purgatory. He urged those who wished to save their soul not to hesitate to follow the way of the Lord. Debtors were guaranteed security, while the pope would protect their property, wives and children during their absence. And if any lacked money, then divine mercy would provide.

There followed a year-long preaching tour of France by the pope's representatives, which caused great excitement throughout the land. Many knights joined the crusade, drawn to it not only by the offer of spiritual benefits, but also by the added attraction of adventure and the prospect of acquiring lands and riches. When they 'took the cross' it was signified by a red cross (hence the title 'crusade', derived from the word 'cross') sewn on the breast or shoulders.

Other preachers took up the call to arms, notably Peter the Hermit, a monk from Amiens, whose appeal was mostly to peasants and townspeople. When he told of the alleged ill-treatment of pilgrims by Muslims it aroused the anger of the masses. Looking forward to the kingdom of heaven which the poor were expected to inherit, large numbers of them joined together to march on the Holy Land. In addition to the many able-bodied men, there were non-combatants such as clerics, women and even children. Their ranks were further swelled by an element of undesirable characters, encouraged by the prospect of immunity from arrest.

The Journey

Over 100,000 pilgrims, including around 10,000 knights who provided the leadership, set off for the Holy Land. Although the starting date set by the pope was 15 August, Peter the Hermit's largely untrained – and unofficial – band made an early departure. Only eight knights and their soldiers, led by Walter Sansavoir of Poissy, joined his party; the remainder consisted of an unarmed crowd carrying palms and crosses on their shoulders. Known as the People's Crusade, the party left Rouen in the spring of 1096, and robbed and pillaged their away across Europe. By August they had reached Constantinople, the agreed meeting point for all the crusaders, only to be massacred by the Seljuk army. The armies of the third wave met with a similar fate.

'CHRIST-KILLERS'

The second wave of pilgrims to set off for the Holy Land was a most disreputable mob. Although the main target of their wrath was the Muslims, the pilgrims felt there was no need to wait until they reached Palestine before beginning their crusade, as there were 'Christ-killers' along the route. There were sizeable Jewish communities in the Rhineland towns of Cologne, Worms, Mainz, Speyer and Trier, and they were attacked without mercy.

At Speyer the Jews were fortunately forewarned of the plan to attack them and only eleven Jews were killed. Around 500 Jews were murdered in their homes at Worms; a further 300 who were given refuge by the bishop were given a choice of either baptism or death: many of them chose to die. At Mainz about 1,300 Jews died in an act of mass suicide. Many paid bribes in the hope of being left alone, but often to no avail.

Throughout the Rhineland around 10,000 Jews were slaughtered, including women and children, as well as others in Hungary and Bohemia. Homes and synagogues were robbed of great sums of money and possessions, then destroyed. Whilst the intention was partly to obtain money and food for the journey, equally compelling was the claim of vengeance for the death of Christ.

This last wave was composed of trained soldiers, and included both French and German knights. They met at Consantinople, from where some 60,000 horsemen, plus a large horde of men on foot, crossed the Bosporus into Asia Minor. Nicaea, the first major city under Muslim control that lay in the path of the Crusaders, was captured in June 1096.

At this point the main party, under the command of Godfrey of Bouillon, son of Count Eustace of Boulogne, divided into two sections. They struggled on towards Jerusalem with increasingly depleted numbers, suffering in the intense heat from constant thirst and hunger, as well as from desertion. The county of Edessa was captured in March 1098 and, at the invitation of the inhabitants, a Crusader kingdom was set up under Baldwin of Boulogne. The remaining forces pressed on towards Antioch, which held out for nine months before a Muslim commander succumbed to bribery and opened one of the gates. Despite the victory, a large number of crusaders lost their lives in the seige, largely due to famine and desertion.

The Holy City

The remnant amounted to less than 40,000 crusaders, most of whom were ordinary men and women still hoping to complete their pilgrimage to the Holy City. By 7 June 1099 they were camped outside the walls of Jerusalem, preparing for a long seige. The numbers were by now further reduced to around 1,500 knights and 15,000 foot-soldiers. Attempts to storm the city failed and seige engines were made with which to scale the walls.

Early on the morning of 15 July an all-out attack was launched on the city. Once over the walls, the Muslim emir (ruler) readily surrendered to the Christian attackers and opened the gates next to David's Tower. The crusaders poured into the city and chased the Saracens[1] as far as the Temple Mount (on which stood the Dome of the Rock), and following their policy of 'taking no prisoners' killed all who crossed their path.

It was here that the Muslims made a last stand, but they were finally overcome by superior forces. Men and women were put to the sword in a most cruel manner, though some managed to escape. In one place Jews were driven into a synagogue and the building set alight. One eyewitness recorded that 'such was the slaughter that we were up to our ankles in their blood'. It is said that 70,000 Muslims and Jews were massacred in the city.

By the end of the day Jerusalem was unexpectedly in the hands of the crusaders, and the pilgrims 'came rejoicing and weeping for joy to worship at the church of the Holy Sepulchre'. Another eyewitness wrote, 'Once the city had been captured it was most rewarding to see the devotion of the pilgrims before the Holy Sepulchre; how they clapped in exultation, singing a new song to the Lord.'

1. Nomadic Arabs of the Syrian desert.

Christian Kingdom

Eight days later Godfrey of Bouillon was elected to rule the new Christian Kingdom of Jerusalem. He refused the title 'king', or to wear a crown in the city where Christ had been crowned with thorns; instead he was known as 'Protector of the Holy Sepulchre'. When he died a year later he was succeeded by his more ambitious brother, Baldwin I, who readily took the title 'King of Jerusalem', and was crowned on Christmas Day, 1100. A new royal palace was built on the Temple Mount and another one near the Tower of David.

Remains of an arched street in the Crusader city of Caesarea, where a great mosque was demolished and replaced by a cathedral.

Three other Christian kingdoms were also established, along the Mediterranean coast: the County of Edessa, the Principality of Antioch and the County of Tripoli. Whilst many of the pilgrims chose to return home after reaching Jerusalem, others settled in the new kingdoms, though only a few of them were knights. They adopted Eastern culture and learned to co-exist with their Muslim neighbours.

For the first time in 450 years Jerusalem was in Christian hands. Immediately a re-building programme was set up to restore the holy places. Despite the Muslim occupation several Churches had maintained a presence in the city: the Armenians, Copts, Nestorians, Syrian Jacobites and – the most powerful of all the groups – the Greek Orthodox. Now a Latin patriarch was established in Jerusalem and Antioch, with a network of bishoprics and Catholic clergy. Churches and monasteries were erected on sites connected with the life of Jesus; others that had been destroyed were repaired.

On the Temple Mount, the Dome of the Rock and the El Aqsa Mosque were taken over as places of Christian worship; the Dome of the Rock, renamed the Temple of the Lord, had a large golden cross placed on the roof. The Church of the Holy Sepulchre was considerably enlarged, a building project that took some fifty years to complete.

From the time of their first conquests in the Near East the crusaders built castles to defend their new kingdoms. Over a hundred are known to have been constructed, most of them entrusted into the hands of two newly established orders of soldier-monks, the Knights of St John and the Knights Templar, founded to fight the enemies of Christendom.

HOSPITALLERS AND TEMPLARS

Support for the Crusades was provided by the Hospitallers and the Templars two military orders which combined chivalry with monasticism. The Knights Hospitaller were founded in the mid-eleventh century, with their headquarters in the Church of St John the Baptist, Jerusalem. Known as Knights of St John, their aim was to provide hospitality for pilgrims and to care for the sick who reached the Holy Land. Its hospital in Jerusalem had beds for 2,000 patients, cared for by four doctors and four surgeons. After the fall of Acre in 1291 they escaped to Cyprus and later conquered Rhodes where they established their headquarters. They moved to Malta in 1530.

The Knights Templar were formed in 1118 by a group of French knights who bound themselves by a solemn vow to protect pilgrims on the road to Jerusalem. They were given quarters on the Temple Mount (hence their title), and their call for moral strength, chastity and integrity made them the most renowned knights of Christ. In the recriminations that followed the loss of the Holy Land, the Templars were falsely accused by Philip IV of France. The pope suppressed the Order in 1312 and gave their lands to the Hospitallers. In England the Hospitallers' property was sequestrated by Henry VIII in 1540, but the Grand Priory was revived in 1831. It led to the foundation of the St John Ambulance Association in 1878 and the St John Ambulance Brigade in 1888.

Later Crusades

Despite the success of the first crusade, the battle for the Holy Land continued until the end of the thirteenth century. A Muslim revival led to the recapture of Edessa and threatened the Kingdom of Jerusalem. A second crusade was launched in 1147, stirred by the preaching of Bernard of Clairvaux, though he disavowed any attempt to put Jews to the sword. It was heavily defeated at Damascus in 1148, leaving a bitter feeling in the West towards the Eastern Empire.

Towards the middle of the century there emerged a powerful Muslim leader, Saladin, a Kurd from northern Iraq, whose forces surrounded the crusader kingdoms. His army of around 30,000 was superior to that of the Christians, and in June 1187 he inflicted a heavy defeat on them at the Horns of Hittim, twin hills to the west of Tiberias, in Galilee. He went on to take Jerusalem, dealing the Christians a more devastating blow and captured over fifty Crusader castles.

Other crusades followed, including the infamous Childrens' Crusade (1212) from France and western Germany, led by a German shepherd boy. Thousands of ten to eighteen year olds set off for the Holy Land, but got no further than the port of embarkation. Further expeditions were a dismal failure, and when Acre, the last Christian stronghold in Syria, fell in 1291 the crusades to the Holy Land were virtually over.

Although the term 'crusade' usually refers to the wars fought to recover the Holy Land, it also embraces the struggle against the Muslims in Europe as well as pagans in the lands of the eastern Baltic, heretical groups,[2] and even orthodox Christians and political opponents of the popes.

After the thirteenth century interest in crusades gradually waned, though they did not finally die out until the eighteenth century. That the crusades did not succeed was due to a number of factors, not least the rise to power of a number of strong Muslim rulers; bad organisation and disunity among the European national armies also contributed to the failure. Yet the crusades were not without their critics, and the thirteenth century philosopher Raymond Lull, who devoted himself to the conversion of Islam, argued strongly in favour of a peaceful mission.

Effects

The crusades deeply damaged the Western Church's relations with other religious groups. Despite Bernard of Clairvaux's plea, Jews were once again made to suffer at the hands of Christians. And the uneasy alliance between the Eastern and Western Churches reached its lowest ebb following the sack of Constantinople by the knights of the Fourth Crusade, in 1204. The importance of the papacy increased, however, as the crusaders were soldiers of the pope who alone could remit their vows.

The Holy Land served as a springboard for missionary activity, and from here the Latin Church sent out emissaries to Asia and, eventually, India and China. Trade with the Near East greatly prospered as a result of

---

2. e.g. the 13th century crusade against the Albigenes (Cathars) of Southern Frace.

the wars, and the cities of northern Italy – particularly Venice and Genoa – enjoyed considerable revenues. Acre and Tyre became centres for exporting textiles, foodstuff and armaments (despite ecclesiastical protests) to the Muslims, while medicaments, silks, pepper, cotton and sugar were sent to western Europe. At the same time, cultural links were established with the ancient civilisations of the East, and interest in travel, map-making and exploration increased.

The most devastating effect was the further deterioration of Jewish-Christian relations, though even worse was to follow – expulsion from their adopted homelands, anti-Semitic laws, the Inquisition, the ghetto, pogroms, the Holocaust. Throughout all these years the Church played a prominent role, for much of the suffering was perpetrated in the name of Christ. It is only in more recent years that Christians have begun to repent for the Church's treatment of their 'blood-brothers' and to make an effort to mend the broken relationship.

16

1173 THE WALDENSIAN MOVEMENT BEGINS

The First Evangelical Church

More than three centuries before the Reformation a movement dedicated to maintaining the apostolic faith was to be found in the alpine valleys of north-west Italy. Sometimes known as the 'oldest evangelical Church', the Waldenses were a group of believers originally within the Roman Church, whose aim was to restore the gospel to its rightful place and bring about a spiritual renewal throughout Christendom. Condemned by Rome as an heretical sect, they endured hardship and savage persecution, but emerged under God as heralds of the Protestant Reformation.

The spiritual life of the Church during the Middle Ages had sunk to a low ebb, and priests and monks were characterised more by moral corruption and idleness rather than by a desire to serve God. From the tenth century there emerged a variety of dissident movements which rejected the false teachings of Rome while endeavouring to return to a simpler form of worship and lifestyle. Not all of them were orthodox in their beliefs.

Foremost among the heretical groups were the Cathars (Greek *katharoi*, 'pure ones'), known in southern France as Albigenses. They flourished in western Europe in the twelfth and thirteenth centuries and emerged as a powerful threat to Catholicism. The Waldenses were another group charged with heresy, a result of their desire to live according to Scripture and to follow the example of Christ and his disciples.

Follow Me

The beginning of the movement owes its origin to Peter Valdes (or Waldo), a wealthy merchant from the French city of Lyons who had made his fortune by money-lending. Early in the 1170s Valdes heard a wandering troubadour singing about St Alexis, a rich fourth century Roman nobleman who had abandoned his wealth and dedicated himself to serving God.

Impressed by the legend, he felt moved to seek after God for himself. 'What is the best and surest way to God?' he asked a theologian. In reply, he was directed to the words of Christ to the rich young ruler: 'If you would be perfect, go and sell what you have, give to the poor and you shall have treasure in heaven. Then come and follow me' (Matt. 19:21). To Valdes, the words came to him as a direct command from the Lord and he determined to put them into practice.

Taking a vow of poverty, he first provided for his wife and family then distributed the rest of his estate among the poor, with the exception of monies he retained for a special purpose. In the Middle Ages, the act of renouncing the world was associated with entering the religious life of a monastic order in order to merit salvation. But for Valdes, after his decision to follow Christ, poverty was an essential element of his Christian discipleship.

Unable to read Latin, Valdes employed two friendly priests to translate Scripture from the Vulgate into his own Franco-provencal language, so that he could know what God had to say to him personally. He then had several books of the Bible translated and began to learn whole passages by heart. As he distributed food in the streets of Lyons, he recited aloud the scriptures he had learned and spoke of his personal experience in finding salvation. People were excited to hear the words of the Bible in their own language, rather than in the Latin heard at mass.

The Poor of Lyons

He soon gathered round him a group of men and women who, like himself, renounced their material possessions and gave themselves to prayer and study. Known at first as 'The Poor of Lyons', they went out in strict observance of Christ's directions to the Seventy, moving around in pairs, wearing sandals, preaching repentance, and exhorting people to return to the purity and simplicity of the first believers.

Hearing of their activities, the Archbishop of Lyons threatened Valdes and forbade him to preach. His reply was the one given by the apostles Peter and John in similar circumstances, that it was better to obey God rather than man. Nevertheless, his refusal to be silent was tantamount to open rebellion and he and his followers were forced to leave Lyons. Some of them reached as far as Germany and Spain, but the majority were scattered around southern France (mainly Provence) and parts of northern Italy (Lombardy), regions where the Cathars were firmly entrenched, Lorraine, Flanders and even as far as England.

Forbidden to preach, in 1179 Valdes went to Rome with some of his followers to seek the help of Pope Alexander III at the Third Lateran Council. The pope accepted a copy of their Scriptures and recognised their vow of poverty. As laymen, however, they were not allowed to preach unless requested to do so by their archbishop, an instruction they were unable to heed. They were consequently excommunicated at the Synod of Verona (1184), presided over by Pope Lucius III.

In Italy, where they became known as the Poor Lombards, Waldensian communities were established in the cities and towns of Lombardy. Around 1230, however, when threatened by the Inquisition, they moved to the valleys of the Cottian Alps of Piedmont, south-west of Turin, where they hoped to live out their faith in peace.

Valdes probably died in 1206, but the movement that bore his name continued to grow. Between the thirteenth and fifteenth centuries it expanded to reach from the Mediterranean to the Baltic, from southern Italy to the Low Countries, becoming strongest in central and eastern Europe, especially Poland and Hungary. The rapid increase in their numbers caused the papacy some alarm. Attempts to reconvert them failed and they were branded as heretics. At the Fourth Lateran Council (1215) they were again excommunicated and became the object of a crusade.

Heresies

From the thirteenth century the movement began to take on a more definite form and ripened into a distinctly organised Church which foreshadowed the Reformation. It divided into three groups: the French, the Italians and the German/Slavs. By the sixteenth century the valleys on the Italian side of the Cottian Alps had become the chief home of the Waldenses. It was here where the greatest suffering was experienced.

The two chief heresies with which they were charged was preaching the Bible without authority and rejecting the clergy's role as mediators. They also repudiated purgatory, indulgences and masses for the dead, holy water and liturgies, and denied the efficacy of sacraments administered by unworthy priests. However, for a time they continued with certain Catholic doctrines, such as the confession, absolution and the mass.

At the heart of their faith was the principle that the Bible – and especially the New Testament – was the sole rule of belief and life. Their chief desire was to be faithful to the words of Jesus and, above all, the Sermon on the Mount.

Each community was under a pastor, trained at a Waldensian college, and supported by a group of laymen. Known as *barbas*, a Piedmontese word meaning 'uncle', they also worked as itinerant pastors, visiting the scattered Waldensian communities throughout Europe. They made two or three visits a year, leaving their home ministry in the care of a lay deputy.

A layman preaching to peasants and shepherds in 13th century France. Based on a painting of 1251 and reproduced here from a 15th century manuscript.

Meeting in secluded woods or caves, the barbas preached to the faithful, instructing them and receiving confessions, and held assemblies to discuss their problems. They were also concerned to preach the gospel. Unable to do so openly, they went about in twos under the guise of pedlars or some other trade,[1] and in this way were afforded opportunities to offer 'the pearl of great price'.

There was an annual synod, composed of an equal number of ministers and lay members. Their function was to hear reports from the barbas and decide where each pair should visit; the barbas brought the money they had collected and it was then decided how it should be distributed. The synod also consecrated candidates to the ministry.

Persecution

As a result of their stand on the Bible, the Waldenses continued to attract the wrath of the Church. The Fourth Lateran Council was responsible for

---

1. One very important 'trade' was the practice of medicine and surgery, which especially opened doors of opportunity for the gospel.

setting up the Inquisition, which called upon bishops to root out heresy and punish heretics. The terms were further enforced at a synod at Toulouse (in 1229), the centre of the Albigensian heresy, while at the Council of Valencia men who were not priests were forbidden to read the Bible.

Over the following centuries the Waldenses were subject to long periods of persecution. From 1380–1393 Waldensian communities on both the Italian and French sides of the Alps were attacked. On Christmas Eve, 1386, an army was despatched to the Valley of Pragelato, Piedmont, where 150 people – including 50 children – were killed in one night and their villages put to the torch. On another occasion, 400 women and children sheltered in a cave while their men were away. When the hiding-place was discovered, a fire was lit at the entrance to the cave and everyone inside perished.

Despite the onslaught, the Waldenses remained firm. In some areas they camouflaged their faith by outwardly remaining Catholics. To avoid suspicions, they attended the obligatory mass three times a year and made an annual confession. At the beginning of the fifteenth century they were encouraged by the movement under John Hus of Prague, who had been influenced by the teachings of John Wyclif. His followers, known as the Bohemian Brethren, became associated with the Waldenses; the two movements joined hands, inspiring each other with a fresh vitality.

Some time after 1518 news reached the Waldenses of the work of Martin Luther and the new reform movement arising in Germany. They recognised that the reformers based their teachings on the Bible, and from their annual reunion in Piedmont in 1526 the barbas sent a delegation to evaluate the movement and to question the leaders. Further contact was made with Swiss reformers, including William Farel, in 1530, when two representatives were sent from Provence. Whilst they discovered that a unity of purpose did exist, especially with reference to belief in the Scriptures, they admitted that in some respects Waldensian biblical interpretation had been faulty.

Watershed

Anxious for a fuller knowledge, a synod held in 1532 at Chanforan in the Angrogna Valley was attended by 140 barbas, along with Swiss leaders of the Reformation, led by Farel. Farel persuaded the Waldenses to accept the principles of the new reformation and to apply them to their own movement. He also urged the synod to commission a translation of the Bible into French, a task completed in two years by Olivetan, a cousin of Calvin.[2] Following a controversial debate, the Confession of Chanforan was drawn up by church leaders of the valleys of the Piedmont, by which the Waldenses became part of the reformed tradition.

By declaring for the reformers, the Waldenses were acknowledging their unity with the search for a faith based on the gospel. The decision also had social and political significance, and marked the beginning of a new expression of independence and autonomy. It was, as the Waldensian Church historian, Prescot Stephens, has observed, 'a spiritual, doctrinal and historical watershed for the Waldensian movement'.

For a while the new-found freedom allowed the Waldenses to emerge from secrecy and begin open-air preaching. Crowds gathered to hear them, so that buildings had to be erected to shelter them from the elements. The first church was built in 1555, the same year that trained pastors arrived from Geneva and began to replace the travelling barbas. Reaction set in, however, as the civil authorities were not prepared to allow this threat to the Catholic Church.

Massacres

Persecutions continued, and the movement was virtually wiped out in Provence in the 1540s and in southern Italy in the 1560s. Largely due to the efforts of a Protestant lady of nobility, they won a limited peace which lasted until 1665. In that year edicts were issued ordering the people to attend mass and to dismiss their pastors. A force of 5,000 troops was sent into the valleys to ensure the edicts were obeyed. On Easter eve, without warning, a massacre of Waldenses took place at Torre in the Pellice Valley, when men, women and children were cruelly put to death. Protestant Europe was horrified by the attack.

Oliver Cromwell, the Lord Protector of England, was outraged. He called for a day of fasting and prayer, and ordered a public collection for the relief of the victims; he also sent an envoy to protest to the Duke of Savoy. His secretary, the poet John Milton, wrote a poem condemning the massacre. Remarkably, the survivors regrouped and, aided by French Huguenots, successfully struck back at the enemy. The Waldenses survived and began to recover.

---

2. One of the greatest Waldensian contributions to the Church was their translation of the Bible into several vernacular languages of the day.

ON THE LATE MASSACRE IN PIEDMONT
By John Milton

Avenge, O Lord, thy slaughtered Saints, whose bones
Lie scattered on the Alpine mountains cold,
Ev'n them who kept thy truth so pure of old,
When all our Fathers worship't Stocks and Stones.

Forget not: in thy book record their groans
Who were thy sheep and in their ancient fold
Slayn by the bloody Piedmontese that roll'd
Mother with infant down the rocks. Their moans
The vales redoubl'd to the hills, and they
To heav'n. Their martyred blood and ashes sow
O're all th' Italian fields where still doth sway
The triple tryrant: that from these may grow
A hundred-fold, who having learnt thy way
Early may fly the Babylonian woe.

Yet a further attempt to enforce the Catholic religion was made thirty years later, although it was motivated more by politics than religion. King Loius XIV of France persuaded the Duke of Savoy to attack the Waldenses, who had been joined by Huguenot refugees, and an army was despatched to the alps. With the cry of 'Death rather than the mass', some 3,000 Protestants were slaughtered and others forced into exile, while many died of exposure during the harsh alpine winter.

In 1689 a band of 900 trained men from Switzerland made a surprise assault on the Waldensian valleys and, despite heavy losses, overcame the Savoy troops. At this point, the Duke of Savoy quarrelled with Louis XIV and signed a treaty allowing the Waldensians a limited religious liberty. Known as the 'Glorious Return', it paved the way for the refugees from Switzerland and Germany to go back to their homeland.

It was not until 1848, the year revolutions rocked Europe, that the Waldenses were granted civil and political rights. And while steps were taken towards religious freedom in 1860, when Italy was united under King Victor Emmanuel, it was not until recent years that full liberty was achieved. In 1979 the Waldensian and Methodist Churches of Italy united to form the Evangelical Waldensian Church.

THE WALDENSIAN CHURCH

The Waldensian Church is part of the family of Reformed Churches which profess the fundamental principle of a living Christian faith based solely on the Bible. The Church is not regarded as an organisation, but rather a community of believers saved by the grace of God. This faith is lived out in individual lives and in dedication to the service of society as a whole, as evidenced – for example – by Waldensian involvement in the Red Cross and Amnesty International.

The Church also runs youth centres, schools, hospitals and old people's homes. It maintains strong links with the Lutheran, Methodist and Baptist Churches, and runs an internationally renowned ecumenical centre called 'Agape'. It is a member of the World Council of Churches and of the Federation of Evangelical Churches in Italy.

Today there are Waldensian churches throughout Italy, from the northern alps southwards to Calabria and Sicily. It has a membership of around 30,000, half of whom live in the valleys of Piedmont. There are some 15,000 Waldenses in South America. It is a free Church, and supports the idea of the separation of Church and State.

17

1215 INNOCENT III ASSEMBLES THE FOURTH LATERAN COUNCIL

Papal Power Reaches New Heights

The Fourth Lateran Council, one of the greatest of all ecumenical councils, marks the high point of the medieval papacy. Convoked by the pope, Innocent III (1198–1216), it issued seventy canons and one crusading decree. While one of its chief objects was the reform of the Church, it is especially remembered for its two chief achievements, the declaration of Transubstantiation as orthodox doctrine and the establishment of the Inquisition as a means of combatting heresy.

Councils were a regular feature of Church life from the second century onwards. They were called to discuss doctrinal questions, to deal with heresies, to exercise discipline and generally be responsible for the good order of the Church. From the time of Constantine the Great, the first emperor to regard himself as ruler of both State and Church, Roman emperors wielded considerable influence over Church affairs. Not only did they claim the right to summon the great Councils, but also to ratify their decrees.

Authority

Over the following centuries the Church began to assume more control over its own affairs. Authority to do so was based on the recognition of the apostle Peter as 'the pillar of the Faith and the founder of the Catholic Church'. The next step was to declare the bishop of Rome as the successor and representative of Peter with the title of pope, first given to Leo the Great (in 451). Despite this regard, the Councils still held it was they, and not the pope, who had the final say in matters of doctrine and discipline.

Following the coronation by Pope Leo III of Charlemagne as the first emperor of the Holy Roman Empire (on Christmas Day, 800), the authority of the papacy was gradually in the ascendency until the pope, rather than the emperor, held power over both Church and State. Pope Gregory VII (1073–1085) claimed the right, as the Vicar of Christ and the representative of the apostle Peter, to give away empires and kingdoms, and to depose kings and to sit in judgment on their sins. But it was under Innocent III that the medieval papacy reached the height of its power and prestige.

In one memorable instance (in 1077), Emperor Henry IV – who had attempted to depose the pope – was forced to ask for clemency. Fearful of being excommunicated, for three days he stood barefoot in the wind and snow outside the papal palace at Canossa (northern Italy), dressed as a humble penitent, waiting to ask the pope's forgiveness. When he was finally allowed in he fell at the pope's feet, confessing his fault and seeking absolution.

Aristocratic Family

Innocent was born into an aristocratic family in 1160 or 1161, and was related to many noble Roman families. His original name was Lothar of Segni. He had a superb intellect and studied theology at Paris and canon law at Bologna. In 1190 Pope Clement III, possibly a relative of his, created him a cardinal deacon, during which time he wrote several theological tracts. Though not an outstanding cardinal, he was active in curial[1] matters and had a shrewd idea of the needs of the Roman Church.

Lothar was unanimously elected pope on 8 January 1198, after only two ballots; he was ordained priest on 21 February, and the following day was consecrated Bishop of Rome. A great administrator and a man with an extraordinary capacity for work, he quickly mastered the affairs of the Curia and during his pontificate wrote more than 6,000 letters, many of which were decretals (i.e., they carried the authority of law). He created a sound fiscal administration, and his pontificate was one of the few that did not experience financial difficulties.

As 'the true Vicar of Christ on earth', he often spoke of the pope's sovereign power as rooted in a spiritual power given to Peter by Christ. He claimed the right to set aside any human actions (since they were rooted in sin) and to intervene in temporal affairs, though only with those kingdoms

---

1. The Curia is the court of the papal see, by which the government of the Roman Catholic Church is administered.

that recognised the papacy. Such was the success of his diplomatic skills that he had as his vassals the majority of the princes of Christendom, though not without a struggle.

Threatened

Within a few years he had re-established effective government over the papal states by reorganising the government, ensuring their independency from secular powers. The attempt by Germany, which ruled north and south Italy, to effect a reunion with Sicily threatened the papal states. To defend his position, Innocent excommunicated the new German emperor, then gave his support to another candidate who shortly afterwards was replaced by a newly-elected emperor.

In England, Innocent successfully disputed the appointment of a new Archbishop of Canterbury (1205). When King John refused to accept the papal nomination and retaliated by seizing Church lands, in 1208 the pope placed the whole of England under an interdict.[2] Three years later John was excommunicated and the throne of England declared vacant; the pope invited the French king to invade the land and take the crown for himself. This move forced King John to accept the pope's terms; he surrendered his crown and the kingdom of England to the papacy and promised to do homage to the pope as his feudal lord.

Within the Church, Innocent's achievements were wide-ranging. They included two crusades, against the Muslims of the Near East and against the Albigensian heresy, and the recognition of two new mendicant (i.e., begging) orders, the Order of St Dominic and the Order of St Francis. But it was the Fourth Lateran Council that constituted the culmination of his work and, indeed, of the whole medieval papacy.

Council

For some years Innocent had in mind calling a Council, but was delayed by the numerous problems that confronted him. It was formally announced in a bull of 19 April 1213, when over 1,200 letters of invitation were despatched to clerics and Christian secular rulers from all parts of the Church, both East and West. In his letter of convocation he announced the objects of the Council as measures for the reconquest of the Holy Land and the reform of the universal Church.

---

2. An ecclesiastical punishment, whereby churches were closed and mass ceased to be said; baptisms and burials were allowed.

When the Council finally assembled in Rome at the Lateran Church of St John (November, 1215), there were present 412 archbishops and bishops, including the Latin patriarchs of Constantinople and Jerusalem, and delegates from Alexandria and Antioch. There were also over 800 abbots and priors, plus the envoys of Emperor Frederick II, the Latin emperor of Constantinople, and of the kings of Aragon, Cyprus, England, France, Hungary, Jerusalem and Sicily.

It was a splendid occasion, with great crowds, processions and various festivities. The Council opened with mass celebrated at dawn by the pope, who also preached a sermon based on Luke 22:15. At the inaugural session, there was a speech from the Patriarch of Jerusalem on the misfortunes that plagued the Holy Land, then by the Bishop of Agde (south-west France) on the problems of the Albigenses, before getting down to business.

Albigenses

The first canon was directed against the errors of the Albigenses; it included a Confession of Faith which contained the following statement on the Eucharist:

> 'There is one universal Church of the faithful, outside which no one at all is in a state of salvation. In this Church, Jesus Christ is himself both Priest and Sacrifice; and his body and blood are really contained in the sacrament of the altar under the species of bread and wine, the bread being transubstantiated into the body, and the wine into the blood by the power of God, so that, to effect the mystery of unity, we ourselves receive from his what he himself received from ours.'

Transubstantiation (meaning 'a change of substance') was not a new idea, for it had been known since the early centuries of the Church.[3] The term was now used for the first time and declared to be the official doctrine of the Western Church. According to this teaching, it was claimed that in the mass the priest became an *alter Christus* ('another Christ'), in that he sacrificed the real Christ upon the altar. This occurred at the consecration of the elements, when the bread and wine were said to become the actual body and blood, together with the soul and divinity, of Christ, though the appearance of the bread and wine remained unchanged.

---

3. It was not recognised in England until after the Norman conquest.

From the twelfth century the great business of both Church and State was the repression of heresy. The Second and Third Lateran Councils (1139 and 1179) had required sovereigns to prosecute heretics and even to use force of arms. But the movement against heretics remained unorganised and further steps needed to be taken. The idea of what was later termed by Innocent as an inquisition was introduced at the Council of Verona (1184). By this decree, bishops were instructed to question suspects and require them to recant. Any who refused were to be handed over to the secular authorities to be punished, though this did not include the death penalty.

THE INQUISITION

The Inquisition owes its name to Innocent III when he instituted a new form of procedure for searching out heretics. Though aimed specifically at the Albigeneses, it also included witches, diviners, blasphemers and sacrilegious persons. Its origins, however, date back to the Second Lateran Council (1139) which required secular princes to prosecute heretics. When this failed, Innocent threatened to depose prelates and obliged secular rulers to assist the Church under pain of forfeiture.

Because none of these moves was successful, Pope Gregory IX (1227–1241) published a decretal which imposed a life sentence on a repentant heretic, and capital punishment for those who refused to comply. In 1233 he gave the task of combatting heresy to the Dominicans, with a mission that covered the whole of France, later extended to Flanders and the Low Countries. Suspected heretics were invited to confess and reaffirm the Faith. Torture was permissible if all the gentler methods of persuasion failed. Failure to repent usually meant death, and in Rome some were burned at the stake.

In 1479 the Spanish Inquisition was established by the Catholic monarchs Ferdinand and Isabella, with the approval of Pope Sixtus IV, specially directed against lapsed Jewish and Moorish Christians.

Spread of Heresy

Innocent had long been disquieted about the continued spread of heresy. In 1204 he sent papal legates to Languedoc (France) to persuade the Count of Toulouse to root out the Albigenses, but without success. Two years later an Augustinian monk, Dominic,[4] set out on a preaching tour to persuade the lost sheep to return to the Catholic fold, but with little success. An army was finally raised against the heretics in 1209, which marched down the Rhine Valley into Languedoc. Several thousands of the inhabitants of Bezier – both Cathars and Catholics – were massacred; and even though other Albigensian strongholds were captured, the crusade failed in its task.

---

4. In 1216 Dominic founded the Order that bears his name. The Dominicans devoted themselves to preaching and were members of the Inquisition.

Determined to continue the fight and – seemingly – to crush freedom of thought throughout the Church, the Fourth Lateran Council restated all previous decrees. Procedural rules were drawn up and crusading privileges, such as complete remission of all sins, were extended to those taking part in the campaigns. Although no new canons were added, Innocent introduced harsh measures and permitted the use of the sword. His argument was that if criminals were convicted of treason and punished with death, how much more should those who had offended the Son of God and deserted the Faith be cut off from the Christian communion.

Following the unsuccessful outcome of the Fourth Crusade (1204), the Council drew up plans for the promotion of a new venture, to start on 1st June 1217. Though the initial response was disappointing, the imposition of a special tax on the clergy of one fortieth of their income helped create the nucleus of a force. To prepare for the crusade, a four-year peace was imposed upon Christian peoples, and bishops were commanded to reconcile all enemies. All prelates and Christian rulers were enjoined to preach and support the crusade, and participants were offered the usual privileges. But as Innocent died before the starting date, the driving force was gone and all interest soon lost.

Further decrees dealt with the order and discipline of the Church, the moral well-being of the clergy, and various matters of spiritual and political interest. Some canons established dogmatic definitions and sacramental obligations that have remained in force to the present day, such as the obligation to attend mass and to confess at least once a year (during Easter time). Other canons included provision for cathedral schools with free instruction, care for the dying, penalties for all forms of simony (i.e., the purchase or sale of a benefice), regulations for the public display of relics and for curbing the abuses on indulgences – plus a prohibition on the blessing of hot water and hot iron for judicial ordeals!

Christians and Jews

The closing canons concerned the religious and social segregation of Christians and Jews, making official what was already common practice. The one exception was canon 68, which stated 'We decree that Jews and Saracens[5] of both sexes in every Christian province and at all times shall be marked off in the eyes of the public from other people through the character of their dress. Particularly, since it may be read in the writings of Moses

---

5. i.e., Muslims or opponents of the crusades.

that this very law has enjoined upon them.' The most common stipulated requirement was the 'Jewish badge', which in England took the form of a piece of yellow taffeta worn above the heart by all Jews above the age of seven. A Jew not wearing a badge was subject to a fine and forfeiture of his garments.

Other decrees stated that no Christian was to have commerce with Jewish money-lenders; Jews were forbidden to appear in public during Holy Week, to avoid risk of insult to Christians, nor could they exercise any public function that involved authority over Christians; and Jews willingly seeking baptism must first abandon their own rites.

Under Innocent's presidency the Fourth Lateran Council served as a model for future Councils. This Council was the first ecumenical Council of the medieval period to summon lay representatives, though they were in no way representative of the laity. They were, in fact, used as a rubber stamp to endorse the pope's decisions, as Innocent had no intention of sharing power with them or in being humiliated, as at Lateran I, which defeated the pope.

Some of the canons passed by the Council decisively influenced Roman Catholic teaching and practice for many centuries to come, especially those dealing with the sacraments. But there were pressure groups within the Church which were concerned at its departure from the gospel and were endeavouring to return to the simplicity of Christ's teachings. It was to be a further 200 years, however, before the revolt sparked off by Luther split Western Christianity in two.

18

1290 THE EXPULSION OF THE JEWS FROM ENGLAND

Anti-Semitism in State and Church

On 18th July 1290, King Edward I ordered all Jews to leave the country by All Saints' Day (1st November), on penalty of death. For over 200 years English kings had overtaxed and exploited the Jews until their money was virtually exhausted. Then because their days of usefulness were over they were summarily expelled from the land. It was nearly 400 years before they were allowed to return.

The first Jews in England were Norman-French and came from Rouen with William the Conqueror in 1066.[1] They settled in London, in the vicinity of what is now Old Jewry. Communities of Jews were later to be found in a number of county towns such as Lincoln, Norwich, York and Oxford. They built houses of stone and founded synagogues, whilst ground was allocated to them for use as cemeteries. And while there were no Jewish ghettoes in medieval towns (for Jews 'lived among the Christians'), their homes were in close proximity to one another.

The Conqueror used the Jews as financial agents in collecting his feudal dues, a work they had undertaken in France. Prevented under the feudal system from holding land and excluded from the medieval trade guilds, which were largely religious associations, many Jews specialised in commerce and trade. Because of a series of discriminatory laws, however, they were forced to employ their capital in the only way available to them,

---

1. There is some evidence that a few had already found their way to Britain before the Conquest.

in lending at interest, a talent enhanced by their facility for languages and their international contacts.[2]

Charter

During the period of the first Norman kings the Jews fared well. As 'servants of the chamber' they belonged to the king and were under the protection of the Crown. Henry I (1100–1135) issued a charter, reissued by succeeding rulers, to confirm their privileged position. By this charter Jews were granted liberty of movement, freedom from ordinary tolls and free access to royal justice, and with provision for fair trials. They became the 'King's men', a position that caused resentment among the nobility.

Monarchs and merchants alike found them useful when in need of finance to maintain armies and to engage in trade. Although Henry II (1154–1189) began his reign by borrowing from them on a modest scale, when he embarked upon the crusades it was from the Jews that he exacted much of the finance needed to fund the expedition. Hence, ironically, the Third Crusade was largely financed by Jews. Known as the Saladin Tithe, they were levied at the rate of one quarter of their property, while the Christians were only taxed at one tenth. Of the £70,000 demanded from the nation, the Jewish contribution was fixed at £60,000.

Because the medieval Church was opposed to usury and decreed it to be contrary to Scripture, Jews were able to secure a monopoly of the money-market, for they were not under canon law.[3] Impoverished churchmen, however, overcame their scruples and used Jewish money in order to build monasteries and cathedrals. At least nine Cistercian monasteries, the Abbey of St Albans, and the cathedrals of Lincoln and Peterborough were partly financed by Jewish money. Rates of interest were high, an average of 43 per cent, but the risks were equally great. Some borrowers ran up high debts and resented having to repay the money. False charges were made against Jews and they suffered frequently from mob attacks.

The riots were usually fuelled by rumours such as the one in Norwich in 1144. A twelve-year-old boy, William, went missing just before Easter (and Passover). His body was found in a wood, hanging from a tree, his head shaved and his body covered with stab wounds. The Jews were accused

---

2. While the vast majority of Jews were far from rich, a few Jewish money-lenders acquired great wealth. When Aaron of Lincoln died in 1185 he was probably the wealthiest man in England and was owed £15,000, equal to three-quarters of the annual royal income.

3. The Jewish Talmud prohibited charging excessive interest, but not lending at a reasonable rate.

of ritual murder, and were said to have crucified the boy on Good Friday in a re-enactment of the crucifixion. They were also charged with 'blood-libel', killing the child in order to use his blood for making matzo for Passover. Afterwards, whenever a child was killed in suspicious circumstances near to a community of Jews, the accusation of ritual murder was levelled at them. 'St William of Norwich' was venerated as medieval Europe's first child martyr.

Exchequer of the Jews

One protective measure taken towards the end of the twelfth century in towns with a Jewish community was the introduction of secure chests (*archae*), with triple locks, which contained records of all Jewish debt-bonds and mortgages. All loans had to be made in the presence of both Jewish and Christian officials, and an Exchequer of the Jews (a department of the Treasury) was set up to oversee the transactions. In this way the king took a cut of all Jewish business deals while at the same time it gave him a firmer hold over Jewish finances.

Following the death of Henry II a number of riots broke out against Jews, on the rumour that the new king (Richard I, 1189–1199) had ordered they should be killed. The first riot occurred at Westminster on the occasion of Richard's coronation. A deputation of wealthy Jews attending the ceremony were refused entry. In the ensuing commotion, they were attacked by the crowd and hostilities quickly spread to the whole of London's Jewry. The following spring, trouble broke out at Bury St Edmunds, Thetford, Stamford and Kings Lynn, where houses were pillaged and Jews murdered. At Dunstable, the Jewish population chose baptism rather than face death.

The most tragic event took place at York in March 1190, when a group of barons preparing for the crusade plundered Jewish homes and massacred the residents. A fire broke out, no doubt deliberately started, at the house of Benedict of York.[4] Bands of robbers joined in the attack on other Jewish homes and the victims fled to the royal castle for protection. Rather than surrender to their attackers and bring dishonour upon their race, some 150 of the Jews committed suicide in what is today called Clifford's Tower. When the remnant surrendered at daybreak they were seized and cruelly put to death. The barons hastened to the cathedral where they destroyed all Jewish debt records against them. It was obvious that the Jews could no longer rely on royal protection.

---

4. Benedict had died during the coronation riot, though his family had continued to live in the house.

Hardships

The onset of the thirteenth century witnessed continuing hardships, persecutions and the revival of restrictive laws combined to bring disaster on the Jewish population. In 1215, when the barons rebelled against King John (1199–1216), more Jewish homes in London were attacked and demolished. The king was forced to sign the Magna Carta, drawn up to secure national liberties; it included a clause limiting the claims of Jewish money-lenders against the estates of landowners who had died in their debt.

A period of respite followed on the accession to the throne of Henry III (1216–1272), who did much to restore Jewish fortunes. The prejudicial clauses of the Magna Carta were dropped, many Jews were released from prison and others had their bonds restored. In this enlightened climate, there was an influx of Jews into England from the Continent, though none were allowed to leave the country without licence.

Unhappily, it was during this more liberal reign that the Church, belatedly, decided to put into effect the discriminatory decrees issued by the Fourth Lateran Council (1215). Of the seventy canons drawn up, four directly concerned the Jews and were inspired by the Church's alarm over the spread of the Cathar heresy,[5] for which it held the Jews responsible. The Council ordered Jews to wear a different dress from Christians, as well as a distinctive badge (or tabula).[6] They were also forbidden to appear out of doors during Passion week. The last canon dealt with Jews converted to Christianity and was intended to ensure that they break completely with the Faith of their Fathers.

Although Henry had hoped to maintain his royal authority over the Jews, he finally complied with the papal decrees. In 1253 he issued an edict, its harsh demands reflected in the opening words: 'No Jew may remain in England unless he do the king's service, and from the hour of his birth, every Jew, whether male or female, shall serve us in some way.'

Tower of London

Hostility towards Jews continued to spread. The charge of ritual murder was raised again in 1255, when the body of a murdered Christian child was

---

5. Whilst the Cathars accepted the New Testament and some Christian teachings, their basic heresy was a belief in a good and an evil god, the latter identified with the God of the Old Testament.

6. After the legendary shape of the two tablets of the Ten Commandments. At least forty Councils throughout Europe approved badge resolutions.

found in a cesspool at Lincoln. Ninety Jews were arrested and sent to the Tower of London for trial; eighteen of them were executed. By this time the ritual murder myth was rife across Europe. A rebellion of barons against the king in 1263 led to a further wave of violence against Jews in London, Canterbury and other cities, and attempts were made to destroy the archae. Then, pandering to popular demand, the king closed down synagogues in London and had them converted into chapels. Meanwhile the oppressive taxes regularly levied upon Jews meant that the king was gradually destroying his greatest source of income. Many Jews applied to leave the country, but their requests were turned down.

The accession of Edward I (1272–1309) marked the final decline of the Jews in England, for there came to the throne a king who was anti-Jewish and who was set on stripping them of their assets. It was already clear that Jewish lending power was exhausted when, in 1275, Edward passed the Statute of Jewry, forbidding Jews to lend money on interest and encouraging them to become merchants and artisans. Other provisions decreed that Jews could only live in certain appointed towns: that all Jews over the age of twelve years old had to pay an annual poll tax at Easter; and that the distinctive badge for Jews had to be worn from the earlier age of seven (originally white, but now of yellow).

The king's repressive actions continued when next he accused Jews of debasing the coinage by coin-clipping. (That is, filing the edges of coins and melting the clippings into bullion.) Over 600 Jews were imprisoned in the Tower, of whom 293 were executed, whereas only three Christians were hanged for the offence. When in 1289 Edward needed money to ransom his cousin, Charles of Salerno, he met the demand by confiscating the property of his Gascony Jews[7] and then expelling them.

DOMUS CONVERSORUM

Early in Anglo-Jewish history efforts were begun to convert Jews to Christianity, by disputations, treatises and by preaching. Any who converted were given Christian names and received into a converts' home (*domus conversorum*) on the grounds that they had left the Jewish fold. Converts could expect to forfeit their property because it had been obtained by the 'sin of usury', but they were granted a pension for daily expenses.

Among the earliest such homes was the one to be found in Bristol (opened in 1154), and another opened in 1213 by Richard of Bermondsey (now a suburb of London) in the neighbourhood of his monastery. In 1221 a group of Dominican friars settled in Oxford and established themselves in the heart of the Jewish quarter. They immediately made efforts to convert their Jewish neighbours and were so successful that a home for converts was opened in Fish Street.

The foremost converts' home was established in 1232 by Henry III, in New Street (now Chancery Lane), London. The king assigned 700 marks annually for the upkeep of the home and its residents. Their pension, in 1290, amounted to 1½d a day for a man and 1d for a woman. In that year there were ninety-seven men and women in the home. Later, a warden and a chaplain were appointed, and houses and a chapel were added. The building continued as a converts' home after the expulsion in 1290 and only closed down in the mid-nineteenth century. From time to time newly converted Jews were admitted into the home, though for a few periods there was no one in residence. There is an abundance of detail about the home in the Close and Patent Rolls, as well as in other records from 1331.

Expulsion

With no further use for the Jewish community, in the summer of 1290 Edward issued an edict expelling all Jews,[8] on the grounds that they had disregarded the Statute of Jewry and had secretly reverted to money-lending. The date was 18 July, which corresponded with the 9th of Av, the fast commemorating the destruction of the first and second Temples in Jerusalem. Writs were sent to the sherriffs of various counties with instructions that no one should 'injure, harm, damage or grieve' the Jews in their departure. The Warden of the Cinque Ports was ordered to see that the refugees were given a safe and speedy passage across the channel on their way to Europe.

The expulsion provided the Crown with one final benefit, in that Jewish houses, synagogues and cemeteries fell to the king, as well as the considerable value of their debts. How many Jews left the country is a matter of dispute, and numbers vary widely between 2,500 and 16,000. The majority of them settled in France, though the following year the French king moved them on to other parts of Europe.

Sadly, England was not alone in its antipathy to Jews, and medieval Christian governments throughout Europe were often faced with 'the Jewish problem' and felt it necessary to take anti-Jewish measures. Although several countries attempted to expel Jews, in England's case it succeeded because of the barrier of the Channel. Pressure was also on Jews to convert to Christianity, sometimes under threat of death or by bribery or a desire to become accepted in society. There were, of course, some genuine

---

7. Edward was Lord of Gascony (France) as well as King of England.

8. An alternative reason for the expulsion is that it was the price demanded by parliament in return for granting the king permission to levy a tax which he badly needed to pay off his debts.

conversions, a step which severely tested their faith as it left them in direst poverty.

Domus Conversorum (Oxford), a house for Jewish converts,
established by the Dominicans in the 13th century.

This period is one of the most shameful in the history of England and the Church, for it further inflamed anti-Semitic attitudes that had existed in Christendom from the second century. Though Jewish people are now fully integrated into British society, anti-Semitism has continued down the centuries, even in the Church. Happily, in recent years an increasing number of Christians have begun to recognise the need to seek reconciliation and ask forgiveness. Both the Roman Catholic Church and the World Council of Churches have repudiated anti-Semitism, whilst the Lutheran Church has acknowledged Germany's guilt in its treatment of Jews during the 1930s and 40s.

One beneficial legacy of the Jewish presence in England was a renewed interest in Hebrew studies. Though there was a barrier between church and synagogue, contact with Jewish people enabled the more learned Christian clergy to benefit from the expertise of Jewish scholars.

After 1290, apart from a few travellers and Jewish Christians there were no Jews in England for nearly 400 years. That they were readmitted in 1656 during the rule of Oliver Cromwell, Lord Protector of England, was partly because of the economic benefits their presence could bring. Jews were allowed to become full citizens, though with the same limitations as those placed upon Catholics and Nonconformists. Although England was the first nation to expel Jews, it was also the first nation where it became possible for a Jewish community to be established, though it was to be a further 200 years before they finally gained complete emancipation.

In 1846 the thirteenth century anti-Jewish statutes were formally repealed.

THE JEWS AND CHRISTIANITY

The long history of division between Jews and Christians dates back to the early years of the Church. Following the destruction of Jerusalem in AD70 the Church began to teach that God had rejected his ancient people. By the time of Justin Martyr (c 150) the attitude prevailed that the Church was now the 'new Israel' and heir to all the promises of God. Increasingly, Christians began to distance themselves from their Jewish roots, which in turn developed into an attitude of anti-Judaism and ultimately anti-Semitism.

During the fourth century, following the Edict of Milan (313) when Christians were granted religious toleration, anti-Jewish laws were passed which aimed at severing all connection between Jews and Christians. And when Christianity became the official religion of the empire (in 381), synagogues were plundered and Jewish homes destroyed. In later centuries Jews were branded as 'Christ-killers'; they were excluded from normal social intercourse and forced to live in ghettoes.

The eleventh century crusades led to the cruel killing of thousands of Jews both in Europe and the Holy Land. Towards the end of the fifteenth century both Spain and Portugal turned against their Jewish subjects; many were forcibly baptised, while others were expelled or put to death. In Eastern Europe, the nineteenth century Russian pogroms destroyed Jewish villages, forcing thousands of Jews to flee the country. More recently, the Holocaust resulted in the deaths of some six million Jews, including over a million children. It is only in recent years that Christians have recognised the great injustice inflicted upon the Jews and attempted to heal the breach.

19

1415 COUNCIL OF CONSTANCE CONDEMNS HUS TO DEATH

Burnt at the Stake for the Sake of the Gospel

The Council of Constance (1414–1418) met primarily in an attempt to heal a breach within the Church, when Western Christendom was divided by the creation by a number of anti-popes. It was also called to deal with charges of heresy, especially with regard to the teachings of John Hus, the leader of a protest movement in the kingdom of Bohemia. The wranglings over the papacy led the Council to declare its supreme authority over all things in the Church, enabling it to resolve the papal dilemma, while Hus was found guilty and burnt at the stake.

In the fourteenth century papal power was on the decline as more and more the pope came to be regarded as a foreign prince rather than the Vicar of Christ. To maintain his authority Pope Boniface VIII (1294–1303) issued the famous bull of 1302, *Unam Sanctum*, in which he restated the papal claim to supremacy over civil powers. It affirmed that temporal powers were subject to spiritual authority and declared there was no salvation or remission of sins outside the one holy, Catholic and Apostolic Church. Following Boniface's death, the French king brought pressure to bear on Rome and between 1308 and 1378 a succession of Frenchmen were elected to the office of pope. The papal court was moved from Rome to Avignon, where it continued until 1377 before being restored to Rome.

Great Schism

No sooner had this been accomplished than once again the Roman Church was thrown into confusion, this time by the Great Schism. It lasted from 1378 to 1417 and split Catholicism into two separate camps. The election of Urban VI as pope in 1378 was the result of pressure from the people of Rome, who were keen to keep the papacy in the city and to have an Italian pope. After four months the hostility of the cardinals towards Urban led them to declare their choice void, since, they claimed, it had been dictated by fear. The same cardinals then chose another pope, Clement VII, who took up residence at Avignon.

The Papal Palace at Avignon where the rival (French) popes lived in the 14th century.

Christian Europe was divided on the issue and nationalist feelings in Italy and France ran high, for both countries wanted the papacy, together with its money, power and prestige. For the next four decades there were rival colleges of cardinals, at Rome and Avignon, who elected different popes. A Council of cardinals, bishops and heads of the great orders met at Pisa in 1409 to seek a solution. As the two popes refused to attend, they were deposed and another pope elected in their place. The problem was not resolved, for there were now three popes where there had been two, but it had at least established that a Council was superior to the papacy.

By now there was an increasing clamour for Church reform 'in head and members' – both papacy and clergy – and for moral and administrative changes as well. The new Holy Roman Emperor, Sigismund (1410–1437), used his influence to call another Council, which met over a period of three and a half years, not in Rome, but in the walled town of Constance, in the south of Germany. One of the great Councils of the Middle Ages, it was attended by cardinals, bishops, doctors of theology and representatives of monarchs, including Sigismund himself.

The Council began by deposing the Italian pope, John XXIII; shortly afterwards a second pope, Gregory XII, resigned. But the third pope, a Spanish prelate, Benedict XIII, could not be persuaded to stand down; he was tried and formally deposed. This action brought the schism to an end, though the opportunity to introduce urgent reforms was postponed and referred to the next pope, Martin V, elected in 1417.

Condemned

On the question of doctrine, the Council condemned the teachings of both the English theologian, John Wyclif, and John Hus, the Bohemian (Czech) reformer. The two men had been responsible for the launch of dissident groups that challenged the corruption of the Church and the papacy, hence the determination of the Council to stamp out these troublesome movements.

John Wyclif had been a priest and a leading theologian at Oxford University, though his early reputation was as a philosopher. His attacks on some of the central doctrines of the Church and the abuses of the clergy brought him many enemies, though his teachings began to find favour on the Continent. This was the result of the marriage between King Richard II of England (1377–1399) and Anne, the sister of King Wenceslaus of Bohemia, in 1382. The union opened the way for the spread of Wyclif's ideas to Bohemia; scholars from Prague were attracted to Oxford where they encountered his theological works, returning home with new ideas for the reform of the Bohemian Church. They found in John Hus a ready and capable leader who was profoundly affected by Wyclif's theological writings.

JOHN WYCLIF (1330–1384)

It was the wealth of the Church and clerical interference in political life that ultimately aroused Wyclif's opposition to Rome. In his lectures at Oxford and through his writings he challenged the Church to return to the simplicity of the gospel. The sole basis for doctrine, he argued, was the Bible, which he distinguished from the teaching of the Church. He maintained that the Church was made up of the whole company of the elect, those predestined to be saved, and not simply the pope and the clergy. The head of the Church was Christ, not the pope, who might not necessarily be one of the elect! His pamphlet, *On the Eucharist*, opposed the Church's teaching of transubstantiation, for he believed the real presence of Christ in the mass to be spiritual and not literal.

Attracted by his ideas, Wyclif gathered around him a band of followers known as Lollards. Like the Waldensians, these men based their teachings on the Bible and went out two by two, preaching the gospel and distributing tracts (which were written in English and not Latin). They attacked false doctrines, and practices such as indulgences and pilgrimages, and held that priestly acts were only valid when evidenced by a priest's moral character.

John Hus (c1372-1415)

John Hus was born about 1372 of peasant stock in the village of Husinecz, southern Bohemia, from where he derived his name. The boy's scholastic gifts were early recognised and a wealthy nobleman paid the expenses for his schooling. About 1390 he enrolled in the University of Prague, gaining a theological degree and where two years later he received his master's degree. In 1401 he was ordained to the Catholic priesthood and became dean of the philosophical faculty at the university.

Meanwhile Hus was becoming increasingly familiar with Wyclif's works, and was especially moved by the message conveyed by two cartoons he saw which aptly commented on the condition of the Church. One depicted the Lord Jesus wearing the crown of thorns, with the pope dressed in clothing of rich purple and silk and wearing a crown of gold. The other was a picture of the woman to whom Jesus said, 'Your sins are forgiven you', with the pope depicted selling indulgences. These impressions inspired him to work actively for the reforms demanded by the English reformer.

Bethlehem Chapel

With a growing reputation as a preacher, Hus was invited to fill the pulpit at the Bethlehem Chapel in Prague, while continuing to teach in the university. This chapel had been specially built in 1391 to give ordinary people the opportunity of hearing sermons in their own language, rather than in Latin. At the centre of the church was not an altar, but a pulpit. Hus proved to be a popular choice, and though continuing to enjoy the favour of King Wenceslaus, his fiery sermons attacking the abuses of the clergy soon incurred the hostility of the Archbishop of Prague.

The Church, already discredited by the Great Schism, owned about a half of all the land in Bohemia; while the higher clergy enjoyed great wealth, the peasants were heavily taxed, causing further resentment. Under Hus, Bethlehem Chapel became the centre of a growing reform movement in Bohemia, though opposition to his ideas was steadily mounting. Like Wyclif, Hus believed in predestination, he accepted the Scriptures as the sole source of Christian doctrine, and that the Church must be subject in all things to the Bible. But he did not share all of Wyclif's radical views and continued to hold to – amongst others – the idea of transubstantiation, purgatory, masses for the dead and the seven sacraments.

Some of the fiercest opposition to Wyclif's teachings came from the German masters who taught at the university. This opposition enraged the king, and in January 1409, induced by Hus, he succeeded in ousting them. The result was a mass exodus of Germans to Leipzig where they founded a new university, while Hus was elected Rector of the now Czech-dominated University of Prague.

Although the Archbishop of Prague persuaded the anti-pope to prohibit teaching in private chapels, the reformer continued to preach at the Bethlehem Chapel. When questioned about his readiness to obey papal decrees, Hus replied that he could assent only in so far as they were in agreement with the doctrines of Christ. 'But when I see the contrary I will not obey them, even though you burn my body,' he declared. (The expression 'to contrary Christ' was an expression used by Wyclif's followers to mark out those who 'contraried' Christ – those who were his enemies, and therefore to be resisted.)

Indulgences

Matters came to a head when a new dispute arose over the sale of indulgences,[1] issued by anti-pope John XXIII. Their sale in Bohemia aroused great indignation and Hus publicly condemned them. In doing so, however, he lost the support of King Wenceslaus, who, as usual, shared in the proceeds. Charges of heresy were once more revived against Hus and he was excommunicated for refusing to appear for trial at the curia. When an interdict was pronounced over Prague in 1411, he left the city in order to spare it the consequences.

He found refuge for two years in southern Bohemia, where he spent his time in writing tractates in Czech, many of which have become classics in Czech literature, and in preaching. His most important work was *De Ecclesia* ('On the Church'), which was later to have an influence on Luther's thinking. His opponents also wrote a large number of treatises against him, maintaining the persecution and preparing the ground for an opportunity to bring him down.

When the Council of Constance met in November 1414, it was an attempt by the German emperor to unite the Church and to put an end to all heresy. Hus was summoned to appear before the Council, to explain his views. He was assured of a safe-conduct for the journey to Constance and back, whatever the outcome. On this basis Hus consented to attend, not as an accused, but on condition that he would be allowed free discussion. The emperor, however, was overruled, when a month later Hus was arrested and imprisoned, from which he never emerged.

As a result of Sigismund's intervention, the accused was – contrary to

---

1. See Box, 'Indulgences', p.178.

canon law – allowed to defend himself in open court. Declared to be a Wycliffite heretic, Hus was interrogated by Dominicans who had not even read his books, so that he was able to refute some of their false charges (such as he claimed to be the fourth person of the Trinity!). Throughout all the proceedings Hus refused to recant, on the ground that they ascribed to him views he did not hold.

Death by Burning

Found guilty, on 6 July 1415 he was degraded from the priesthood and condemned to death by burning. Kneeling down in the court room, he prayed, 'Lord Jesus, pardon all my enemies for the sake of thy great mercy. Thou knowest that they have falsely accused me, brought forward false witnesses, and concocted false charges against me. Pardon them for the sake of thine infinite mercy.'

Hus was straight away led out of prison to the place of burning on what was a glorious summer's day, followed in a procession by the entire town. A mock crown was placed on his head, depicting three dancing devils and with the words, 'This is an arch-heretic'. As the fire was lit, he prayed, 'Into they hands, O Lord, I commend my spirit.' And, 'I am willing patiently and publicly to endure this dreadful, shameful and cruel death for the sake of thy gospel and the preaching of thy Word.' As the wind blew the smoke into his face, his lips were still moving in prayer as he expired without a groan. To prevent his being honoured as a martyr, his ashes were collected and scattered on the River Rhine.

While Hus had been in prison, his followers in Prague, who held that all believers should receive both the bread and the wine at the Lord's Supper (contrary to the Catholic practice of the mass), had begun the practice of administering the elements to the laity. When the Council of Constance put Hus to death, the people of Bohemia were outraged; but when it forbade the bread and wine to the laity, thousands of townspeople took to arms. Under the command of a one-eyed leader, John Zizka, a revolution broke out which lasted for over twenty years.

The Hussites had their headquarters on a mountain which they named Tabor,[2] from where they fought for their cause against Emperor Sigismund, whom they blamed for Hus' death. But when Zizka died in 1421, a sharp contention arose among the Hussites, some of whom were prepared to compromise with the papacy and return to the Roman Catholic Church.

2. Hence they were sometimes called Taborites.

The Waldenses, who had been established in Bohemia for many years, joined forces with the Hussites, and from about 1453 they were together known as the Unitas Fratrum, or Bohemian Brethren.

In 1436 the autonomous Hussite Church became the first national reform church to exist outside Rome. Though overwhelmed in 1620 by the Hapsburgs, a remnant remained and, despite persecution, persisted in Bohemia and maintained its witness. Two hundred years later it influenced the emergence of the German Pietist movement and the rebirth of the Moravian Brethren, which in turn helped kindle the fires of the Wesleyan revival.

20

1456 THE MODERN PRINTING MACHINE INVENTED

The First Printed Bible

The invention of printing in the fifteenth century not only brought about a wider diffusion of culture and learning, but also made possible the production of a vastly increased number of Bibles and other books and tracts. Whereas previously books had been copied by hand, the new art of printing opened a floodgate of literature, so that by the beginning of the sixteenth century some 40,000 titles had been published throughout Europe.

As with so many other inventions, the process of printing was not the result of a flash of genius, but the culmination of many years of experimentation. The basic materials, paper and ink, had been in existence for centuries, as had various primitive methods of printing. It was the development of a movable type that revolutionised the operation and made possible the production of books on a grand scale.

From the third millenium BC the Egyptians began to use papyrus as a writing material. It was made from the fibrous pith of a water-plant which formerly grew in the marshes of lower Egypt, but is no longer to be found there. Thin strips of the plant were laid in two layers and glued, then polished to produce a smooth surface. They were made in sheets of various sizes, glued or sewn together and fastened to a wooden rod to produce a scroll, the ancient form of a 'book'.

Scrolls varied in size. The longest known scroll (to be seen in the British Museum) is 133 feet, and the greatest known height 19 inches. For practical purposes, however, a scroll would not usually exceed 35 feet in length, with a height of around 9 or 10 inches. A scroll of 32–35 feet would normally contain one of the longer Gospels, a factor which suggests that each of the Gospels and Acts must originally have circulated separately. Certainly there was no possibility of getting the Epistles of Paul, let alone the New Testament, on a longer scroll.

The writing on papyrus manuscripts was generally rather small, the letters separately formed though occasionally linked together. It was in two columns, usually about 2½–3 inches wide, allowing space in the margins for notes. There was a blank space at the beginning of the scroll to give the reader something to hold when reading the first column.

Normally, writing was only on one side of the scroll, though where papyrus was scarce it might be used both 'inside and out' (cf. Ezek. 2:10) i.e., on both sides. Words were not separated, there was hardly any punctuation and paragraphs were rare; without chapter divisions it could be difficult to locate a specific passage.

Developments

In the early years of the second century some writings were presented in codex form (our modern book, with leaves and pages) rather than a scroll. Whilst this may not necessarily have been a Christian invention, it was chiefly employed by the Christian community. In this way, much more material could be included without it becoming too cumbersome, thus making it possible for the Gospels to be circulated together.

An equally significant development was the switch from papyrus to the use of vellum. Papyrus was a perishable material which became brittle with age if dry, or rotted when damp. Consequently, the life span of a papyrus manuscript in most climates was limited. One exception was the dry soil of parts of Egypt, which has yielded a great number of early papyri. Otherwise few papyrus manuscripts have survived from the first centuries of the Church's history.

Vellum was produced from the skins of cattle, mainly calves, lambs and kids, and had a durable quality. The skins were washed, scraped with pumice and dressed with chalk, leaving a white surface; it was possible to write on both sides of the skin, and the ink could easily be removed to allow for corrections. Writing on vellum manuscripts was in capital letters known as uncials, a style which later made the codices rather cumbersome.

First used at Pergamum[1] (Asia Minor) in the second century BC, the

---

1. The new material was hence called pergamene, from which we get our word parchment.

superior advantages of vellum were not generally recognised until the fourth century AD. Following the demand for more copies of the Scriptures to replace those destroyed during the third century persecutions of Decius and Diocletian, vellum became the principal writing material. When Constantine, for example, ordered fifty copies of the Scriptures for his newly built churches, he expressly commanded that they should be on vellum.

In the ninth century a new, smaller form of writing developed known as miniscule or cursive, from the fact that the letters were often linked together so as to make a running hand. The result was that the books were smaller and, therefore, easier to handle. From the tenth to the fifteenth century virtually all manuscripts were written in this way. With the advent of monasteries, copying Scripture became one of the chief occupations of monks.

It was the introduction of paper that finally made printing possible. Originally invented by the Chinese early in the second century, the art of paper-making reached Europe in the twelfth century when the earliest paper mills were set up in Spain and Italy. Paper gradually became the chief literary writing material in Europe, replacing parchment. Thus before the invention of printing with movable type the necessary basic requirements for the development of mass-produced books were in place.

PAPER-MAKING

Paper was invented by the Chinese, though our word for it is derived from its predecessor, papyrus. The Egyptians wrote on papyrus as far back as the third millennium BC, and it was in use for a thousand years in the Greco-Roman world. Vellum (parchment) was the literary writing material of the Middle Ages. It is thought that paper was the invention of Ts'ai Lun, chief eunuch to the Chinese Emperor Ho Ti, around 105.

The earliest extant documents on paper belong to the early fourth century. Discovered in the Caves of the Thousand Buddhas, in Kansu province, they were made entirely from rags of fabric woven of Chinese hemp. The Arabs learned the craft of paper-making from Chinese prisoners, captured at Samarkand in 751. Arabic manuscripts, made of pure rag, still exist from the ninth century onwards. Soon, Baghdad and Damascus became important centres of paper manufacture. By the beginning of the twelfth century there were paper mills at Cairo, Fez (Morocco) and Valencia (Spain). Good paper was not made in Christian Europe until the end of the thirteenth century, when Italy led the world. Paper-making reached Germany the following century, when it was cheap enough for the printing of books to be a practical business proposition.

Printing

No single person can be credited with the invention of printing. Its origins can be traced back to ninth century China, perhaps even earlier, to the efforts of Buddhist monks. The monks made a print from a wooden block on which Chinese characters were carved to stand in relief, and the earliest known printed book is dated 868. By the eleventh century a simple kind of movable type, made of clay, had been developed, though the idea appears not to have survived. Chinese handwriting, with its vast number of ideograms requiring many thousands of symbols, was difficult to handle, and the system never came into general use.

In the West a method of printing similar to that of the Chinese was being used in the first half of the fifteenth century, but it was a slow and laborious method. The real breakthrough came when Johann Gutenberg (c1397–1468) of Mainz, Germany, invented printing by movable type. Though other men in Holland and Italy were simultaneously working along the same lines in the search for a faster and cheaper way of producing books, credit is usually given to the German.

Little is known of Gutenberg's early life, except that his family were expelled from Mainz for political reasons when Gutenberg was a young man. They settled in Strasbourg where he was apprenticed to a printer and became a recognised industrial artist, skilled in engraving and metal working. He set up a printing business with the offer of teaching his partners some 'secret arts', presumably a reference to his new ideas.

It seems that he was at work on several innovations and by the 1440s had perfected a number of new techniques. One was a hand-held mould that could be adapted to cast metal letters of exactly the same height and in large quantities, and another was a tin alloy that melted and solidified quickly. In addition he made modifications to his press and the printing process.

New Business

Gutenberg returned to Mainz around 1448 to further the cause of his inventions. He set up a new business and borrowed a large some of money 'for the making of books' from a Johann Fust, a rich goldsmith, who became his partner. In 1455 when Fust demanded repayment of the loan, Gutenberg was unable to comply. His printing equipment, which had been offered as security, was forfeited to Fust and his former partner took control of the business.

Movable Type

It was in the early 1450s when Gutenberg began operating his new movable type. His first production was a single sheet Letter of Indulgence, but it is likely he was also at work on his first book, Jerome's Latin translation of the Bible, the Vulgate. Printed simultaneously on six presses, it had two columns to a page, each with forty-two lines, and used both sides of each page. The typeface resembled the ornate letters often used by scribes when copying manuscripts; each chapter began with a large illuminated initial and was adorned with richly-coloured embellishments.

The Gutenberg Bible is known to have been in circulation by 15 August 1456, for this is the date inscribed by the rubricator (the artist who added the coloured initials). It has been acclaimed as 'one of the most beautiful books ever printed'. Of the 200 copies produced, about forty still exist. Since the seventeenth century it has also been known as the Mazarin Bible, from the fact that the copy that first attracted the attention of scholars was in the library of Cardinal Mazarin at Paris.

Although credit for this edition is usually given to Gutenberg, by the time of publication his business had been taken over by Fust. Hence the Bibles that came off the press did not bear Gutenberg's name, though he quite likely set up the type. Some scholars believe this edition was actually printed by Fust and his partner Peter Schoeffer, who later became his son-in-law.

Despite continued financial difficulties, Gutenberg succeeded in setting up a new printing business in 1458, but was never able to prosper materially from his invention. He died in Mainz where he was buried in the Franciscan church.

Gutenberg's invention remained a trade secret until 1462, when Mainz was plundered and the city's printers fled to other parts of the Continent. Within decades similar printing presses had been set up throughout Europe: Rome (1467), Paris (1470), Cracow (1474) and Madrid (1499). In London, William Caxton set up a press in the Westminster Abbey Almonry, and in 1477 at the *Sign of the Red Pale* published the first dated book printed in England.

Revolution

The new developments within printing made possible the sale of large quantities of relatively cheap literature. There was a great demand for new reading material, encouraging ordinary people to learn to read and thus creating a wider interest in education, while authors began to write books in plainer language. Within the next fifty years more copies of books were produced than in several previous centuries together.

Many literary and scientific works were published, contributing greatly towards the spread of knowledge and new ideas. By means of books, pamphlets and broadsheets, information of all kinds reached all levels of society, bringing about changes – for better and for worse – that would not otherwise have happened.

Since the previous century, the Renaissance – the rebirth of ancient (secular) learning – had meanwhile been gathering momentum. When Constantinople fell to the Turks in 1453, many scholars fled to the West, carrying their books with them. The new invention provided a timely impetus to the revival of learning, and Europe was deeply influenced by the writings broadcast by the press.

RENAISSANCE

The Renaissance was one of the most important factors that paved the way for the Reformation. The term means 'rebirth' or 'renewal', and is used to describe a revival of ancient learning in literature, art and science. The followers of the new learning were known as Humanists, though not to be confused with the modern usage of the term.

The first stirrings of the Renaissance began in the Italian city states during the latter years of the fourteenth century, with a new appreciation of Latin and Greek antiquity and the rediscovery of the ancient world. When the Byzantine city of Constantinople was captured by the Turks in 1453, many of the Greek scholars fled to Italy. They took with them not only their learning but also their valuable ancient manuscripts, contributing to the furtherance of Greek studies in Italian universities. The revival spread north of the Alps, penetrating Germany and Holland, where it assumed a more religious expression, and reached England, France and Spain.

Scholars now turned their attentions to the study of the texts of sacred literature, prompting Christians to re-examine the Greek New Testament. The leading Christian Humanist of the time was Erasmus (1469–1536), the first professor of Greek at Cambridge, whose Greek edition of the New Testament was used by reformers for Bible translation work.

The chief book to be produced, however, was the Bible, though a variety of other religious material, such as the Psalter and other church service books, was also published. Reading the Scriptures was no longer the prerogative of the clergy, as lay people also had access to the Word of God, albeit (for the time being) in Latin. When Luther nailed his ninety-five theses to the door of the church at Wittenberg, printing was well established throughout Europe. Within a short space of time his ideas were known in both Paris and Rome, hastening the onset of the Reformation.

For scholars, the printing press proved a great aid to biblical studies. Now, instead of the wide variety of manuscripts in use prior to the fifteenth century, all copies printed from a single setting of type could be counted on to be identical. There would be no more variations caused by the errors of human scribes; scholars could avail themselves of a reliable text. Henceforth the way was open for the production of accurate Greek texts of the New Testament and for the Bible in the language of the people. 'As the apostles of Christ formerly went through the world announcing the good news,' wrote one patriotic German, 'so in our days the disciples of the new art (i.e., of printing) spread themselves through all countries, and their books are as the heralds of the gospel'.

Thus Western society, and especially the Church, experienced a revolution that soon reverberated around the world. The quest for innovation continues; but in spite of the modern development of audiovisual technology, the printed word continues to hold its place as an indispensable means of communication.

21

1517 MARTIN LUTHER POSTS HIS NINETY-FIVE THESES

Salvation By Faith Alone

The day Martin Luther nailed his ninety-five theses to the door of the castle church at Wittenberg marked the beginning of the religious revolution known as the Reformation. Although the gesture was intended as the opening salvo of an academic disputation, it sparked off a conflict that engulfed the whole of Europe and divided Christendom. From this upheaval emerged the Protestant renewal movement in which the Bible was once again restored to its rightful place and Christianity entered a new period of expansion.

In the centuries prior to the Reformation the Church had become increasingly marked by a spirit of wordliness. The papacy accumulated large holdings of land and amassed great wealth, patronising the arts rather than caring for the faithful. Popes and priests alike were guilty of bringing the Church into disrepute by unholy living, and doctrines and practices were introduced that were contrary to Scripture. Whereas the papacy had once been a uniting force within the Church, it lost its spiritual and moral authority and became the cause of its own undoing.

One of the most unhappy doctrines held by the medieval Church was that of purgatory, which was the cause of considerable torment and fear. The Church maintained that every one had to face the consequence and punishment for every sin ever committed before finally being admitted to heaven. These punishments were said to be meted out in purgatory, where those who had died in the grace of God atoned for their unforgiven sins and were purged before entry to their eternal abode. As purgatory might last for thousands of years, it caused considerable anguish of soul. It was held, however, that this period of time could be shortened by means of an indulgence, which remitted some or all of the punishments due.

In the centuries leading up to the Reformation voices were increasingly raised in protest at widespread abuses within the Church. There was a call for a return to a more spiritual and inward religion, and to restore the simplicity of the gospel. Although aware of the problems, the great Councils of Pisa (1409) and Constance (1414–1418) failed to introduce any reforms. When Luther posted his ninety-five theses in 1517, the rising tide of disquiet surfaced and the Church found itself faced with a revolt.

Behind the Walls

The young Martin Luther (1483–1546) was endowed with considerable intellect, and fortunately his father was able to afford him a university education. At the age of eighteen he matriculated at the university of Erfurt (Saxony) in 1501, where he went on to earn a Master of Arts degree (1505). While his father wanted him to become a lawyer, to his fury Martin entered the Order of Augustinian Friars at Erfurt, though he did not inform his parents until he was behind the walls.

Luther entered the Order because of his concern for his soul, for he was anxious to be at peace with God. Taught that despite the Fall, man had power to earn salvation by his own good works and efforts, he observed all the rules of his Order and spent much time in Bible study and prayer. But at confession he was never sure that he had confessed all his sins or that he was forgiven. He believed that one day he would have to face the wrath of a righteous and angry God, but did not know how he could love a God that condemned him. In the monastery, Luther was prescribed a course of study, attending lectures and reading the works of leading theologians of the day. Though the books did not supply him with the answers he was looking for, they directed his attention to the Scriptures.

The following year (1508) he was appointed lecturer in moral philosophy at the new university of Wittenberg, a post he held for a year; he returned there in 1511 as a professor, with added responsibilities for preaching and with a view to working for his doctorate. It was shortly before this second appointment that Luther undertook a memorable journey to Rome, sent to the papal office on business relating to the monastery. For Luther, it offered the prospect of a pilgrimage with the hope of unburdening his soul and possibly finding some answers.

He spent a month in the eternal city, only to return home disillusioned, concluding that 'the Church had lost the key to the kingdom'. During his stay, Luther ran 'like a mad saint through all the churches and catacombs'. He seized every opportunity to make his confession and one day he saw seven masses performed in one hour; on another occasion he visited the seven main pilgrimage churches in a single day. He crawled up the twenty-eight steps of the Scala Sancta, saying a Pater Noster (the Lord's Prayer) on each step.[1] When he reached the top, he asked himself, 'How do I know all this is true?' Apparently this pious observance was said to free a soul from purgatory at one fell swoop, but Luther had no assurance of any such release.

Search for Peace

Back at Wittenberg his search for peace continued. He began to study Greek and Hebrew, to read Augustine and the early Church Fathers; he lectured on the Psalms and the Pauline epistles. It was in 1513, while preparing a lecture on Psalm 31, that he read the words 'deliver me in your righteousness', which suddenly began to take on a new meaning for him. He searched for other Bible uses of this term and came upon Romans 1:17: 'For in the gospel a righteousness from God is revealed, a righteousness that is by faith from first to last, just as it written, "The righteous will live by faith."'

At this, the realisation struck him that it was not the anger of a holy God against sinful man, but rather the loving righteousness of a God who was prepared to show mercy and to forgive. It was not earned by good works, but was a gift to be received by faith. He was straight away released from his state of despair as it dawned upon him that he was made right with God by faith alone. This phrase, *sola fide* ('faith alone'), became the watchword of the Reformation, recapturing the gospel of salvation that had been neglected for centuries.

Writing afterwards of his spiritual awakening, Luther declared, 'When I had realised this I felt myself absolutely born again. The gates of paradise had been flung open and I had entered. There and then the whole of Scripture took on another look for me'.

For the next four years he pursued his theological studies with renewed vigour, gaining new insights into biblical truths and imparting them to his students. As he began to understand the full implications of the doctrine of

---

1. This staircase was said to have been the one ascended by Jesus at Pilate's residence, but now removed to Rome. Many years later, Luther's son told how, when his father was ascending the steps a text from Habbakuk came to his mind – 'The righteous shall live by his faith', though it was to be some time before the full impact of this verse dawned upon his soul.

justification by faith, he found himself arguing against the Church and quarrelling with the papacy. His reading of the New Testament, for example, led him to the rediscovery of the priesthood of all believers, and with it the realisation that the only mediator between God and man was Christ Jesus, and not the Church.

Holy Trade

By 1517 Luther had become increasingly concerned about the scandal of indulgences. The matter was brought to a head when a Dominican friar, John Tetzel, acting on behalf of the Archbishop of Mainz, attempted to ply his 'holy trade' in Saxony. The proceeds of the sale were to be divided between the pope, to help build the new St Peter's at Rome, and the archbishop whose pressing debts needed to be met. Whilst the papal bull made it clear that absolution depended upon the purchaser's genuine repentance and confession, this thought tended to get overlooked.

INDULGENCES

The idea behind indulgences (from the Latin *indulgenta*, 'permit') can be traced back to the third century, when certain 'satisfactions' had to be made by lapsed Christians who wished to be readmitted to the fellowship. Penances were imposed by a priest, but when indulgences were introduced they were granted by the pope. In 1095 Pope Urban II offered an indulgence granting total remission of the pains of purgatory to anyone engaging in the crusade against Islam. As indulgences became recognised as a useful source of income, their scope was widened; in 1476 it became possible to purchase them on behalf of the dead, thus creating a huge demand for the certificates. The holder of an indulgence (or a deceased relative) could be excused all works of penance, and anyone who died forgiven by the priest was still guaranteed entrance to heaven.

The theory was that Jesus, the Blessed Virgin Mary and the saints had built up a 'credit balance' of good works, which were available to all. The pope, holding the keys of the kingdom, was empowered to draw upon this treasury of merit and distribute it at will, so that an indulgence transferred enough merit to deliver the holder from some or all penalties due.

Tetzel was refused permission to sell indulgences in Saxony, as the Elector, Frederick the Wise (1486–1525), wanted people to spend their money on viewing his 5,005 relics at the castle church of Wittenberg. These relics, which included thorns from Christ's crown, fragments of the true cross and some straw from Christ's manger, were reckoned to earn a penitent 1,902,202 years and 270 days remission in purgatory. As it was possible, however, to acquire an indulgence in the adjoining electorate, many citizens slipped over the border to make their purchase. They were no doubt

Luther (1483-1546) standing at the door of the
Wittenberg Church where he posted his 95 theses.

persuaded by Tetzel's appeal on behalf of dead souls languishing in the agonies of purgatory, crying out for relief. He promised them...

'As soon as the coin in the coffer rings
The soul from purgatory springs.'

Aware that indulgences were no substitute for repentance and faith in Christ, and anxious that true doctrine should prevail, Luther threatened to 'knock a hole in (Tetzel's) drum'. He decided to draw the Church's attention to the degree to which it had strayed from New Testament doctrine by the customary method of an academic discussion, and nailed a list of ninety-five theses, written in Latin, to the church door at Wittenberg. He also sent printed copies of the document to his bishop and archbishop. The theses were posted on the 31 October, the eve of All Saints' Day, the day the university officially attended church and when the Elector's relics were on view to the crowds. Although no one took up Luther's challenge, within four weeks the list had been translated into German and circulated all over Germany and Switzerland.

Dispute

The publication of the theses caused a furore, which the papacy at first regarded simply as a 'monkish dispute'. But when Luther continued his campaign, preaching and writing tracts, attempts were made to persuade him to recant. At every stage of the dispute Luther maintained that he taught nothing contrary to Scripture. He even attacked the papacy, accusing the pope of being the Antichrist; he argued that the pope was not above Scripture and that his claim to supremacy was based on false decretals and not on the Bible. 'A single layman armed with Scripture is to be believed above the pope or a council without it,' he declared.

Following a failed attempt to excommunicate him in 1520, when Luther publicly burned the papal bull, he was summoned to appear before Emperor Charles V, a devout Catholic, at the Diet of Worms (April 1521). When he again refused to recant, he was given twenty-one days in which to return to Wittenberg, after which he was to be regarded as a convicted heretic. Protected by his ruler Frederick the Wise as long as he remained in Saxony, his break with Rome was now complete. A further attempt was made to secure the sole supremacy of the Catholic Church at the Diet of Speyer (1529), a move that would have stopped the spread of the new movement. But six German princes and fourteen cities, who had rejected Rome in favour of Luther, drew up a 'protest'. From then on the reformers were known as 'Protestants' and the movement referred to as 'the Reformation'. The reformers formerly declared their articles of faith in the Augsburg Confession (1530).

The Catholic hierarchy was unable to recognise the extent to which it had strayed from the Scriptures and rejected any attempt to usurp its authority. With the accession of a new pope, Paul III (1534–1549), Catholic overtures were made to bring about a reunion between the two groups. Both sides endeavoured to reach an understanding, but failed. A last effort was made in 1545 at the Council of Trent, though ultimately neither side could concede the other's demands. With the door closed, the Council launched a counter-reformation. Catholic doctrines and practices disputed in the Reformation were reaffirmed, a blow aimed at the Protestant religion, and a number of disciplinary measures were introduced. A wave of missionary enterprise was set in motion, spearheaded by the Jesuits, which recaptured some of the ground lost to Rome.

CHURCH REFORMS

The change over from a Roman to an evangelical faith took some time to affect. Soon, however, Luther began to receive requests for guidance from parishes on how to conduct their worship services. He wrote a tract setting out a new liturgy, in which the Word of God was to be central to the worship; anything that was of human invention was to be set aside. He dropped the daily mass and instructed that services were to last no longer than an hour: they included reading and exposition of the Bible, using the German translation that he had made, which was to last about half an hour, to be followed by prayers and thanksgivings.

Attendance of the whole community was expected only on Sunday, when services were to include preaching of the Word, as well as a revised form of the mass (in Latin). But he replaced the central act whereby the elements were transmuted into the body and blood of Christ with the words of the institution of the Lord's Supper. In 1526 he introduced a new mass in German, a simple service for the uneducated laity. Hymns were included, some of which were written by Luther.

Luther's Legacy

Germany was now divided into two great religious parties. Luther had not intended starting a new movement, but aimed rather at reforming the Church from within, introducing changes in co-operation with the rulers and magistrates. Frederick, the Elector of Saxony, was a pious man who supported Luther, as did his successor, Elector John the Steadfast (1535–1532); they took responsibility for securing church discipline. Other

German princes and cities accepted this principle and were brought into league with Saxony. Wherever the Reformation was established, this system was copied – with modifications – whereby rulers in alliance with evangelical clergy took charge of the new emerging churches.

The Reformation developed along two main paths, from Germany and from Switzerland, though united in a recognition for the need to return to scriptural Christianity. By the end of the sixteenth century, the Lutheran (or Evangelical) Church had been established as the state religion throughout most of Germany. It also became the official religion of the Scandinavian countries, Sweden, Norway and Denmark, from where it was carried by emigrants to the United States and Canada. Its Confession of Faith, originally prepared for the Diet of Augsburg, was largely composed by Luther's lieutenant, Melanchthon.

The movement arising in Switzerland had much in common with Lutheranism, such as belief in the Bible as the only rule of faith and the doctrine of justification by faith alone. These Churches, which followed the theology of Calvin as formulated in his Institutes of the Christian Religion, were known as the Reformed Church. This arm of the movement took hold in France, where those who adopted the reformed religion became known as Huguenots, and spread to Scotland where under the leadership of John Knox it became the Presbyterian Church. In Holland, Christians were martyred for their Lutheran beliefs as early as 1523, though by the following century (1622) the Reformed Church had become the state religion.

Splinter Groups
A number of splinter groups also developed, such as the radical Anabaptists who rejected the old Church and advocated a return to the New Testament pattern. The Reformation took a different form in England, where Henry VIII simply made himself head of the Church. He wanted an English Catholic Church rather than a Roman one, a change the people of England readily accepted. It was not until after his death that changes were made that gave birth to the Anglican Communion.

The Reformation proved to be the greatest revival in the Church since Pentecost, and Luther's rediscovery of the doctrine of Scripture as the sole basis of faith led to a renewed interest in the Bible. New translations were produced in the vernacular and personal Bible reading was encouraged. This generated a growing interest in unfulfilled prophecy and with it the hope of the Second Coming. It also awakened a concern for the conversion of the Jews, who for centuries had been neglected by the Church.

Although Luther rejected papal authority, he continued to cling to certain unscriptural doctrines and practices he had inherited from Rome: he maintained the doctrine of the real presence of Christ's body and blood in the Lord's Supper (though refuting the idea that the bread and wine became the body and blood of Christ), he retained the practice of infant baptism and the use of the crucifix, candles and vestments. And despite his evangelical faith, he failed to promote any missionary enterprises for the furtherance of the gospel, relying rather on state rulers to bring their peoples into the Protestant fold.

For nearly five centuries the Reformation has continued to influence the development of the Church, giving rise to a number of movements and denominations, missions and revivals, whose spiritual ancestry can be traced back to Luther's revolt. But in every age and generation the Church needs to rediscover the truths of the Bible for itself, lest like the medieval Church it falls again into error.

22

1525 THE ANABAPTIST MOVEMENT BEGINS

The First 'Free Church' of Modern Times

On 21 January 1525 a group of six men met together for Bible study and prayer in a house in Zurich, near to the Great Minster. In defiance of a ruling made that day by the city Council and with the threat of persecution hanging over them, the men baptised one another and then commissioned each other to build Christ's Church on earth. This gathering marked the launch of the sixteenth century Anabaptist movement and the beginning of the first 'free church' of modern times. It proved to be the most radical attempt within the Protestant Reformation to renew the Church, aimed at furthering the reforms begun by Luther and Zwingli.

The Anabaptist movement proper consequently had its roots in the Swiss city of Zurich, where in 1518 the reformer Ulrich Zwingli (1484–1529) was elected People's Preacher at the Great Minster. Zwingli, for the most part independent of Luther, had come to recognise the Protestant doctrine of the supremacy of the Scriptures, and his evangelical preaching in Zurich prepared the people for the introduction of far-reaching reforms. Not wanting to proceed without the authority of the cantonal government, he delayed taking action.

By 1523, however, the city Council was still not prepared to carry out the reforms expected of them by the Church.[1] A disputation on images and the mass was held in Zurich in the October of that year, but without making any progress. Some of Zwingli's close supporters, whose ideas were even more radical than his own, urged him to go ahead 'without tarrying for

---

1. A state Church was regarded as having the divinely appointed task of guarding the Church's doctrines and punishing offenders.

any.' They exhorted him to remove or destroy all images, abolish the mass and set up a Church composed only of 'saints'. His refusal to accede to their demands led to a break between the two parties in 1524.

New Ideas

The leaders of this separatist group were Conrad Grebel, a young man of an aristocratic family, trained at Vienna and Paris, Felix Manz, an excellent Hebrew scholar, and George Blaurock, a priest. They held private Bible study meetings where the new ideas were discussed and developed. By the end of that year they had reached a conclusion on two matters, concerning infant baptism and the relationship between State and Church.

They held that the true Church was composed only of believers, those who had deliberately entered it by way of free choice. As baptism was both the symbol and the means of entry, it could only be administered to adult believers. Infant baptism, they contended, was unscriptural, and only an adult was able to repent and make a deliberate commitment to Christ. After the failure of a public disputation with Zwingli, the rebels began re-baptising those who had been baptised in infancy, hence the nickname 'Anabaptists' ('rebaptisers').

Baptism, however, was not the most important issue for them; more crucial was that of the link between Church and State. Zwingli, like Luther, held to the ideal of a Christian state in which all its citizens were baptised into the one Church, joined by the same creed. In contrast, the radicals believed in the complete separation between Church and State, and rejected the idea of a state Church to which everyone should belong. The Church, they argued, was made up only of true believers, those who were committed disciples of Christ. They should have nothing to do with the 'sword' (i.e., the civil authority), neither should they take up arms, swear oaths or take part in government.

Nevertheless, they regarded the state as ordained of God, but it was to be obeyed only where its obligations were not in opposition to conscience. They denied it had any authority over the Church, nor could it be expected to carry out reforms; it was needed only to protect the good and punish the wicked.

Radical Teachings

For a time, Zwingli was almost persuaded by the arguments against infant baptism, but held back. He realised that if there was to be a state Church, then infant baptism should be retained. The city Council finally decided to act against the radical teachings, for they posed a threat to the unity of the Church, as well as presenting a challenge to the Council's authority. On 21 January 1525 it was decreed that all children not yet baptised had to undergo the rite within eight days, that private religious meetings were prohibited, and that all foreign Anabaptists had to leave the country.

That evening the rebels met secretly at the house on Neustadtgasse, no doubt to discuss the way forward. After prayer, and believing they should be faithful to the Word of God, they held a simple communion service, then took a dipper and baptised one another by affusion (i.e., pouring). Within a few weeks, a great many people from the surrounding towns and villages – more especially from among the peasantry – had been rebaptised (some by immersion in rivers), thus anticipating the practice of the Baptist Church by almost a hundred years. Congregations consisting of believers only were set up, in which they elected their own pastor.[2] Evening gatherings were held in each others' homes, which can be said to be the first Baptist Church meetings. There was an informal celebration of the Lord's Supper, which contrasted greatly with the ritual of the mass.

SCHLEITHEIM CONFESSION (1527)

Whilst the Anabaptists did not have any generally accepted doctrinal statement, they did have a code of seven articles. It was for the most part written by Michael Sattler, an ex-Benedictine prior, in February 1527, at Schleitheim on the Swiss-German border. The document outlined certain points about which it was felt there could be no disagreement:

* Baptism is not for infants, but rather for those 'who have been taught repentance' and who consciously decide to follow Christ.
* Those who fall into error and sin shall be warned twice privately, and the third time be publicly admonished, at the breaking of bread.
* The breaking of bread is a memorial service and is only for the baptised.
* Believers should have no fellowship with the devil and his affairs, including Catholic and Protestant state Churches, and must renounce warfare.
* Pastors are to read the Scriptures, exhort, teach, warn and admonish the congregation.
* The sword is for use by wordly magistrates to punish the wicked; it must not be used in self-defence by Christians.
* The swearing of oaths is forbidden.

Sattler was captured that same year in Rothenberg and charged with a number of heretical beliefs. It was his refusal to engage in the war against the Turks for which he was burned at the stake.

---

2. These were known as 'gathered' churches.

Several of the leaders were consequently arrested and thrown into prison, warned as to their future conduct, and then released. Their persistent disobedience led to their rearrest, though most of them managed to escape. They made their way to other cantons in Switzerland where for a while they were able to resume their preaching. But renewed attempts in the cantons to stamp out the new sect meant that the leaders were forced to leave Switzerland, making for either Austria or Moravia.

Persecution was stepped up in Zurich (in January 1526) when the Council laid down heavy fines for anyone rebaptising, or for those who aided and abetted them in the act. As it failed to check the movement, eighteen men were thrown into prison and ordered to be fed on bread and water until they 'die and rot'. Blaurock was beaten through the streets and banished from the country. Others were threatened with death[3] by drowning (in hideous parody of their belief), which was the fate of Manz the following January.

Missionaries

By 1527 the movement in Zurich had been stamped out, though the only real consequence was to disperse the Anabaptists to other countries. They saw themselves as missionaries, and within a few years their influence had spread through Europe as far east as Poland, mainly among the German and Dutch-speaking peoples. The refugees from Switzerland who fled to Austria found themselves under a Catholic government which hunted them down. Among the leaders were George Blaurock of Zurich, and Hans Hut, a charismatic preacher and successful Anabaptist missionary, who prophesied that Christ's return would be at Pentecost 1528. Large numbers of converts were made and congregations established all over Austria. One contemporary account put the total number of adherents at around 12,000. Hut was captured and died in his prison cell in December 1527, while Blaurock was martyred two years later.

In 1529 Jacob Hutter became the leading Anabaptist in the Tyrol, where he built a congregation on the apostolic model of the community of property. Everyday, however, there were imprisonments and burnings; property was abandoned and children left without parents. He moved with some of his flock to the comparative safety of Moravia, where he joined other missionaries. Despite constant quarrels in the community he brought

---

3. This decision had legal precedent, for it was based on a fifth century Roman law drawn up against the Donatists, another breakaway group.

stability to the work; he introduced a common ownership of goods and gave this branch of the movement a tradition of communal farming. But in 1536 he too was arrested, tortured, whipped, immersed in freezing water, dowsed with brandy and publicly burned. The work, nevertheless, continued and the community sent out waves of missionaries throughout Europe.[4]

Martyrs

The price of their faith was high and large numbers of them perished for their beliefs. According to one account, between 1527 and 1530 some 1,000 Anabaptists were burned in the Inn Valley alone, while the Hutterite Chronicle states that 2,169 were martyred in the Holy Roman Empire during the reign of Emperor Charles V. Rather than stamping out the movement, persecution had the effect of spreading Anabaptist teachings, and more congregations were established in Germany and the Netherlands.

In Germany, as early as 1521 Anabaptist ideas and teaching about the Lord's imminent return had been circulating in the university town of Wittenberg during Luther's absence.[5] Although an ardent reformer, Luther had retained some elements of Roman ritual. Among them was that of infant baptism, which he felt infused 'a kind of faith' into infants. A group of radical prophets had arrived from Zwickau, in Saxony, and begun teaching that infant baptism was unscriptural, winning over many of Luther's disciples to the need to be rebaptised as adults. Concerned that this teaching could ruin the reform movement, on his return Luther took firm steps to suppress the new ideas and bring the converts back into the fold. The revolt ended and the prophets were driven away.

In the late 1520s Anabaptist missionaries moved into the region of the lower Rhine. The city of Strasbourg, already a meeting-place for the different branches of evangelical reform, became home to a number of Anabaptist refugees from Switzerland. They were joined by Melchior Hoffmann from Swabia, a zealous itinerant preacher with a remarkable knowledge of Scripture and determined Lutheran views. His powerful preaching often aroused opposition, which sometimes led to riots and even bloodshed. Forced to move on from one town to another, he arrived in Strasbourg in 1529. It was here that for the first time he came into contact with Anabaptists; he was won over to their views and baptised into their fellowship.

---

4. The descendants of this community are today known as Hutterites, and their descendants survive in the USA.

5. Luther was a wanted man and was in hiding at the castle at Wartburg, Thuringia.

Not all his teachings, however, were orthodox, and he taught – for example – that the Second Coming would be at Strasbourg, the New Jerusalem, in 1533. Possibly because of his extreme views, in May 1530 he fled the city and moved up the Rhine towards the Netherlands. Both here and in East Friesia, his fervent evangelical preaching brought large numbers of believers – largely from among the lower classes – into the Anabaptist fold. Such was his success that it has been claimed that the majority of Evangelicals in the Netherlands from 1533 to 1566 were of the Hoffmannite type. But in order to be present when the Lord came to take up his reign in Strasbourg, he returned to the city to await the occasion. His arrival coincided with a decisive turn in the city against Anabaptism; he was arrested and thrown into prison, where he died ten years later.

Sinister Events

It was at this point that the movement was disturbed by a much more sinister turn of events. In 1529 the German city of Munster, in Westphalia, close to the Netherlands' border, had welcomed the Reformation. A Lutheran city Council was set up and the ruling prince-bishop was driven away. Towards the end of 1533 Jan Matthys, the new Anabaptist leader in the Netherlands, sent two missionaries to Munster to introduce their teachings, winning many over to their cause.

Announcing Munster to be the New Jerusalem, Matthys arrived and took over control of the city and invited all Anabaptists to join them. Thousands made the exodus from the Netherlands to Munster, ready for the return of Christ. Whereas Hoffmann had urged his followers to peacefully await the kingdom of God, Matthys taught that it was necessary to use force. He introduced communal ownership of all property and allowed polygamy; there was no place for the magistrates or the law, and all books except the Bible were to be burned. Those Lutherans and Catholics who refused baptism were driven out of the city, replaced by thousands more oppressed Anabaptists looking for security.

The expelled prince-bishop gathered an army of both Catholic and Lutheran forces, and supported by neighbouring princes beseiged the city. Matthys, believing himself to be invulnerable, was killed in a sortie; his successor, Jan of Leyden, who thought of himself as a new messiah, proclaimed himself king, complete with robes and court attendants. A fanatic who ruled with an iron discipline, he managed to hold on to the city even though it was being starved to death. In June 1535 Munster fell to the beseiging armies; King Jan was tortured and then executed and hundreds of his followers were massacred.

The Munster tragedy was disastrous for the Anabaptists, as their opponents claimed here was evidence that, despite their insistence, the movement was a violent one and could only be contained by persecution. Wherever the name was mentioned, it was associated with the troubles at Munster, and all around Europe measures against them were sharpened. Luther, who had earlier on confronted the Anabaptists at Wittenberg, went so far as to state that they should be put to death. For many of the Anabaptists, they saw the episode at Munster as a perversion of the gospel and endeavoured to disassociate themselves from it.

A New Face

The leading figure responsible for re-organising the Anabaptists and giving the movement a new face was Menno Simons (1496–1561), a former priest from Friesland. Often under threat of death, for twenty-five years he travelled northern Germany and the Netherlands, preaching and baptising at night. It was Simons who helped rebuild the image of Anabaptists as a pious and gentle people; he stressed the idea of a community of believers and encouraged pacifism. His name has lived on in the Mennonite sect, the name by which most Anabaptist descendants are known today.

MENNONITES

The original Mennonites (Anabaptists) considered themselves to be the true heirs of the Reformation, and felt betrayed by Luther and Zwingli and their idea of a state Church. They advocated a return to New Testament Christianity in both faith and practice, and expected the brethren to literally follow the teachings of Christ.

Continued persecution forced many of them to leave for the New World. The first colonists were Dutchmen who settled in New Amsterdam (New York) about 1650. In 1683, thirteen families from Germany emigrated to America; they bought 8,000 acres of land from William Penn and founded Germantown (now part of Philadelphia). More families followed in 1683, and the exodus continued through into the nineteenth century.

In 1788, during the reign of Empress Catharine II, large numbers of Mennonites left Prussia and settled in Russia, on the understanding they would be able to live according to their religion. When in the 1870s danger threatened this arrangement 15,000 of them left for America.

Mennonite communities are today for the most part to be found in America and Canada, but also in Switzerland, the Netherlands, France and Germany, as well as Brazil, Paraguay and Mexico.

Anabaptism was never a unified movement, for the congregations differed in spirit, aims and doctrines, though agreeing in their ideas about baptism and the state Church. Their views caused fear and alarm in some rulers and theologians, and they were denounced by the leading reformers of the day. Yet in 1608 John Smyth and a group of English exiles in Amsterdam came under Mennonite influence, and four years later one of his associates formed the first Baptist congregation in England.

While the movement in south Germany and Austria was stamped out, small enclaves were still to be found in Switzerland; the Hutterite brotherhood survived in rural congregations in Moravia, and the Mennonites lingered on in the Netherlands. During the seventeenth century small groups made their way to America, where they became part of a large number of European pilgrims who crossed the Atlantic in order to enjoy freedom of worship in the New World.

23

1534 ACT OF SUPREMACY PASSED

The Church of England Established

The Reformation was slow in gaining a foothold in England. Initially, the impetus for reform had more to do with the political manoeuvrings of Henry VIII (1509–1547) than with any desire for the new teaching. In his quarrel with the papacy concerning a divorce from Queen Catherine, Henry made himself head of the Church in England. By the Act of Supremacy, the powers of the papacy were transferred to the king and the Archbishop of Canterbury, and Henry's marriage to Catherine was annulled. With the bonds between Rome and England severed, the way was open for the introduction of Reformation ideas and the advance of Protestantism.

When the seventeen year old Prince Henry succeeded to the throne of England in 1509, it seemed as if he were just the monarch to support the new learning that was filtering through from the Continent. The young and handsome ruler was a gifted scholar, an accomplished musician and poet, skilled at sport, and a devout churchman. But he was already a headstrong and impatient young man, determined to have his own way; throughout his reign he ruthlessly crushed anyone who crossed him.

Shortly after his accession Henry married Catherine of Aragon, the daughter of Ferdinand and Isabella of Spain, a union made possible only after the pope had granted a special dispensation. This was necessary because Catherine had formerly been married to Henry's older brother, Prince Arthur, who had died seven years previously. Of the five children born to Henry and Catherine, only Mary (born 1516) survived, hence the king's concern for a male heir to succeed to the throne. But Catherine's failure to give him a son seemed to him as God's judgment for having contracted an unlawful marriage. Even though Catherine was a popular and respected queen, it did not deter Henry from seeking a divorce.

Difficulty

In 1527 finally Henry determined to be rid of the queen in order to marry Anne Boleyn, a young lady-in-waiting. All that was needed was for the pope to declare his marriage to Catherine null and void, on the ground that the papal dispensation had been *ultra vires* (i.e., beyond the pope's authority), as it was contrary to the law of God.[1] Normally, for someone in Henry's position this would not have been an impossible task, but there was a major difficulty in the way, for Catherine's nephew was the emperor Charles V who at that time imprisoned the pope. To further his cause in what he began to call his 'Great Matter', he placed his divorce proceedings in the hands of Cardinal Wolsey, who had been appointed a papal legate (a personal representative of the Holy See).

By 1529 no decision had been taken and Henry's patience had become exhausted. Wolsey was dismissed for failing to make progress in the matter and the king took affairs into his own hands. If the pope would not agree to the divorce, then he would defy him and the clergy as well. To make the matter legal, he needed to persuade parliament to back him against the pope and throw off papal jurisdiction over the English Church. What became known as the Reformation Parliament sat over a period of seven years, from 1529 to 1536 (meeting for only a few weeks each winter), passing a series of laws by which Henry secured the obedience of the clergy, made himself head of the Church in England and achieved his divorce.

With Wolsey out of the way, Henry was able to work through parliament rather than through Convocation, the Church's assembly, so that questions of church discipline and order were discussed by the secular government. The king's first step was to secure the obedience of the clergy to himself, for he recognised that the most powerful man in the land was not himself but the archbishop. He made two moves which went a considerable way towards achieving this objective.

Threatened

Under the Act of Praemunire,[2] the clergy were accused of having accepted Cardinal Wolsey as a papal legate (even though the king had asked for the appointment), and were threatened with punishment. After discussion, Convocation agreed to buy its immunity from under the act; Canterbury paid Henry the sum of £100,000, and York contributed £19,000.

---

1. Leviticus 20:21, which actually refers to childlessness.
2. Statutes passed in 1353, 1365 and 1393 to protect the rights of the English Crown against papal claims.

Convocation also recognised the king as 'Protector and Supreme Head of the English Church and Clergy', though adding the clause, 'as far as the law of Christ allows'.

The outcome was that the clergy accepted the Crown as an essential part of the constitution of the English Church and they were not allowed to take any action not approved by the king or the king in parliament. Though there was no reference to a repudiation of papal jurisdiction nor any suggestion of a separate Church, Henry had prepared the way for assuming leadership of the Church in England.

Aware that his worst enemies were among the Protestants, the king determined to defuse the opposition while at the same time winning over the disgruntled clergy. In 1531 he gave the clergy permission to hunt down, imprison and burn any who were disciples of Luther. The first to receive the martyr's crown was the godly Thomas Bilney of Norwich, one of a number of Cambridge reformers; others burnt at the stake included Richard Bayfield, an evangelist, John Tewkesbury, a respected merchant, and James Bainham, a distinguished lawyer. Catholics who opposed the king's plans also met with the same fate.

Reformation Hope

A development took place around this time that marked the beginning of a reformation hope, for in 1533 Henry appointed Thomas Cranmer to be Archbishop of Canterbury. When Henry first met Cranmer, in 1529, the Cambridge don had suggested the king might consult the universities of Europe on the legality of the divorce. Cranmer was despatched on a tour of European universities to sound them out; he succeeded in gaining their support. When the need arose for a new archbishop Henry turned to the one who had furthered his cause. Cranmer was reluctant to accept the offer and would have preferred a more peaceful life, but the king insisted on having his way. Once he accepted, Cranmer remained a faithful servant of the king; though often given to compromise in matters of religion, he was the one who gently opened the door to the new teachings.

Time, however, was pressing. Henry had secretly married Anne Boleyn in January 1533, and they were living together at Greenwich. As she was already with child, then his marital affairs needed to be straightened out quickly if the child was to be recognised as legitimate. It was to his new archbishop that Henry looked to bring the affair to a satisfactory conclusion. Both parliament and Convocation accepted that the pope had exceeded his authority in giving Henry a dispensation, and that the marriage to Catherine was null from the first. Cranmer agreed and pronounced the king's marriage to Anne valid; she was crowned queen on Whit-Sunday at Westminster Abbey and the young Princess Elizabeth was born in the September. The pope attempted to annul the marriage and threatened to excommunicate the couple if they did not separate, but to no avail.

Henry's next task was to remove the pope's prerogatives and powers over the English Church, and further acts were passed to secure his ambition of becoming Supreme Head. Parliament passed the Act for the Restraint of Annates, forbidding the payment of the first year's income of a bishop, abbot or parish priest to the papacy; it was, instead, to be paid to the Crown. (It was calculated that since the accession of Henry VII, in 1485, the sum had amounted to £160,000.) The act also stated that in future all bishops should be consecrated in England by the archbishop.

Of greater importance, however, was the Act for the Restraint of Appeals, passed in February 1533, which forbade English law cases being taken to Rome. This frustrated Catherine's attempt to submit her case to the pope. The law went on to declare that the realm of England was an 'empire' (i.e., an independent, sovereign state), and that the king was Supreme Head of both Church and State. Further, it laid down that ecclesiastical matters were to be dealt with by Church courts.

Other acts completed the work of separation from the papacy: bishops were to be elected by the king, acting through the cathedral chapters; Peter's Pence (an ecclesiastical tax paid to the pope) was abolished; and the archbishop was authorised to grant dispensations and licences instead of appealing to the pope. Meanwhile, Convocation finally agreed to make no new ecclesiastical laws without the king's permission, and accepted that all existing canons should receive his approval.

Supreme Head

Henry's efforts were crowned with success when, in November 1534, the Act of Supremacy declared that the king and his successors should be 'accepted and reputed the only Supreme Head on earth of the Church of England', without any saving clause about 'the law of Christ'. In addition, the act gave him power to define the Church's doctrine and to punish heresy. This was followed by an Act of Succession, under which the marriage to the Lady Catherine was declared null and the marriage to Anne was decreed legitimate. In this way, Henry and Anne's children were to succeed to the throne. What is more, it required all nobles, both spiritual and temporal, to take an oath acknowledging the king's new position. Both Sir Thomas

More and Bishop Fisher of Rochester refused the oath and were executed in 1535. Then under an Act of Treason, anyone plotting against the king, calling him a tyrant or a heretic, was liable for the death penalty.

Within the space of three years, Henry had carried through a major revolution; all allegiance to Rome had been severed and the powers transferred to the king or the archbishop. This was not brought about by the Church, but was rather a constitutional change, legally effected by the king through parliament. As yet the Reformation had not begun, though there was an increasing desire for reform within the hearts of many English people. What is more, there was a strong feeling among the laity against papal abuses and a rising tide of nationalism that resented interference of Rome.

Monasteries

By this time Henry's extravagances had left him short of money and he needed to replenish the dwindling royal coffers. His eyes lighted on the country's 800 religious houses, which he realised could provide him with a source of income. It was widely recognised that many of the monasteries were sadly in need of reform, an excuse used by the king to appropriate their estates and incomes. His Vicar-General, Thomas Cromwell, Earl of Essex, carried out a survey of all monastic properties, returning with a damning report for parliament which paved the way for the Dissolution.

Titchfield Abbey, dissolved by Henry VIII in 1536,
though the tudor gateway was left standing.

Under the 1536 Act for the Supression of the Lesser Monasteries, the last act of the Reformation Parliament, the process began of closing down all religious houses, with the seizure of their estates and incomes for the Crown – all carried out under the guise of reform. Some of the properties were sold or leased, others were given to the king's supporters as political rewards. All monastic treasures were sent to the king's jewel house, while buildings were partly dismantled and the materials used for other purposes. In the space of four years one of England's most ancient institutions was virtually wiped out and many of its notable buildings thrown into disrepair.

DISSOLUTION OF THE MONASTERIES

In April 1536 there were some 800 religious houses scattered throughout England and Wales; four years later there were none. The first wave of suppression of the monasteries centred on those houses with a net income of less than £200 a year. Of the 600 smaller abbeys and priories, only 243 were affected; others escaped under various discretionary clauses in the Act.

Protests were raised in Lincolnshire and Yorkshire, and Heads of the larger abbeys who aided the rebels were tried for treason and condemned. As a result, some who had expressed sympathy for the revolt decided it more prudent to yield their properties to the Crown. All the remaining monastic houses surrendered voluntarily, until there were none left in England or Wales.

The 10,000 inhabitants of the religious houses were given the choice of either taking a life pension or receiving a dispensation from their vows. All monastic treasures were seized. The bells were taken to be recast as canon, lead stripped from the roofs was used for shot and the timbers taken for the furnaces. With no roof, buildings started to deteriorate, a process considerably hastened by the removal of large quantities of stones for other building purposes.

Throughout his reign Henry remained a staunch Catholic and was hostile towards Lutheran doctrines. Incensed by the reformer's attack on the sacraments, in 1520 he wrote a treatise, *Assertion of the Seven Sacraments*, defending the Catholic position. A copy of the book was presented to Pope Leo X, who rewarded him with the title of Fidei Defensor – 'Defender of the Faith'. In 1554 Parliament acknowledged this title as officially belonging to the English monarch, and has since continued to be used by all British sovereigns.

Articles of Faith

Despite the king's opposition to Protestantism, Reformation ideas were gaining ground in England. There were now two rival movements within the land, creating a constant tension between the opposing parties. Lutheran doctrines, which were being discussed in the English universities in the

1520s, had many adherents, some of whom were to suffer martyrdom for their cause. In an attempt to bring stability into a confused situation, in 1536 Convocation under Archbishop Cranmer adopted the Ten Articles of Faith. With a preface by the king, the articles represented a compromise between the old and the new teachings; whilst reflecting the Lutheran Confession of Augsburg (1530) they also retained elements of Roman doctrine and practices, such as purgatory and the veneration of the saints. Perhaps more important, the king permitted the publication of the Great Bible[3] (so named because of its size), a copy of which was ordered to be placed in every church that it might be read by the laity.

CRANMER AND THE REFORMATION

One of Cranmer's most important contributions to the Reformation was the introduction of English into church services. The Great Bible was already available in every church, and in 1542 Convocation ordered that in all services a chapter of the New Testament should be read in English, but without exposition; two years later prayers in English were introduced. The use of English, and not Latin, was a revolutionary move.

On the accession of Edward VI (1547), the pace of reform increased. In that year, Cranmer and Bishop Ridley produced a Book of Homilies – evangelical sermons to be read in parish churches. In 1549 Cranmer replaced the Roman Catholic Missal (service book) with the Book of Common Prayer; the aim was to simplify and condense the Latin missal, and to produce a service book in English for priest and people. It was a compromise between Catholic and Reform, so phrased that it would not unnecessarily offend Catholics. A music edition was issued, which was an adaption of plain chant to the new liturgy. A government proclamation ordered all pictures and images in churches to be destroyed, especially those of the Virgin Mary.

The BCP was revised in 1552, when a truly Protestant version was produced, amended under Elizabeth in 1559 and was again revised in 1662, remaining almost unchanged until recent times.

Cranmer was arrested when the Catholic Queen Mary came to the throne in 1553. Two years later he was burned at the stake.

Despite these hopeful signs, Henry continued to be something of an enigma. In 1539 the reformers received a setback when an act, introduced into the House of Lords by the Duke of Norfolk and backed by the king, approved a new statement of doctrine. The Six Articles laid down what doctrines were to be believed: transubstantiation, communion in one kind only (bread), clerical celibacy, vows of chastity for the laity (i.e., ex-nuns and lay-brothers), private masses and compulsory auricular confessions.

---

3. The first recognition of the Bible in English.

Denial of transubstantiation was heresy and was punishable by death.

Whilst Cranmer showed signs of leaning more and more towards Reformation views, he continued to lend support to the king, who protected his archbishop from calls to have him sent to the Tower. Overtures from German theologians towards England, to embrace Lutheran doctrines, were firmly rejected by Henry. And though Cranmer was sympathetic, his belief in a 'godly prince' remained firm and his uneasy relationship with the king held throughout the remaining years of the reign.

When Henry died in 1547 he was succeeded by his nine-year-old son, Edward VI (1547–1553), who had been tutored by an avowed reformer. The young king's uncle, the Duke of Somerset, also anxious to further the Protestant cause, became Protector. Thus the way was open for the introduction of the changes many longed for. Under Cranmer a foundation was laid down whereby the Church of England underwent a reformation which, despite having to endure the fiery ordeal of Catholic Queen Mary's reign (1553–1558), emerged a reformed Church which was finally secured under the rule of Elizabeth I.

24

1536 CALVIN PUBLISHES FIRST EDITION OF HIS *INSTITUTES OF THE CHRISTIAN RELIGION*

The First Systematic Exposition of Reformed Theology

Calvin's *Institutes of the Christian Religion* was his crowning achievement and has been described as a 'masterpiece of Protestant theology'. When the work was first published in 1536 it was quickly recognised as an outstanding contribution to the cause of the Reformation. It went through several editions before reaching its final form in 1559, emerging not only as a complete summary of Christian teaching but also a synthesis of Calvinist thought.

John Calvin (1509–1564) was born into a Catholic family in the cathedral city of Noyon, France, some sixty miles north-east of Paris. His father, Gerard Cauvin,[1] an ambitious and self-made man, had risen to become secretary to the Bishop of Noyon and procurator of the cathedral chapter. On the understanding that he would one day join the priesthood, by the age of twelve Calvin had obtained an income from two benefices, a result of his father's influence, which enabled him to pursue a scholastic career.

Early Years

Details of Calvin's early years and his life as a student are sketchy, as he appears to have been reluctant to place them on record. He first entered the College des Capettes in Noyon, where among his companions were a number of young noblemen from the district. Two years later, at the age of

---

1. The son Latinised his surname Cauvin to Calvinus, and became known as Calvin.

fourteen, his father sent him to the College de la Marche in Paris, where he studied philosophy and dialectics, and also enjoyed instruction in Latin under the renowned Mathurin Cordier. This was the beginning of a life-long friendship between the two, and years later Calvin acknowledged that the foundation of his fluent style in Latin had been laid down by his tutor.

In 1523 he moved to the College de Montaigu where he completed his undergraduate studies in 1528. Though his father had originally wanted his son to read theology, he changed his mind following a quarrel with the Noyon Chapter, feeling that a career in law would be more remunerative. In obedience to his father's wishes, Calvin moved to the University at Orleans where in 1533 he was awarded his doctorate. It was at Orleans that he met a Lutheran, Melchior Wolmar, the leader of a group in which Reformation ideas were discussed, who considerably influenced his thinking. He became interested in Christian humanism, and under Wolmar took up the study of Greek.

When Calvin was converted is not at all clear, though after his father's death (in 1531) he felt able to renew his interest in theology. There is no doubt, however, that by the year 1533 he had accepted the truth of Lutheran doctrines and had undergone a conversion experience. A hint is given in his *Commentary on the Psalms*, published in 1558, where he writes of his being taken from the study of philosophy in order to learn law, 'from which ... God in his secret providence finally curbed and turned me in another direction. At first, although I was so obstinately given to the superstitions of the papacy, that it was extremely difficult to drag me from the depths of the mire, yet by a sudden conversion he tamed my heart and made it teachable, this heart which for its age was excessively hardened in such matters.'

It seems as though it was during these years, whilst studying law, that he first tasted of 'the pure religion'. Yet even before he met Wolmar, his cousin, Robert Olivetan,[2] had already spoken to him of 'papal superstitions', probably in 1528. At first he stubbornly resisted this 'different form of doctrine', though he was 'grievously troubled ... on account of the wretched state into which (he had) fallen ... (and) of the knowledge of the eternal death' which hung over him. He read the works of Luther and other evangelical writers, but found their doctrine hard to receive.

---

2. It was Olivetan who translated the Bible into French for the Waldenses.

Sound Doctrine

By now, however, Calvin was beginning 'to emerge somewhat from the darkness of popery … having acquired some little taste for sound doctrine'. Faced with the struggle of leaving the Church of his childhood, he was nevertheless able – like Luther before him – to repent of his sin and give himself up to God's way. From then on, he recognised he had a calling from God to proclaim the truth, which he did both by preaching and by his writings.

His conversion could quite likely have taken place a year or so before the usually accepted date of 1533, perhaps between the publication of his first book in the spring of 1532, and the autumn of the following year. Even so, his tenuous links with the Roman Church continued for another two years, when he finally relinquished his benefices. By this time he was firmly established within the Protestant fold.

The date of 1533, nevertheless, turned out to be one of significance for Calvin, for the threat of persecution forced him to leave Paris, travelling around France under an assumed name. It was the consequence of an address delivered by his friend Nicholas Cop, the newlyelected rector of the University of Paris. The inaugural sermon, written in language borrowed from Luther and Erasmus and seemingly penned by Calvin, aroused the anger of both King Francis I and the Parlement of Paris. The king, writing to the Parlement, commanded that a search should be made for members of this Lutheran sect and that proceedings should be taken against them.

Following the flight of Cop to Basel, Calvin also made his getaway. He escaped through the window of his room and left Paris in the borrowed clothes of a vinedresser, with a beggar's sack on his back and a hoe on his shoulder. Invited by his friend Louis du Tillet to stay in Angoulême, north-east of Bordeaux, he spent several happy months in retreat working in the long gallery of St Peter's Cathedral. It seems that his studies and researches during this period formed the basis of his Institutes, for which he had begun to draw up plans.

Imprisoned

The following year, in April 1534, Calvin was again on the move. Whether it was because of the threat of persecution or that he wished to consult with others concerning the Scriptures, is not entirely clear. It seems more than likely that during this period he would have continued to work on his manuscript. At Nerac, he met with Jacques Lefevre d'Etaples, 'one of the most learned men of his century', a former professor and author of commentaries on the Psalms and the Epistle to the Romans. He returned briefly to Paris, then went to his native Noyon where he resigned his benefices and was, for a short while, imprisoned.

But France was now too dangerous for him, especially since in the October a Protestant pastor had publicly attacked the abuses of the mass by nailing strongly worded placards and books at several crossroads around Paris. Calvin hastily moved to Poitiers and then to Orléans, and early in the New Year of 1535 travelled via Strasbourg to Protestant Basel, where he was safe from the clutches of the French king.

CALVIN AT GENEVA

During the course of his journeyings, Calvin visited Geneva in 1536, when he was invited by the reformer William Farel (1489–1565) to join him in establishing the Reformation in the city. He lectured on the Bible and was later appointed preacher. In January 1537, in an attempt to make Geneva a model community, he and Farel laid before the city Council a series of recommendations to impose church discipline upon the people of the city. However, an attempt that was strongly was resented. The two men were expelled and Calvin moved to Strasbourg where he became the pastor of a congregation of French refugees.

In 1540 the party in Geneva that was favourably disposed towards Calvin was restored to power, and the following year he reluctantly accepted an invitation to return. His aim was to build a 'City of God', a model Christian community, based on the New Testament, though it could only succeed with the imposition of a rigorous discipline. Like Luther and other reformers, he believed that both Church and State derived their authority from God, and that the two should co-operate with each other.

The city was ruled by a Consistory Council, made up of pastors and elders approved by the magistrates, and was entrusted solely with matters of ecclesiastical discipline. However, they relied on the civil magistrates to enforce the rules and maintain the cause of religion. But the magistrates of the city had no intention of allowing Calvin to infringe upon the prerogatives of the civil power, and they laid down that civil offences were outside the jurisdiction of the Council.

Rules were introduced governing the details of everyday life, such as a prohibition of dancing and regulations concerning clothing and even food. Penalties were laid down for defaulters, including excommunication, which also involved the loss of citizenship. The conflict between the civil and religious authorities persisted for many years, though in the end Calvin won the battle. Geneva became a transformed society and a haven for persecuted believers who found refuge within its walls. Later, the Scots reformer John Knox described the city as 'the most perfect school of Christ that ever was in the earth since the days of the apostles'.

Basel was one of the chief intellectual centres of Europe and was widely known for the excellency of its printers. He took lodgings under the assumed name of Lucanius, in order to protect his identity. No doubt he was reunited with his old friend Cop, who had taken refuge there, and he met the Swiss Reformer, Henry Bullinger, who had succeeded Zwingli as chief pastor of Zurich.

This respite in Basel gave him the opportunity to continue his studies in theology, and to work on a Latin catechism as well as his Institutes. But the publication of his Institutes was hastened by the sad events taking place in France, where a number of Evangelicals – including a personal friend, a merchant from Paris – had been arrested and, on the king's orders, burnt at the stake. The outburst of persecution was further inflamed by the news of the wild excesses of a group of fanatical Anabaptists at Munster,[3] where Jan Mathys, a 'prophet' from the Netherlands, had stirred up his followers to forcibly expel all those who would not accept his teachings. As a result of this action, the normally peaceable Anabaptists and Evangelicals were alike lumped together and branded as 'political agitators'.

Evil Charges

Calvin, incensed by this 'infamous shedding of innocent blood', voiced his strong opposition to the killings. He later wrote (in his Commentary on the Psalms), 'it seemed to me that unless I were strongly opposed to this, as far as in me lay, I could not exonerate myself from the charge of disloyalty if I remained silent.' It was for this reason that he was spurred on to publish his Institutes. 'Firstly', he continued, 'in order to reply to these evil charges which others were sowing and to clear my brothers, whose death was precious before the Lord.'

His intention was to give a summary of the Faith held by Evangelicals, which was the work he had already begun in Angoulême. He prefaced it with a letter dedicating the Institutes to the French king, hoping to convince him that he was wrong to persecute those of the Reformed Church. It was addressed 'To the most Christian king of France, Francis the First of this name, his Prince and sovereign Lord'. It goes on to express the author's aim, which was 'to serve our French people of whom I can see many who are hungry and thirsty for Jesus Christ and few who have gained a right knowledge of him'. The letter, courteous and dignified, was a clear presentation of the Protestant position and has been recognised as 'one of the literary masterpieces of the Reformation age'. Dated August 1535, the book was not actually published until the following March.

---

3. See p.192.

Written in Latin, the Institutes ran to 516 pages, though its small format was such that it could easily be slipped into the large pockets of the clothes then worn. The book was, in effect, a catechism; it consisted of six chapters, of which the first four followed the plan of Luther's Little Catechism; these were: (1) concerning the law, including an explanation of the Ten Commandments, (2) concerning faith, in which the Apostles' Creed is expounded, (3) on prayer, together with a commentary on the Lord's Prayer, and (4) on the sacraments, covering baptism and the Lord's Supper.

The remaining two chapters are in a quite different vein: (5) deals with the five other rites, previously called sacraments by the Roman Catholic Church, and (6) sets out Calvin's ideas on Christian freedom, as well as the relation between Church and State in a society influenced by the gospel. This last section was a reply to the condemnation of the placards of 1534 in Paris and of the French king's attitude to the Reformation.

Further Editions

Although this first publication was successful – it was speedily translated into the languages of Europe and was completely sold out in less than a year – Calvin was not entirely satisfied with the work. A second edition, again in Latin, appeared three years later, with an added eleven chapters and included an expanded treatment of the Trinity. A French translation of this edition was published in 1541, no doubt intended for the reformed of France and for those who could not read Latin.

Calvin produced a further edition in 1543, which increased the number of chapters by four, bringing the total to twenty-one. The additional material was based on the Apostles' Creed, which served as a framework for the work when it was recast in 1559. A French translation of this edition appeared in 1545. In the edition of 1550, the chapters were for the first time subdivided into paragraphs in order to help the reader more easily find his way through the work. The French translation, in 1551, contained supplementary sections which were incorporated into the 1559 edition.

By the time Calvin decided to produce a definitive edition of his work, he was ill and not expecting to live long. Despite severe pain, he worked with his brother and some friends to clarify passages that did not seem clear and to make minor additions. There is some doubt whether the French translation of 1560 was actually written by the reformer, or whether it was dictated.

Calvin's *Institutes of the Christian Religion* published

John Calvin (1509-1564)

CALVIN AND PREDESTINATION

Some theologians have claimed – quite wrongly – that the central theme of Calvin's doctrine was predestination. In fact it was hardly mentioned in the 1536 edition of his Institutes, and it was not until later editions that it assumed a more important place in his writings.

As with the later Westminster Confession (1647), the starting point of his Institutes was the sovereignty of God, omnipotent and omnipresent, who had created the world in order that man might know him. Since the Fall of man, however, there had been a barrier between man and God; as man had no goodness or power of himself, so all men were in a hopeless condition. Redemption was only available through the grace of God, mediated through the work of Christ on the cross.

But from before creation, God had a plan for man (a 'decree') by which he predestined some men to be saved through faith in Jesus Christ (election), and others to be condemned (reprobation); it was by God's choice alone that some were imputed to eternal life and others to damnation. Despite his strong emphasis on 'double predestination', as it is known, he appears to avoid the idea of a limited Atonement whereby Christ's death does not have a universal application.

However, the doctrine brings into question the love of God, for if God could save, why did he not? Why leave any to perish? Perhaps it is only as it is recognised that God's love was behind the plan of salvation, and that his purposes were to bless others rather simply to affect the salvation of individual people. Thus Calvin perceived it not as an arbitrary act of God, but as according to his own 'good pleasure'.

207

By now, the Institutes were composed of eighty chapters, broken down into four sections, just as the Apostles' Creed has four parts. The four sections deal with (1) the knowledge of God, who is the Creator and sovereign governor of the world; (2) the Fall of Man and God's work of redemption through Jesus Christ; (3) the work of the Holy Spirit in the life of the believer; and (4) the Church and the means of grace, including the sacraments.

Whilst Calvin owed much to the work of Luther before him, especially his concept of justification by faith and of the sacraments, at the relative young age of twenty-six the Institutes had placed him at the forefront of the Reformation movement. Like Luther, he was not proposing a new creed but was rather attempting to bring the Church back to its historic beliefs and practices. The Institutes were recognised as the most orderly and systematic popular presentation of doctrine and the Christian life yet produced by the Reformation, and probably no book published in the sixteenth century had such far-reaching effects.

Calvin was the greatest biblical theologian of his age and the leading reformer of the second phase in the development of the Reformation. His theological works gave the movement an added impetus, helping to shape the Reformed churches and providing the basis for their confessions of faith. Though both men and movements were profoundly influenced by his ministry, he left no successor of equal status.

25

1609 SMYTH BAPTISES SELF BY AFFUSION

The Emergence of the Baptist Movement

During the early years of the seventeenth century there emerged in England a group of Christians known as 'Baptists'. Their roots can be traced to events in Holland, when in 1609 John Smyth (1570?–1612) baptised himself and then members of his congregation. But the origins of the new movement, however, more correctly belong to the European Anabaptists of the previous century, who helped pave the way for the rediscovery of believer's baptism. Despite persecution, baptist convictions began to spread: the first Baptist church was formed in London in 1612, and in 1639 a Baptist congregation was organised in Rhode Island, America.

When the Anabaptists rejected the practice of infant baptism in favour of believer's baptism they were often branded as fanatics. Over the sixteenth century thousands of them suffered martyrdom at the hands of both Protestants and Catholics. Following the tragedy of the massacre at Munster in 1535,[1] the survivors fled to Holland and, later, to England only to meet with a similar fate. Between 1535 and the end of the century, a number of Dutch and English so-called heretics were either burned at the stake or hanged after refusing to recant of their new-found beliefs.

By the end of the century the Anabaptist movement in England had virtually disappeared. At the same time, the Puritan revolt in the Church of England continued to gain in strength, though alongside them developed a second dissident movement, the Separatists,[2] who dissociated themselves

---

1. See p.192.
2. This move was based on 2 Corinthians 6:17. Separatists were also known as Dissenters, because they dissented from the Established Church. Later, when dissent was tolerated, they became known as Nonconformists and eventually the term Free Churches was substituted.

from the Church of England. Whereas the Puritans remained within the established Church, anxious to 'purify' it of its Roman elements, the Separatists rejected the idea of a state-controlled Church; they consequently withdrew and set up their own independent congregations.

Independent Church

Led by Robert Browne (c1550–1633) and Robert Harrison (d 1585), in 1581 a group of believers formed an independent church at Norwich. Like the Anabaptists, they believed the local church should be composed of a body of regenerate members, united to God and each other by a voluntary covenant; it should be self-governing, and having no authority over any other church. Despite Anabaptist leanings, however, they did not reject the practice of infant baptism. The followers of Browne became known as 'Brownists', and this move towards independent gatherings marked the beginning of what was later to become the Congregational Church.

Browne openly preached his views in Norwich and soon found himself arrested and was twice imprisoned. As the harassment continued, he finally decided with Harrison and other members of his congregation to take refuge in Middelburg, Holland, where religious nonconformity was now tolerated. Yet he did not stay there for long, as dissension in the congregation persuaded him to renounce his position and return to England, where he spent the rest of his life within the Anglican fold.

The movement continued to gather momentum, however, and despite persecution others joined the Separatist cause. In London, Henry Barrow and John Greenwood were arrested in 1587 for holding Separatist meetings; their followers continued to meet in secret though they were never safe from arrest. The two leaders were finally arrested and hanged at Tyburn in 1593 for defying the Queen's supremacy and saying 'there was not a true church in England'.

What proved to be a work of far-reaching consequence, however, was begun in 1606 by John Smyth, a Fellow of Christ's College, Cambridge, and an Anglican clergyman who had adopted Separatist principles. Dismissed from his post in Lincoln as lecturer and chaplain to the mayor, he joined a group of Puritans meeting at the old hall in Gainsborough, in the lower Trent valley, on the boundaries of Lincolnshire, Nottinghamshire and Yorkshire. They had seceded from the established Church and formed a gathered independent congregation, joining themselves together by a covenant of the Lord, 'as the Lord's free people ... to walk in all his ways ... whatever it might cost...'

Haven

By 1607, however, the congregation had split into two, quite probably on theological grounds. One group was based at Gainsborough and they chose Smyth as their pastor. Among the members was Thomas Helwys, a wealthy lawyer and a landed gentleman of Broxtowe Hall – a haven for dissenters – near Nottingham, who was later to establish the first Baptist Church in England. The second group met at nearby Scrooby Manor and was led by John Robinson, a former Fellow of Corpus Christi College, Cambridge. William Brewster, lord of the Manor and bailiff of the Archbishop of York, and the seventeen year old William Bradford, the future Governor of the Plymouth colony of New England, were members of this congregation.

As the threat of persecution and imprisonment was an ever-present one, the Gainsborough group decided to leave England for a place where they could freely worship God. In 1608 Smyth took his wife, family and congregation to Holland, which had recently overthrown its Spanish (Catholic) overlords and established a republic, where freedom of religion was permitted. They settled in Amsterdam where they joined a gathering of other exiles, pastored by Francis Johnson, once a Fellow of Christ's College, Cambridge, and where the teacher was Henry Ainsworth, formerly Smyth's tutor. The Scrooby congregation followed later and also took refuge in Amsterdam before moving to Leyden.

Smyth, however, was a man of forthright views, and his arrival soon produced controversy within an already troubled congregation. Anxious to have a church 'according to the New Testament pattern', Smyth raised two issues with Johnson's 'ancient Separatist church'. The first concerned the reading of translations of the Scriptures which, maintained Smyth, were only inspired in their original tongue. He contended that it was only permissible for church officers to read the Scriptures in the original Hebrew or Greek, then to translate them 'by voice'. It was on this matter that Smyth and his followers left Johnson's church, calling themselves 'the brethren of the separation of the second English church at Amsterdam'.

The other dispute concerned the matter of church government. Whereas Johnson kept discipline in his fractious church in his own hands and those of the elders, Smyth argued in favour of democracy in the church, whereby the elders could do nothing without the approval of the body of believers. Ainsworth, Johnson's assistant, later came to see the force of this teaching and in 1610 seceded from Johnson's church. At this point Smyth's congregation appears to have been given hospitality by the Mennonites and they took over a room at the back of a 'great cake-house' for their place of worship.

Believer's Baptism

One other matter that had begun to trouble Smyth was the practice of infant baptism. While the Separatists had declared that the Church of England was not a true Church, they had continued the practice of baptising infants. Possibly as the result of having contact with the Mennonite group in Amsterdam, and certainly through his own search of the Scriptures, Smyth came to the conclusion that adult believer's baptism was the New Testament norm. He rejected infant baptism on the grounds that an infant had no awareness of sin and could not repent. A true Church, he held, was composed of those who had been baptised on profession of their personal faith in Christ.

THE SACRAMENT OF BAPTISM

The Greek verb *baptizein* has given rise to the English words 'baptise' and 'baptism', and means 'to dip, soak or immerse'. The Christian practice of baptism owes its origins to the Jewish idea of ceremonial washing or purification, where self-immersion in a *mikveh* (ritual bath) was necessary for ritual cleansing.

John the Baptist adopted the practice, but linked it to repentance from sin – a revolutionary step for Jews – in preparation for the coming of the Messiah. Later, Peter and the apostles preached the same message on the Day of Pentecost, when some 3,000 people were baptised, no doubt in the *mikvah* of which there were several located at the foot of the Temple steps.

During the early years of the Church converts were admitted to the Christian community by a public confession of faith and baptism. Some scholars, however, accept that there may have been occasions when children were baptised together with their parents (e.g., Acts 16:33). Tertullian (c150–c225) and Origen (c185–254) were familiar with child baptism, though it was not a universal practice; in fact rather the opposite, as some Christians left it until their deathbed before accepting the rite, as did the emperor Constantine.

In the fifth century the custom of baptising infants by affusion became the rule rather than the exception, and it had by now acquired some sort of 'magical' quality. Because infant mortality rates were high, the ceremony usually took place shortly after birth, and if a child died unbaptised then it was thought it would not go to heaven.

That infant baptism became the norm was in part due to Augustine, Bishop of Hippo (354–431), and other Church Fathers who taught that baptism dealt with the condition of original sin and was therefore necessary for salvation. At the Reformation, infant baptism was retained by the Lutheran, Reformed and Anglican Churches on the basis that 'a kind of faith' was bestowed through baptism. It was taught that child baptism was the equivalent of Jewish circumcision, by which the child was included in the family of Faith.

When he brought the issue before his own congregation his arguments were accepted and they decided to act upon their decision. Smyth first baptised himself, not by immersion but by pouring water out of a basin over his face. He then baptised Thomas Helwys and some forty other members of his congregation. The decision to adopt the rite of adult believer's baptism, as they saw practised in the New Testament, brought them into line with the Anabaptists (though not with their mode of baptising), as well as with the Hutterites and the Mennonites. Yet all of the groups were denounced at various times by Luther, Zwingli and Calvin, and persecuted by both Catholics and Protestants.

Not all Smyth's congregation was in agreement with his teaching, and one critic from among them pointed out that if Smyth baptised himself then 'any man could do likewise and churches could be established of solitary men, which would be absurd'. By the February of the following year Smyth had also begun to express doubts about the validity of his second baptism. He came to the decision that they had all been in error to 'church themselves', as he put it, and that only the Mennonites, not being heretical, had the authority to administer baptism. Furthermore, he had reached the position – possibly influenced by the Mennonites – whereby he had rejected the Calvinist doctrines of original sin and predestination, and accepted the Arminian view that Christ died for all and not simply for the elect.

Disagreements

The congregation was still split by disagreements, which led some seven or eight of them, under Helwys, to withdraw from the fellowship. Helwys declared he could not follow Smyth in accepting certain Mennonite practices, such as forbidding oaths and their refusal to enter civil or military service. But he reaffirmed his belief in original sin and the Arminian view that Christ's redemption was for all men and that God 'had predestinated that all that believe in him shall be saved'. These views were incorporated into *A Declaration of Faith*, drawn up by Helwys and his supporters in 1610, which was the basis for later General Baptist confessions.

The split between the two leaders was hurtful to them both, as they had been firm friends. The breakaway group moved from Amsterdam to Leyden, where they formed a separate church. Smyth and the rest of the congregation attended the services of a Mennonite group, where they applied for membership. Because of the doubt concerning their baptism, however, it was not until 1615 that they were admitted into the fellowship.

By 1612 Helwys had become convinced that they had been wrong to leave England and that it was better 'to lay down their lives in their own country for Christ' than to flee from persecution. He also concluded that the 'days of great tribulation spoken of by Christ' had arrived, and that he must return to England in order to appeal to James I for an end to the persecution of believers.

London

That same year he led a small group of supporters back to England where at Spitalfields, just outside the City, he founded the first (General) Baptist church on English soil. It was based on principles inherited from Smyth, especially that of believer's baptism[3] and the Arminian doctrine that the atonement was 'general', that Christ died for all, and rejected the Calvinist idea of a 'particular' atonement specifically for the elect only. In addition to the London congregation, others were later founded at Lincoln, Salisbury, Coventry and Tiverton; but by 1626 the five congregations only numbered some 150 members.

True to his word, Helwys wrote an address to James I entitled '*The Mystery of Iniquity*', in which he appealed for toleration not only for dissenters, but also for Turks and Jews as well, for 'men's religion ... is

Baptist Chapel, Monksthorpe (Lincolnshire), built in 1701,
is one of the oldest in England – it had an open-air baptistry.

---

3. This was a radical step in England, for infant baptism had been an established practice since the fourth century. Any attempt to challenge this view was considered to be heresy, hence Baptists became a persecuted people.

betwixt God and themselves'. He went on to say, 'The king is mortal and not God; therefore he hath no power over the immortal souls of his subjects to make laws and ordinances for them and to set spiritual lords over them.' For this audacious rebuke he was thrown into Newgate prison where he died, sometime before 1616.

The Particular Baptists[4] emerged in the 1630s. They were descended from a strong Calvinistic independent church formed in Southwark, London, in 1616, led by Henry Jacob (1553–1624). Their concept of a local church was similar to that held by the Independents, but they were convinced that infant baptism was not scriptural. In 1633 a group from among the membership formed a new congregation under John Spilsbury (1593–c1668) and received believer's baptism (though not yet by immersion). They were joined by others who had seceded from independent churches, while similar congregations sprang up outside the capital, sometimes by way of a church plant.

Immersion

In 1640 one of their number, Richard Blunt, became convinced that baptism ought not to be affusion, but 'by dipping the body into water, resembling burial and rising again', as implied by Romans 6:4 and Colossians 2:12. Blunt was sent to Holland to see how the Anabaptists – who were here accustomed to immerse believers – carried out their rite of baptism. He accordingly received immersion. When he returned home he baptised his fellow elder and they baptised the other fifty-three members of the congregation. Spilsbury's church became the first immersed believers' church in England, and both the Particular and the General Baptists adopted immersion as their form of baptism. At first most believers preferred to be baptised in 'living waters' (i.e., a flowing river or stream), as opposed to a pond or baptistry.

> HYMN-SINGING
> Although Luther had introduced hymns at the Reformation, in England both Anglicans and Nonconformists followed Calvin in dismissing their use. Anglican, Presbyterian and Scottish Presbyterian congregations sang metrical versions of the Psalms, and while General Baptists did not object to individuals singing Psalms during worship, they regarded hymns as 'carnal formalities'.
> The practice of hymn-singing did not take hold until towards the end of the

---

4. To avoid being labelled 'anabaptist', the simpler name of 'Baptists' was adopted, first in Holland and then in England, where they called themselves 'The baptised church of Christ worshipping at...' (followed by a geographical location).

seventeenth century. The passing of the Toleration Act in 1689, which gave Nonconformists a measure of religious freedom, meant that it was safe for them to sing hymns without the fear of being detected. At first, hymns were only sung at the end of the communion service, following the pattern of the Last Supper. The practice was only extended after many prejudices had been overcome. Several collections of hymns were available, but it was Isaac Watts' *Hymns and Spiritual Songs* (1707) – which included 'When I survey the wondrous cross' and 'Join all the glorious names' – which led the way for the increasing popularity of hymns in worship services.

The Wesley brothers greatly encouraged the singing of hymns, and in 1780 produced *A Collection of Hymns for the People Called Methodists*, ranked by one scholar alongside the Psalms and the Book of Common Prayer. Hymn-singing among Anglicans did not become established until the nineteenth century, following the publication of *Hymns Ancient and Modern*.

There was steady growth among the Baptists during the seventeenth century. By 1660 there were about 130 Particular Baptist churches, while the General Baptists had 115. Whilst the Particular Baptists were strong in their doctrinal beliefs, the General Baptists were not so soundly based and by the end of the eighteenth century a number of congregations had moved to a Unitarian position.

Though the title 'Baptist' might appear to suggest that this ritual is central to the Church's teaching, this is not the case. Behind the rite of baptism lies a deeper truth – the need for regeneration, to enter into a personal relationship with God through Christ. This is not arrived at by undergoing any particular ritual, but rather by a work of God's Spirit in the life of the individual.

26

1611 KING JAMES VERSION OF THE BIBLE PUBLISHED

The High-water Mark of Bible Translation

It was not until towards the end of the fourteenth century that the first English[1] translation of the Bible appeared. For the most part it was the work of John Wyclif (1320–1384), an Oxford philosopher and theologian, who spearheaded an attack on Church abuses. 'If the ordinary man was to understand the Faith for himself,' he argued, 'then he must have access to the Scriptures … and he should be taught them in whatever language is best known to them.' It was this impetus given by Wyclif that led to a surge in Bible translations and ultimately to the production of the King James Bible.

Over the centuries there had been a long-standing desire in England for a translation of the Bible in the vernacular. A number of Scripture portions in local dialects had been made, but it was not until Wyclif's efforts that there was an attempt to produce a complete Bible in English. Once a breakthrough had been achieved it eventually opened the door to a number of other translations, often made at great personal cost to the translators.

Wyclif's Bible was not entirely his own work, for he was assisted by a small group of followers, known as Lollards. They translated the Latin Bible into a Midland dialect, published in 1382. A revised version was made later, written this time in a more common dialect of the day; it was finished in 1388, four years after Wyclif's death.

Up to this point the clergy had shown no concern at the translation of

---

1. Following the Norman conquest in 1066, French became the dominant language in England. Latin remained as the language of religion and learning, while the ordinary people spoke dialect English.

the Scriptures into the vernacular. But this latest trend challenged the authority of the Church. To maintain its hold on the Bible and its interpretation, rendering the Scriptures into English was henceforth forbidden (1407), and anyone found reading the Scriptures in the mother tongue would have 'to forfeit lands, cattle and life'. This prohibition forced a number of scholars to move to the Continent in order to continue their endeavours; for the next hundred years or so most translation work was accomplished abroad.

EARLY TRANSLATIONS

The movement in England to translate the Word of God into the language of the people had its origins in the seventh century. At that time there were only a few portions of Scripture translated into Anglo-Saxon, including John's Gospel, translated by the Venerable Bede (673–735). Towards the end of the tenth century there appeared the earliest English translation of the four Gospels (the Wessex version) and an interlinear version of the Lindisfarne Gospels in the Northumbrian dialect.

As very few people outside the monasteries could read, manuscripts were both costly and scarce. Thus the Church retained its prerogative over the Scriptures, and Jerome's Vulgate continued in use throughout the Middle Ages virtually without rival.

No further translations were made during the period from the Norman Conquest of 1066 until the time of Wyclif. This was partly because French culture began to dominate the English scene, but also due to the lack of a uniform English language. (There were many dialects in use throughout the land, making a common translation impossible.) That English survived this struggle was in some measure due to the work of Chaucer (1340–1400), whose poetry laid a foundation for the native tongue.

Renaissance

Tremendous changes, however, were taking place throughout Europe during the fifteenth century which greatly assisted the cause of the translators. The invention of printing made possible the production of Bibles on a scale not previously imagined. Before the end of the century Bibles had been printed in the national languages of the major European countries, except England. Around the same time a revival of ancient learning – the Renaissance – created a renewed interest in the original languages of the Bible. In 1516 the Dutch scholar Erasmus published his corrected Greek New Testament, which provided a more accurate rendering of the Scriptures.

In England, the first man to use the original biblical languages for translation purposes was William Tyndale (1494–1536). He was determined to produce an English Bible that 'even the ploughboy' could read and understand. 'It was impossible to establish the lay people in any truth,' he contended, 'except the Scriptures were plainly laid before their eyes in their mother tongue.' Hostility forced him to leave the country in order to achieve his ambition – first to Germany, the land of the Reformation, then to Belgium. Despite opposition, his New Testament was published in 1525. He next turned his attention to the Old Testament, but was betrayed before his task was completed. Condemned as a heretic, he was publicly strangled and his body burned at the stake. His final prayer was, 'Lord, open the King of England's eyes.'

The tide of opinion in England was meanwhile beginning to change. Thomas Cranmer, appointed Archbishop of Canterbury in 1532, and Thomas Cromwell, Henry VIII's Vicar-General and a strong advocate of Protestantism, both supported the idea of an authoritative rendering of the Bible into English. Cranmer's appeal to the king, 'that the Holy Scriptures shall be translated into the vulgar English tongue', met with approval. Tyndale's prayer was answered.

Tyndale's Work

Over the next decades several versions of the Bible were published, all of them founded on Tyndale's translation. Matthew's Bible, printed abroad in 1537, was sanctioned by the Church and licensed by the king; it was sold publicly in England, even though a great part of it was Tyndale's work. Its controversial marginal notes, however, alarmed Cromwell and a new edition was brought out in 1538.

Edited by Myles Coverdale, the new 'Byble in Englyshe' was actually the Matthew's Bible but without the notes. These had been banned by Royal Proclamation, which decreed that any Bible in the English tongue should have only the plain text. Though warmly commended by Cranmer, it was viewed with disapproval by many conservative churchmen because it was based on the work of the 'heretic' Tyndale. Known as the Great Bible because of its size, it was the first Bible to be formally authorised for public use, and Thomas Cromwell issued an order that a copy should be placed in every parish church throughout the realm.

During the reign of the Catholic Queen Mary (1553–1558) a number of Protestant leaders were forced to flee to the Continent, finding a refuge in Geneva, the home of the reformer Calvin. Here, in 1560, a new English translation of the Bible was published that was considered more accessible to the ordinary man: it was smaller in size, the old-fashioned type was replaced by a clearer, Roman type – making it more legible – and the verses were now divided and numbered.[2] Sometimes referred to as the Breeches Bible (because of its translation of Genesis 3:7), the Geneva Bible immediately gained in popularity, threatening to oust the Great Bible.

The Geneva Bible, showing the reference to Adam and Eve making themselves 'breeches' (Gen. 3:7), so that it became known as the Breeches Bible.

When Queen Elizabeth I came to the throne, a revision of the Great Bible was made in the hope that it would replace that from Geneva. Known as the Bishops' Bible– because it was prepared by a panel of bishops – and published in 1568, it was the only version recognised by Convocation.

Hampton Court

Without a doubt, however, the translation that most endeared itself to the nation and gradually won supremacy over all the other versions was the one authorised by King James I (1603–1625) in 1611. Although the idea of a new Bible was a Puritan proposal, credit must be given to James who was the driving force behind the undertaking.

James became King of Scotland on the abdication of his mother, Mary Queen of the Scots. He succeeded to the throne of England on the death of

---

2. The Hebrew New Testament was divided into verses by a Rabbi Nathan (1448). The first Bible that has the present verse division in both Testaments was Stephanus' Vulgate of 1555.

Elizabeth I by virtue of his mother's descent from Henry VII. The religious parties in England eagerly anticipated his accession – the Catholics on account of his parentage, the Anglicans because of his high ideal of 'the divine right of kings' and the Puritans by reason of his Presbyterian education.

On his way to London in April 1603, James was met by a delegation of Puritans who presented him with the so-called Millenary Petition.[3] Led by Dr John Rainolds, President of Corpus Christi College, Oxford, the Puritans were anxious to 'purify' the Church of all 'the rags of popery' – the Romish practices and abuses that remained after the Reformation. The petition expressed a desire to be rid of bishops, requested changes to the Prayer Book and prayed to be relieved from the 'common burden of human rites and ceremonies'.

Although brought up Presbyterian, James gladly embraced the principles of the Church of England and especially the king's title, Defender of the Faith. In an attempt to put down the Puritans, he agreed to meet them in conference along with the bishops. It was held at Hampton Court palace in January 1604, with the king in the chair. James quickly showed where his sympathies lay and made it clear that there would be no changes in the Elizabethan Church Settlement.

Whilst no concessions were made to the Puritans, Rainolds' idea – that 'there might be a new translation of the Bible, because those which were allowed in the reigns of Henry VIII and Edward VI were corrupt and not answerable to the truth of the original' – was readily received. For the king, here was a chance to get rid of the popular Geneva Bible which had Calvinistic leanings, and to produce a more acceptable version.

Translation

A panel of fifty-four translators was appointed from both Oxford and Cambridge Universities, without regard to their theological or ecclesiastical bias, divided into six committees. A set of rules was drawn up for their guidance, with the stipulation that the text should not be 'prejudiced' by the use of marginal notes, though cross-references and explanations of Hebrew and Greek words were permissible.

Each committee was assigned a portion of the text and three years were given over to preliminary research. They used the Hebrew and Greek Testaments, but also referred to previous Protestant and Catholic

---

3. Because it was said to have been signed by a thousand clergymen.

translations, including those in French, Spanish and Italian. Working individually and in conference, the work took two years to complete. A committee of twelve required a further nine months to scrutinise the whole text, and it was edited by Dr Miles Smith (who also wrote the Preface) and Bishop Bilson. There is no actual proof that it was formally authorised by King James, though it was ascribed to him.

Behind it all was the inspiration of Tyndale's original version, for such was the excellence of his work that many of the passages in the KJV's New Testament remained as he wrote them. While the actual number of new renderings was small, the engrafting of the various sources was done in such a masterly manner as to make it 'a work of art'. For a time the KJV competed in popular use with the Geneva Bible, and did not gain the ascendency until the restoration of the monarchy (1660). In the end it prevailed and, with the exception of the Catholic Church, was acknowledged as the Authorised Version of the English-speaking people.

Discoveries

The outcome of the Hampton Court Conference served only to widen the gap between the Puritans and the Anglican Church, and the king's threat to 'harry them out of the land, or do worse', was a serious one. Unable to wait for reform within the Church of England, many of them – known as Separatists – had already withdrawn and joined the Anabaptists. Some had emigrated to Holland before James had ascended the throne, and others now joined the stream of refugees leaving the country. In 1620 the Pilgrim Fathers, as they later became known, sailed to America, determined to build a 'New England' where they could worship in freedom.

While no other authorised versions were made for nearly three centuries, later developments finally made a revision necessary. One reason relates to the changes that had taken place in English usage. Many forms of expression used in the KJV had become outdated and generally unintelligible to the public. In addition there were words still in use that had changed in meaning. For example, the KJV used the word 'prevent' to mean precede, 'communicate' for to share and 'allege' for prove. Many other examples could be quoted.

Another compelling reason was the discovery of a large number of ancient Greek and Hebrew manuscripts, including a great many fragments. These finds were helpful in two ways. In the first place, they provided a more reliable biblical text from which to work, as scholars were able to determine how the books of the Bible had been transmitted since they were originally composed. Then, the discovery of a large number of Greek

TRANSLATIONS OF THE BIBLE

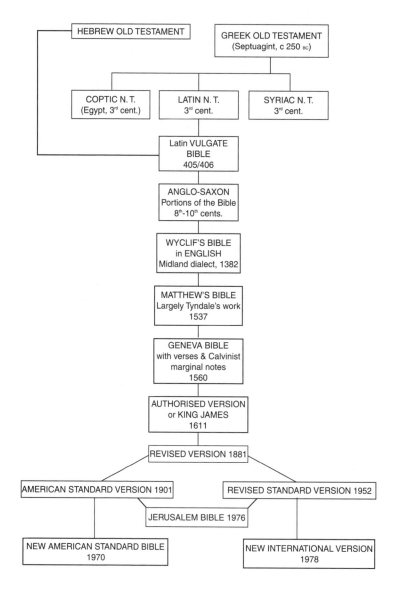

papyri, which included private letters, official reports, business accounts and other everyday items, shed new light on the meaning of Greek words that helped to give a better rendering of the text.

ANCIENT MANUSCRIPTS

Since the publication of the KJV in 1611 a large number of ancient manuscripts have come to light. The first discovery was the early fifth century manuscript of the Greek Bible, the *Codex Alexandrinus*, a gift from the Patriarch of Constantinople to the English monarch in 1627. The arrival of a manuscript of such antiquity created a sensation and a search was begun throughout the libraries of Europe. Between 1627 and 1830 over a thousand manuscripts were catalogued. The oldest was the *Codex Vaticanus*, a fourth century Greek Bible which had been in the Vatican library since at least 1481. There was also the *Codex Bezae*, a fifth century Graeco-Latin manuscript of the Gospels and Acts, presented in 1581 to the University of Cambridge.

The most amazing find was that made by Count Tischendorf (1815–74) who, after graduating in theology at Leipzig University, set himself the task of searching out and publishing every fragment of uncial manuscripts he could locate. At the St Catherine monastery, Mount Sinai, he one day saw in a basket a number of vellum leaves with fine, early uncial writing on them. He rescued them, for they were about to be destroyed (as had already happened to similar leaves). On succeeding visits he made further finds, until eventually he had the whole of the New Testament and nearly half of the Old Testament. Now known as the *Codex Sinaiticus*, it was a hundred years older than any extant manuscript, except the *Codex Vaticanus*. At Tischendorf's suggestion, the monks presented the fourth century codex to the Tsar of Russia. In 1933 it was sold by the Soviet Government to the British Museum for £100,000.

An English revised version was consequently published, by authority of the Church of England, between 1881–1885. (Some 80 per cent of this version was taken from the work of Tyndale, which included phrases such as 'salt of the earth' and 'the spirit is willing but the flesh is weak'.) An American Standard Version was produced in 1901. Since then a wide variety of Bibles and New Testaments have been made available – some authorised, others a result of the endeavours of private individuals.

The King James Bible, however, represented more than any other the high-water mark of translation, superior in literary merit to all other versions. Its acceptance by English-speaking peoples has commended the teachings of the Bible to ordinary men and women, making its mark upon the character of the nation in a way that no other book can claim.

27

1662 THE ACT OF UNIFORMITY

The Emergence of Nonconformity as a Force for Good

The 1662 Act of Uniformity was a deliberate attempt by parliament to oust the Puritans from the Established Church. By insisting that all clergymen should subscribe to the Prayer Book and submit to episcopacy, nearly 2,000 ministers, who preferred to preserve their independence, were forced to surrender their livings. Whilst some of them expected this would only be a temporary move and that a change of circumstances would enable them to return, it ultimately drove them further into dissent. Rather than bringing the rebels to heel, the act highlighted the division that existed in England between the two groups.

The root of the problem can be traced back a hundred years or more, when in 1534 Henry VIII declared himself to be Supreme Head of the Church of England. Henry was still a Catholic at heart and until his death remained an opponent of the Reformation. While many in England were open to the new ideas, it was not until the reign of the young King Edward VI (1547–1553) that the Reformation was finally introduced. The leading architect of the movement was Archbishop Cramner, supported by a number of leading scholars of a Calvinistic leaning, some of whom were later martyred under the Catholic Queen Mary (1553–1558). As it turned out, Mary's attempt to reintroduce the Catholic religion into England served only to advance the Protestant cause, for many were repulsed by her ruthless methods.

It was left to Elizabeth I (1558–1603) to establish Protestantism in the land, beginning in 1559 with the introduction of two acts of parliament. By the Act of Supremacy Elizabeth proclaimed herself Supreme Governor of the Church of England, then by the Act of Uniformity[1] she reintroduced the 1552 Prayer Book of Edward VI's reign, albeit with a number of modifications. Among them were additions that some regarded as popish and unbiblical: wearing clerical vestments (including the surplice and square cap), kneeling to receive communion, bowing at the name of Jesus, making the sign of the cross at baptism and the laying on of hands at confirmation. Severe penalties for disobedience were drawn up, as well as for failure to attend church on Sundays and holy days.

Disunited

The religious leaders of the day were disunited and gradually three distinct groups developed within the Church. There were the Anglicans who looked back to the ideals of Cranmer, wanting the Church to be Catholic and yet reformed. A second group consisted of those who looked to Calvin for their inspiration; they wanted a Church where both doctrine and practices were based on Scripture, but organised on a Presbyterian basis. Whilst they welcomed the reforms already set in hand, they believed that the Reformation in the Church of England had not gone far enough and worked from within to 'purify' the Church of its popish tendencies – hence the term 'Puritan'.[2]

The third group consisted of those who wanted a Church free from state interference. Their leader was Robert Browne and they became known as 'Brownists' or 'Separatists'. Whilst both Presbyterians and Separatists looked to the Word of God as the source of their authority, they held to fundamental differences. In contrast to the Established Church, the Separatists recognised only a 'gathered' church, that is, one made up of true believers (rather than the idea of the nation being the Church, ruled over by parliament), while Presbyterians were more concerned with matters of church government and discipline.

Separated Churches

As the Act of Uniformity was not at first rigidly enforced, a small number of Puritan ministers felt able to remain within the Church without fulfilling the obligations of the Prayer Book. When in 1566 the rebels were threatened with expulsion, 37 out of 110 ministers in London refused and were

---

1. There were four Acts of Uniformity in all: 1549, 1552, 1559 and 1662.
2. During the reign of Elizabeth, Puritans in communion with the Church of England were also known as Nonconformists. It was not until 1662 that the term was applied to those who had separated from the Church.

deprived of their livings; others accepted the terms for staying within the Church. Those who would not conform were forced to meet secretly in 'separated' churches; they gathered in private houses, in the open air, brew-houses, even in ships. The first recorded instance of a Separatist congregation was in 1567, when around 100 people gathered for worship in the Plumber's Hall, in the City of London.

Attempts to suppress the Separatist movement led to further arrests; both men and women were thrown into jail, where a number of them died. Efforts to contain the movement within the Established Church failed. Increased persecution served only to widen the gap between the two, and other breakaway groups were soon formed. In 1572 the first Presbyterian Church was set up by Nicholas Crane in Wandsworth, London. Crane was one of the leaders of the Presbyterian movement launched by Thomas Cartwright, a Cambridge Professor of Divinity.

East Anglia at this time was a stronghold of the Puritan movement. In Norwich (in 1580 or 1581) Robert Browne, a Cambridge graduate, formed an Independent church,[3] the first of what later became known as Congregational churches. When Browne was arrested and imprisoned after preaching at Bury St Edmunds, others of his church became 'fully persuaded that the Lord did call them out of England'. In the autumn of 1581 they left for Holland where religious dissent was tolerated, and where Thomas Cartwright had already fled.

In England, the Conventicle Act of 1593 was passed to deal with all those who refused to attend the Established Church or who attended unauthorised religious meetings. Catholics were fined, imprisoned or executed, and extreme Puritans were banished, forcing whole companies of believers to leave the land for Holland. Even so, further Separatist churches were formed in England, including the first General Baptist Church at Pinners Hall, London, while members continued to be imprisoned or executed.

Opposition

The accession of James I to the throne raised the hopes of many Puritans, as the new king had been brought up in the Presbyterian Church of Scotland and was Calvinist in his doctrine. But James saw in the Puritans a real danger to his throne and he vowed to 'harry them out of the land'. Such was his opposition that some 300 Puritan ministers left the Church of

---

3. i.e., a church that recognised the independence or autonomy of each congregation.

England. Others were ejected and fled either to Holland or to the New World, forcing them into Separatism. Among the emigrants were the Pilgrim Fathers who in 1620 left from Holland for New England.

James was succeeded by his son, Charles 1 (1625–1649), who with Archbishop Laud – an avowed opponent of the Puritans – embarked on an attempt to purge the Church of Puritans and Separatists. The Act of Uniformity was enforced in a way that Elizabeth had never done, and between 1628 and 1640 over 20,000 emigrants crossed the Atlantic to the New World.

When Charles and Laud attempted to impose the Prayer Book and episcopacy upon the Church of Scotland, however, it provoked a violent reaction throughout the land. An army of Scots marched south and the king was forced to accept a truce at Berwick. By now there was a large representation of Presbyterians in the Commons, as well as Independents. Laud, accused of altering the true Protestant religion into popery, was arrested and sent to the Tower, where in 1646 he was executed. Pressure was put upon the king to abolish episcopacy in England and accept Presbyterianism. He refused and fled the capital in an attempt to save this throne. On 22 August 1642, Charles raised his banner at Nottingham, and the Civil War – the struggle between king and parliament – began.

In order to reach some kind of religious settlement in the land parliament convened an assembly of Divines. It was held in a large room at Westminster Abbey, meeting from July 1643 to February 1649. Though it included a few Episcopalians and Independents, it was overwhelmingly Presbyterian and Puritan, some of whom were from Scotland. A Solemn League and Covenant, which aimed at the abolition of popery, prelacy and anything else 'contrary to sound doctrine and the power of godliness', was drawn up. This was followed by the more famous Westminster Confession of Faith, which ultimately became the definitive statement of Presbyterian doctrine in the English-speaking world. It was adopted by the General Assembly of Scotland in August 1647, by the English parliament in June the following year and by the Scottish parliament in 1649. The work is a clear expression of Calvinist theology and is widely recognised as a model Confession.

WESTMINSTER CONFESSION
The earliest confessions were brief phrases of faith expressed by individuals, some of which are to be found in the New Testament. Later, longer statements were drawn up, known as creeds, prefaced by the words 'I/we believe...' (e.g., the Apostles Creed). These were eventually replaced by more detailed, systematic statements of faith, which after the Reformation assumed an even greater

importance in defining the positions taken up by different religious groups.

The aim of the Westminster Confession was to unify the churches of England, Scotland and Ireland. It began by revising the thirty-nine Articles, then went on to propose a presbyterian form of church government, whereby each parish was governed by a presbytery, i.e., the minister and elders, and to abolish the Prayer Book. But its main achievement was the Confession of Faith, based upon the thirty-nine Articles.

The Confession extends to thirty-three chapters, each doctrine liberally supported by Scripture references. Beginning with the recognition of Scripture as containing the whole counsel of God, the articles cover the complete spectrum of Christian doctrine. The Confession, in fact, is ranked among the most notable expositions of Calvinism and is reckoned to be a worthy child of Calvin's Institutes. However, whilst one of its better-known teachings is that of 'limited atonement', that Christ died for the elect alone, this is not quite what Calvin believed.

Confusion

Presbyterianism was now the religion of the nation, and between 1645 and 1653 the Presbyterians remained in power in both parliament and Church. Following the end of the War and the execution of Charles I, the religious life of the land was generally in a state of confusion. From 1653 until the end of the Commonwealth period England was ruled by Oliver Cromwell, an Independent, who took the title of 'Lord Protector'. Cromwell was both broad-minded and tolerant; he did not expect uniformity, nor did he wish 'to meddle with any man's conscience'. Toleration, however, stopped short at Anglicans, Unitarians and Roman Catholics. It was during this period that the Quaker movement under John Fox was founded and a variety of religious sects were formed.

After Cromwell's death in 1658 there was a growing feeling that to avoid anarchy in the land, the monarchy should be restored. In 1660 Charles II, waiting in exile in the Netherlands, was invited to take the throne. Though Catholic in his sympathies, Charles issued a declaration prior to his return promising freedom of conscience in matters of religion, which made him more acceptable to the Puritans. But the first parliament chosen after the Restoration was fiercely royalist and Anglican; the king was easily won over and parliament voted to restore episcopacy.

The Savoy Conference, held in 1661 between Anglicans and Puritans (Congregationalists and Baptists were not invited) met to discuss differences. The bishops refused to yield to Puritan proposals concerning the Prayer Book, though a later committee made some 600 minor alterations. With its Anglican majority, between 1661–1665 parliament was able to pass a

Statue of Cromwell outside the Palace of Westminster,
with a sword in his right hand and a Bible in the other.

number of measures aimed at re-establishing the Church of England.

Known as the Clarendon Code, after Charles' chief minister, the new laws decreed that anyone other than Church of England communicants was prohibited from holding any official or ecclesiastical office. All dissenting gatherings for religious purposes of five or more persons over sixteen were illegal; and Nonconformist ministers were forbidden to live or visit within five miles of any place in which they had previously worked.

Nonconformity Created

But it was the Act of Uniformity (1662) which had the most far-reaching consequences, for it finally split the Church in two and created Nonconformity as a powerful factor in the life of the nation. The bill required all clergymen, on pain of ejection from their livings for disobedience, to publicly declare their 'unfeigned assent and consent' of the Prayer Book in its entirety, as 'in all things agreeable to the Word of God'. Any clergyman who would not declare that he conscientiously believed every sentence printed in the Book was to be deprived of his living in the Church of England. Added to this, all ministers who had not already been episcopally ordained were to be re-ordained, and they were required to renounce the Solemn League and Covenant which aimed at reforming the Church of England.

The intention of the Act was to drive the Puritans from the Church of England. It demanded that they deny everything they had struggled for over the preceding century. On 19 May the bill received the royal assent, and the date for the ejection of those refusing to comply was set at St Bartholomew's Day,[4], 24 August, thereby depriving incumbents of the tithes which they had earned by nearly a year's work. Of the 2,000 clergy deprived of their posts, all except about 400 were Presbyterians. Many of them were driven into poverty while others were forced to become beggars.

The Puritan hope of reforming the Church from within was ended. From 1662 onwards those excluded from the Church of England were referred to as 'Nonconformists' or 'Dissenters' and the emerging denominations and sectaries gradually assumed their individual identities. In Scotland, the Presbyterian Church was once again established, taking the Westminster Confession of Faith as its creed. Despite continued persecution, the existence of Nonconformity was now officially recognised and eventually became a force for good throughout the land.

---

4. By an embarrassing coincidence, the anniversary of the day when in 1572 thousands of Huguenots (Protestants) had been massacred in Paris.

Toleration

Within a few years the idea of toleration began to gain ground when it was recognised that Nonconformity was here to stay. Following the Glorious Revolution (1689), when William III of Orange ascended the throne of England, an Act of Toleration was passed which gave Nonconformity a limited freedom, though it was still illegal.

> **TOLERATION ACT (1689)**
>
> The Toleration Act granted freedom of worship to Dissenters, though Roman Catholics and Unitarians were excluded from the terms. Special arrangements were made for Quakers, who did not take oaths.
>
> Any Trinitarian Dissenter who swore an oath of allegiance and supremacy, and who also accepted the declaration against transubstantiation (thus proving himself not a Catholic), was exempt the penalties. Nonconformist places of worship had to be licensed by the bishop, and ministers had to subscribe to thirty-six of the thirty-nine Articles of the Church of England. (Baptists were exempt with regard to the article on infant baptism.) Dissenters were banned from holding public office and from the two universities. No one could be forced to attend the parish church or be prosecuted for worshipping in another licensed place of worship, though attendance at public worship was still compulsory. Anyone who disturbed worship or caused damage in Nonconformist premises could be prosecuted.
>
> It must be noted, however, that toleration is not the same as liberty, nor is it the same as religious equality; it was nearly a further 200 years before such a stage was reached.

The new era of religious toleration, however, did not lead to a revival of faith in the land, and before the turn of the century a decline in the religious life of the nation had set in. An attempt to unite Presbyterians and Independents failed. Meanwhile, there was a growth of anti-Trinitarian views. The movement spread widely, especially among the Presbyterians and General Baptists, even though Unitarians were penalised under the Toleration Act. It was not until 1773 that the Unitarian denomination was founded and a church established in London.

Whilst the Toleration Act gave relief to Nonconformists, it did not allow complete freedom or give equality in the eyes of the law. In 1811 a Protestant Society for the Protection of Religious Liberty was founded which over succeeding decades secured the repeal of a number of parliamentary acts, enabling Protestants to enjoy the same privileges accorded communicants of the Established Church.

The right to religious freedom in England was achieved only by the sufferings of the first Dissenters, many of whom died a martyr's death in an attempt to build a Church that was true to what they believed was the New Testament pattern. Yet the need to maintain biblically based doctrines and standards and 'to contend for the faith that was once for all entrusted to the saints' is no less urgent now than it was 300 years ago.

28

1675 SPENER'S *PIA DESIDERIA* PUBLISHED

House Groups Breathe New Life into Dead Churches

The publication in 1675 of Philip Jacob Spener's book, *Pia Desideria* ('Holy Desires'), heralded the emergence of a renewal movement within the Lutheran Church in Germany. Known as Pietism, it is sometimes regarded as a second phase of the Reformation. Its aim was to promote the practice of true religion by preaching the need for a new birth experience that issued in godly living. Beginning in Germany, it soon permeated not only parts of Europe, but was also a contributing factor to the spread of revival in both Britain and America. It influenced the growth of overseas missions and motivated Christians to become involved in the social and ethical concerns of the day.

Following the sixteenth century Reformation there emerged three major Protestant denominations: Lutheran, Reformed and Anglican. All three strands were national (i.e., state) Churches, under the rule of civil governments, and to which the whole population belonged irrespective of personal beliefs. The result was that political and ecclesiastical issues were often blurred and church appointments made for the wrong reasons. Frequently pulpits were filled by clergy who had little concern for the needs of their flock, so that moral and spiritual guidance were lacking.

Though the Reformation had refocused attention on the Scriptures, emphasis in Germany had gradually shifted from a heart religion to one of the intellect. While all citizens were baptised as infants and believed to be regenerate, this was obviously not the case. There was an absence of real Christianity, of a living and personal faith. Added to which, the laity appeared to be driven more by fear and superstition rather than by godly desires. As one pastor complained, 'Old and young can no longer tell what is of God or of the Devil, poor widows and orphans are counted for dung, like dogs they are pushed into the street, there to perish of hunger and cold.'

Wars of Religion

A further blow to the cause of religion in Europe was the Thirty Years' War (1618–48), which plunged much of the Continent into a period of turmoil and misery. It arose out of a dispute between Protestants and Catholics in Bohemia concerning the successor to the throne. The war spread until most European states were involved, though the chief centre of conflict was in the German Empire. Fighting continued with great ferocity and resulted in widespread devastation: whole villages were wiped out, the sick and needy were forgotten, crime was rampant, and starvation and disease were widespread. At the end, the population of Germany had been reduced from sixteen million to less than six million. Tired of war, the Peace of Westphalia was made in October 1648.

Though spiritual life was at a low ebb, there were sporadic pleas for a return to right living and a love for God. The greatest influence at that time was exerted by a Lutheran pastor, Johann Arndt (1555–1621), who exhorted his people to seek after a new life in Christ. Arndt – recognised by some as the true father of Pietism[1] – was the author of the widely read book, *True Christianity*. He wrote that true Christianity consisted 'in the proving of true, living, active faith through genuine godliness', and emphasised the need for 'true repentance' and 'renewal of the individual from the inside out'.

There were other Protestant voices from further afield also appealing for a religious renewal. Both in England and the Netherlands, movements arose within the Church which aimed at promoting a strong and active faith. During the reign of Elizabeth I of England, the Puritan revolt had begun by protesting against popish practices being taken on board by the Anglican Church. Attention was then switched from ecclesiastical matters to a need for godliness, which it was felt should be exhibited by all those who professed the Christian Faith. Richard Baxter's *Call to the Unconverted* and John Bunyan's *Pilgrim's Progress* influenced both the Lutheran and Reformed Communions in calling for a return to biblical standards. As William Perkins, the Cambridge theologian, expressed it, 'The body of Scripture is a doctrine sufficient by which to live well.'

---

1. The term Pietism was first applied as a term of derision at Frankfurt, in 1674.

PIETIST MANIFESTO

The *Pia Desideria*, ('Heartfelt Desire for God-pleasing Reform'), is both a devotional work and a textbook on Church renewal. In the key section of the book, Spener sets out his six measures for reform:

1. The Word of God should be made more widely known. Pastors should preach from the whole Bible – not just from isolated texts – and Christians should engage in private Bible reading, as well as study groups and family devotions.

2. The Lutheran doctrine of the priesthood of all believers should receive a new emphasis. This includes recognising the rights of the laity, and everyone's responsibility towards one's fellow men.

3. More attention should be given to the cultivation of individual spiritual life, and that love for God should take priority over all else.

4. Try to avoid religious controversies with unbelievers and heretics; truth is established through prayer and holy living.

5. Candidates for the ministry should be 'true Christians', and training should include small groups for devotional life and personal Bible study.

6. Preaching should aim at edifying believers, strengthening their faith and cultivating inner piety.

Frankfurt

Spener's book, *Pia Desideria*, was published while he was the senior Lutheran pastor at Frankfurt-on-Main (1666–1686), and was an appeal for Christians to lead a holy life. Distressed by the wordliness of the city and an over-emphasis on the sacraments in the Church, each Sunday he preached repentance and renewal to his congregation. In 1670 he put into operation an idea he had previously tried whilst a preacher in Strasbourg, where he had encouraged his congregation to come together for fellowship on a Sunday afternoon, rather than spend their time in drinking, playing cards and gambling.

Following a request from a few of his parishioners he instituted his famous *collegia pietatis* ('religious colleges'), which were cell-groups where congregations could meet informally for mutual edification and encouragement. Gatherings were held at Spener's home on a Sunday afternoon (and, later, on a Wednesday as well), where they reviewed the Sunday sermon and studied the Bible. As the idea of home-groups spread to other churches they became the hallmark of the new movement. The idea of house groups[2] was not entirely new, as Spener had received his inspiration from Johann Arndt, though he must be credited for having promoted the collegia and set in motion the wheels of renewal.

When invited by a publisher to write a preface for a new edition of Arndt's book, Spener's contribution received wide acclaim. Within six months he had published the preface separately under its own title, *Pia Desideria*, which is acknowledged as the classic statement of Pietism. His chief concern was the 'scandalous wordliness' of the churches and his hope for a spiritual renewal, for which he put forward a six-point plan for reform.

Opposition

The new work was received with enthusiasm, yet despite Spener's apparent success there was opposition from his more orthodox colleagues. Some clergy felt threatened by the emphasis on the laity, and academics resented his attack on their theological stance; he was even accused of heresy and fanaticism. But Spener's influence continued to spread and his methods were imitated by other pastors, bringing a new vitality to the Church.

Weary of opposition, in 1686 he accepted a call to be chaplain at the Saxon court at Dresden, only to meet further resistance from orthodox clergy. Before long he was again on the move, when in 1691 he responded to a call from the Elector of Brandenburg to become rector of St Nicholas' Church, Berlin. The elector was intent on building up Berlin as a strong spiritual centre; he brought in other Pietists and welcomed French Huguenots to his court to further his plans. Spener's name became well known throughout Germany, and he spent the remaining years of his life at Berlin where he was truly honoured and appreciated. His success was due in part to his ability to combine the Lutheran stress on the Scriptures with the Reformed Church's insistence on right conduct.

Spener's mantle as leader of the Pietist movement fell on Auguste Hermann Francke (1663–1727), who built on Spener's work. Laying great stress on practical theology, Francke was responsible for developing the philanthropic institutions at Halle (near Leipzig) for which Pietism became renowned, while his leadership and vision for foreign missions marked him out as one of the century's great leaders. At Leipzig University, where he graduated in 1685, he founded the *collegium philobiblicum* ('assembly of Bible lovers'), though it concentrated on an academic rather than a devotional approach to the Bible. But following a conversion experience in 1686 and then a meeting with Spener, he was won to the Pietist cause and brought to a commitment to holy living.

---

2. Pietists in the Netherlands were probably the first to use the term '*huis kerk*' ('house church') for their renewal meetings.

EARLY PROTESTANT MISSIONARY ACTIVITY

The credit for being the father of the modern (Protestant) missionary movement is usually given to William Carey of the Baptist Missionary Society (1792), though missionary endeavours had actually begun some hundred years earlier.

Despite the Reformation's emphasis on the authority of Scripture, Protestants failed to communicate the gospel beyond their own borders. The reason was in part the result of having a state Church, where the religion of a region followed that of its ruler. This meant that a ruler had no concern for regions beyond his control – that was another's responsibility.

There were, however, early exceptions to the rule. The Anglican Society for the Propagation of the Gospel in Foreign Parts was founded in 1701 by Thomas Bray (1656–1730), chiefly to evangelise non-Christian races subject to the Crown. In 1705 King Frederick IV of Denmark (1699–1730) invited two Halle-trained young men to open a mission at Tranquebar, a Danish settlement on the coast of south-east India. A Norwegian Pietist started a work among the semi-pagan Lapps of northern Norway, and around the same time one of his compatriots pioneered missionary work in Greenland.

Meanwhile, the Roman Catholic counter-reformation had begun and missionaries sent out to India and the East, and (as early as 1520) to the New World, where they gained large numbers of converts.

Halle

Francke afterwards considered himself to be Spener's 'dutiful son in the faith'. It was on his advice that Francke was appointed to the chair of Greek and Oriental Languages at the newly established Halle University, and took up the position as pastor of a church at Glancha. This move marked the beginning of Francke's remarkable life's work for which he is best remembered. Fired with a truly practical Pietism, he set about creating a model educational institution at Halle, based on intensive Bible study.

The work began modestly with a ragged school in his own home; as numbers grew, he acquired a property in which to house the orphans. Schools were established, catering for between 2,000 and 3,000 poor children, and a boarding school was opened for boys of well-to-do parents who lived at a distance.[3] Other institutions followed – a printing and publishing house, hospital, library, farm, brewery and a laboratory. He also founded a teacher training college, and a Bible Institute for training pastors and where missionary candidates could receive linguistic training. It was here that a foundation was laid for Pietism's pioneer missionary activities.

Appointed Professor of Theology at Halle in 1698, Francke remained at

---

3. One of the pupils was Nikolas Ludwig (later, Count) von Zinzendorf, son of an Austrian nobleman and godchild of Spener.

the university until his death in 1727. A learned and saintly man and genuinely concerned for his parishioners' problems, it was said that the whole town followed his funeral cortège to the graveside. With the death of Francke, the activities of Pietism in Germany began to wane, though it continued to exercise an influence throughout the northern and central parts of the empire.

Moravians

That the influence of Pietism spread beyond the borders of Germany was in part due to the witness of the Moravians (also known as Bohemian Brethren or Unitas Fratrum), the spiritual descendants of the Czech martyr, John Hus. Driven from their homeland during the Thirty Years' War, in 1722 a group of them settled on Count Zinzendorf's estate in Saxony, east of Dresden, where there was already a fellowship of believers influenced by Pietism. Zinzendorf organised the colony into a community of Bohemian Brethren at a village named Herrnhut ('The Lord's Protection'), which became a haven for Protestant refugees.

In 1727 the community experienced a Pentecostal visitation of the Holy Spirit during the course of a communion service, which transformed the whole group. Their hearts were 'set on fire with new love and faith towards the Saviour and with burning love towards one another'. No longer was it a haven for religious refugees, but a fellowship of Spirit-filled believers now with a firm commitment to foreign missions. Before long, missionaries had been despatched to both the West Indies and Greenland, and a leprosy hospital was set up outside Jerusalem. In 1736 Zinzendorf himself embarked on a missionary journey which included England and America, where he ministered at Germantown and Bethlehem in Pennsylvania.[4]

Early in the eighteenth century there were Moravians to be found in London, and it was their witness which influenced the beginnings of the Evangelical Revival. Following the counsel of a Moravian, John Wesley came to saving faith at a Moravian meeting in Aldersgate Street. To learn more of his benefactors, Wesley paid a visit to Germany where he met Count Zinzendorf and stayed for some time at Herrnhut. The encounter strengthened his new-found faith and he caught the Pietist vision for making Christ known to the unconverted. Like the Pietists, his emphasis on the necessity of a new birth and sanctification were key features of his preaching during the Evangelical Revival.

---

4. It was Zinzendorf who coined the revivalist slogan, 'Come as you are. It is only necessary to believe in the atonement of Christ.'

New World

Among the many emigrants who left Europe for the New World towards the end of the seventeenth century were Pietists from Germany and the Netherlands, who settled mainly in the middle colonies of New York, New Jersey and Pennsylvania. As the Puritan religion of earlier colonists had become increasingly formal and respectable, the spiritual life of the New World churches had correspondingly waned. With the arrival of the Pietists a new work began, and two men especially contributed towards a revival along the eastern seaboard. They were Theodore Frelinghuysen (1692–1748), the son of a German Reformed (Calvinist) pastor, who was educated in the Netherlands, and Henry Mühlenberg (1711–1787), educated by Lutheran Pietists in Germany.

From 1726, Frelinghuysen ministered to the Dutch settlers of the Raritan River Valley, New Jersey, where he warned his parishioners of the dangers of a formal religion. He preached the need for a new birth accompanied by holy living, and demanded evidence of conversion as a requirement for communion. Although he met with stiff opposition from well-to-do farmers and lawyers, his message bore fruit and many of the people in the churches in his charge came to a personal faith. Before long the Dutch Reformed churches were experiencing revival, which proved to be a foretaste of the Great Awakening. Mühlenberg, who arrived in Philadelphia in 1742, ministered among the Lutherans. And though he initially met with ridicule, he strengthened the Lutheran churches and brought about a spiritual renewal.

Whilst in Germany Pietism had restored vitality to Protestant churches, Spener's collegia were not always in the hands of the right people and some of them gained a reputation for promoting fanaticism and even heresy. Further, the lack of organisation led to an element of division, as groups developed into *ecclesiolae in ecclesia* ('little churches within the church'), which Spener protested was contrary to the teachings of the Church.

Despite its failings, the Pietist contribution to Protestantism cannot be overestimated. Its re-emphasis on the experience of the new birth, coupled with its call to holy living restored an element of the gospel that had for some time been lacking. Though in the eighteenth century the influence of the Pietist movement gradually declined, it was not before it had laid a foundation for revival that made a profound impact on both sides of the Atlantic.

29

1681 WILLIAM PENN FOUNDS PENNSYLVANIA

Search for Religious Freedom in the New World

The founding of Pennsylvania was a landmark in the seventeenth century Protestant settlement of the eastern seaboard of North America. Based on the Quaker principle of civil and religious toleration, it soon became established as a force for good and a leading colony in New England. Its founder, William Penn (1644–1718), a devout Quaker, was the moving inspiration behind this 'holy experiment'. He framed its constitution, known as the Great Law, which embraced both European settlers and native Indians alike, and stoutly defended the Quaker cause.

Christianity in North America is essentially of European origin. When Columbus rediscovered the continent in 1492 on the behalf of Catholic Spain, he opened up the way for exploration of the New World. Though his mission was to seek new opportunities for trade, his hope was also that the natives might be converted 'to our Holy Faith'. Other nations followed his lead, and Portugal, England and Holland all joined in the search for new conquests across the Atlantic. In the following century Catholic missionaries made considerable gains in North America, but it was not until nearly a hundred years later that the English colonisation of Virginia opened up the way for Protestant refugees from England and Europe.

The sixteenth century Reformation had initiated a time of religious renewal in Europe, which tragically divided the nations into two camps. As religious affiliation was often determined by political forces, it caused considerable turmoil. Princes and kings aligned their states according to their own religious inclination, whether their subjects should be Catholic or Protestant. By the following century, a number of Protestant splinter groups had emerged in both England and Europe, many of them anxious to find a safe haven in America where they could worship according to their beliefs.

NEW ENGLAND

The name New England was first used by a Capt. John Smith who explored the region in 1614. The first settlers were the Pilgrim Fathers, Puritans who fled to Holland in 1608 before finally emigrating in 1620 to the north-east of America. They landed at Cape Cod, at a spot they named Plymouth. In 1620 English colonists settled in New Hampshire, while more Puritans, together with Congregationalists and Presbyterians – who were of similar theological persuasion to the Puritans – arrived in 1628. Between then and 1638 the colonies of Massachusetts, Connecticut and New Haven were founded. New England became a Puritan stronghold and exerted a profound influence in the life of the nation.

In the 1620s Dutch settlers of the Reformed (Presbyterian) Church also crossed the Atlantic, settling in New Jersey, at a trading colony they called New Amsterdam. Both these territories were handed over to the British in 1664, the latter being renamed New York (in honour of the Duke of York). The Dutch established a settlement in Delaware in 1631, followed by the Swedes, but it was captured by the English in 1664. Further south, Maryland was chartered to Lord Baltimore, a Roman Catholic, to secure freedom for his fellow believers, though full religious toleration was offered to all. North and South Carolina were both established Church of England, though were also settled by Hugenots, Scotch-Irish Presbyterians, Baptists and Quakers.

The oldest English colony, however, was that of Virginia (1607). Though a commercial venture, King James I insisted that the colony's charter provide for propagating the Christian religion, and the Church of England was established by law as the recognised Church of Virginia.

Persecution

The intensity of the persecution led to an increasing surge of immigrants to America. The first refugees were English, beginning in 1620 with the Pilgrim Fathers, who were Separatists, followed by other dissenting groups such as Congregationalists and Presbyterians. There was also a substantial number of Puritans who made the journey, anxious to make a new start and form a more 'pure' Church. Driven from England by both State and Church, they settled in the north-east (New England) where some 20,000 refugees had arrived by 1640. The Europeans were not far behind, with Dutch Reformed, French Hugenots, German Pietists, Mennonites, Anabaptists, Lutherans and Catholics joining the quest for freedom.

Among these groups was a number of Quakers, members of a movement founded by George Fox in 1647 and otherwise known as 'Friends of Light'. Fox went about preaching, teaching the spiritual experience of the Inner

Light, the 'Light of Christ' within Man, whereby it was possible to have a direct relationship with God. Those who live up to this principle were the People of God, and those who lived in disobedience to it were not God's People. Puritans were offended by this preaching, for they believed that divine revelation was given only through the Scriptures. Fox and his followers were frequently attacked, their meetings broken up and members of their congregations brought before the magistrates.

So fierce was the persecution that in 1656 a small group of Friends emigrated to New England, only yet again to meet with hostility. Their preaching was made a capital offence in Massachucetts, for which four of them were hanged on Boston Common. Nevertheless, in 1677–1678 some 800 other Friends emigrated to West Jersey, on this occasion aided by the wealthy and influential William Penn, the foremost Quaker leader after Fox. Although since his student days at Oxford Penn had dreamed of a safe haven for religious refugees, it was not realised until 1681 when he was enabled to purchase the territory to be known as Pennsylvania.

Upper Class

William Penn was born into a privileged upper-class home and was the eldest son of Admiral Sir William Penn who in 1655 had captured Jamaica from the Dutch. As a young man the younger Penn had moved in court circles and was the friend of a number of titled people, including the Duke of York, the king's son. At the age of eleven he began a spiritual pilgrimage that was remarkable in one so young. His family had moved from London to County Cork, Ireland, where in 1656 he heard a Quaker preacher, Thomas Loe of Oxford, who profoundly affected the lad. Afterwards, when alone in his room, 'he was suddenly surprised with an inward comfort, and, as he thought, an external glory in the room … he believed that he had been awakened … or called to a holy life.' This awareness of the presence of God stayed with him for the rest of his life.[1]

At the age of sixteen Penn went up to Christ Church College, Oxford, where he maintained his religious practices. He led a devout life, though he withdrew from 'the national way of worship'. Instead he joined a group of friends for exhortation and prayer, and was consequently fined for his refusal to conform to the Anglican Prayer Book. In the spring of 1662, to the considerable annoyance of his father, he was finally sent down because of his persistent nonconformity.

---

1. *William Penn*, John W Graham, p.20.

William Penn (1644-1718)

To allow the student time for further thought, his father arranged for him to tour the Continent and he was away for nearly three years. He returned home to find the strained relationship with his father had not eased and the two were still at odds. Over the next two years he spent time studying law at Lincoln's Inn, followed by a spell in the army were he had a brief but distinguished career.

Still hoping to divert his son's attention, in 1667 his father despatched him to the family estate in Ireland, where once again he heard Thomas Lowe preach. The sermon reached his heart and he left the meeting 'convinced'. Immediately he began to take a stand for his new-found faith. His resolution brought him into conflict with the authorities by his refusal to doff his hat to his social superiors.[2] This act of defiance caused his father to expel him from home, with the added threat of disinheriting him. He became an itinerant minister for the Friends, visiting meetings around the south of England and defending any who had been imprisoned. Over the

---

2. Even to the king. Quakers reserved this deference for God alone.

next fifty years he wrote numerous books and pamphlets in defence of Quakerism, and his collected works included fifty-eight original volumes.

In Prison

On a number of occasions Penn was arrested and brought before the magistrates. Five times he was imprisoned in the Tower of London and was twice committed to Newgate. His first spell in the Tower, in 1668, was on a trumped-up charge of blasphemy, for which he spent nearly nine months locked up in harsh conditions. It was during this confinement that he wrote his greatest work, *No Cross, No Crown*, which focused on the Christian duty of self-sacrifice. His release was finally achieved by his father through the mediation of the Duke of York.

The persecution of Friends in England was probably far worse than many realise. Hundreds endured far greater suffering than Penn, who had those in high places who could plead for him. At the restoration of the monarchy (1660), Charles II had promised religious toleration for all, though this was not forthcoming. Dissenters were subject to the Conventicle Act of 1664, whereby all meetings for worship of more than five persons, other than the Church of England, were declared illegal. To avoid arrest, Dissenters met in secret, though Quakers maintained their usual meeting places and times of worship. They were consequently more easily arrested and brought to trial.

Between 1647–1661 no less than 3,179 Friends were imprisoned, while between 1650 and 1689 nearly 400 of them met a painful death in prison, the result of living in filthy and unhealthy conditions. Homes were confiscated and children left without parents; some suffered at the whipping post or were locked in the stocks, whilst others were heavily fined. When in 1686 a pardon was finally granted them, some 1,300 Friends were released from prison, many of whom had been inside for twelve or even fifteen years. In 1680 Penn produced a statistical list of sufferings they were undergoing, appealing to the Short Parliament then sitting to redress their grievances, but to no avail.

> ## QUAKER BELIEF AND PRACTICE
> The correct title of the Quaker movement is the Religious Society of Friends. The founding principle of the movement, put forward by the founder, George Fox, was the spiritual experience known as the Inward Light, the Light of Christ that he claimed is within every man. Through this Light, and through the Scriptures, God reveals his word to those he chooses. Thus all true believers, men and women, are channels through which God's grace can flow.

Quakers (or Friends, as they prefer to be called) give no place to outward forms of religion, and therefore do not have an ordained ministry, nor do they hold with vestments or practise baptism or partake of the Lord's Supper. They have a strong social conscience with a concern for the underprivileged, such as refugees, mental patients and old people.

Quakers describe themselves as 'seekers for truth', and individuals have to find their own way to that truth. Unlike mainline churches, Friends do not place any emphasis on creeds or the importance of theology, though they emphasise the need to follow the teachings of Jesus. They are well known as pacifists and believe that war is unlawful for Christians.

Their worship meetings are for the most part held in silence, to allow for individual contemplation, though any who feel led to give a Bible reading (or read from any other suitable book), or to speak a brief message, or to offer a prayer, may do so.

Safe Haven

During the 1670's Penn had been increasingly turning his mind towards the idea of a haven for Quakers in the New World. Following the death of his father he had become a wealthy man and began to use his newly acquired fortune from his father's estate to set up such a scheme. In 1674 the Friends were enabled to purchase the western half of New Jersey (previously a Dutch colony) for £1000, and two years later he assisted 800 Quakers to settle there. He drew up a constitution for the new colony based on civil and religious liberty, which provided for a democratic assembly with manhood suffrage and vote by ballot.

When Penn's father died in 1670 there remained an outstanding claim from his estate against the Crown, consisting of loans and arrears of pay which together with interest added up to £16,000. Penn decided to proceed with a claim against the Crown for a grant of land 'lying north of Maryland, bounded on the east by the Delaware river ... to extend north as far as plantable'. It was pretty country which reminded him of Wales, a land of mountain ridges, rolling hills and narrow valleys. Rather than meet this claim, the king was more disposed to let Penn have the land in lieu of the debt. At the king's insistence, the new colony was named Pennsylvania ('Penn's Woods') in honour of the Admiral.

As proprietor and governor of the province, Penn was invested with legislative power, subject to the assent of the 'freemen' (any who professed the Christian religion and held and cultivated a minimum acreage of land). In order to raise money for government, the land was to be offered for sale. First, however, he bought it back from the Indians, at a fair price, as Penn considered it 'an ill argument to convert (Indians) to Christianity'.

Shares were then offered to the settlers: 5,000 acres each for £100, or plots at nearly 5 pence per acre. Those who could not afford to purchase land could join with others to take up a share. Otherwise, it was possible to rent up to 200 acres at a penny an acre.

Government

In May 1682 Penn drew up a constitution, or Frame of Government, which reflected the principle of civil and religious liberties. Under the terms, Penn was to exercise power as Governor, with a counsel chosen by ballot by the freemen; there was to be a Provincial Council of 72, with an annual election of one-third, and a General Assembly of not more than 200 members was to be chosen by ballot. Judges, treasurers, justices of the peace and coroners were to be nominated by the Governor. Other clauses laid down that prisons were to be provided with workshops, while murder alone was to be treated as a capital offence; and children over the age of twelve were to be taught a trade. All modes of religious worship compatible with monotheism and Christian morality were to be tolerated and Sunday was to be a day of rest.

Slavery was an accepted practice in the New England provinces, but a beginning of a movement towards abolition was made under the Pennsylvania constitution. Slaves were to be given their freedom after fourteen years. They were to receive land, stock and tools, but had to pay two-thirds of their crop to the Company. Some owners, however, were uneasy about holding Blacks as slaves whilst recognising them as fellow Christians.

In 1688 it was proposed that owning slaves should be made illegal, though nothing became of the matter. By 1696 opinion among Friends had moved clearly against bringing any more slaves into the colony. In 1712 an Act was passed on the import of slaves which levied a tax of £20 per head, but it was vetoed by the Home Government. Despite its frustrated attempts to control the trafficking, Friends continued in the vanguard of the abolitionist movement.

Brotherly Love

In the autumn of 1682 Penn sailed to take up his new responsibilities in Pennsylvania, landing at the site chosen for his newly planned town, Philadelphia ('city of brotherly love'). It was to be located on the Delaware River, at a place where there was deep water for ships to unload at the

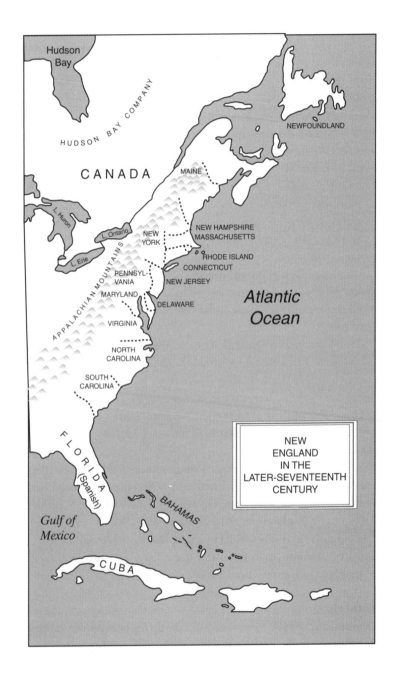

Hudson
Bay

HUDSON BAY COMPANY

NEWFOUNDLAND

CANADA

MAINE

L. Huron

L. Ontario

NEW
YORK

NEW HAMPSHIRE
MASSACHUSETTS

L. Erie

RHODE ISLAND
CONNECTICUT

APPALACHIAN MOUNTAINS

PENNSYL-
VANIA

NEW JERSEY

MARYLAND

DELAWARE

Atlantic
Ocean

VIRGINIA

NORTH
CAROLINA

SOUTH
CAROLINA

FLORIDA
(Spanish)

BAHAMAS

Gulf of
Mexico

CUBA

NEW
ENGLAND
IN THE
LATER-SEVENTEENTH
CENTURY

quay- side. The town was to be a 'green, country town', covering 10,000 acres (the size of London in Penn's time!), with space around the houses for gardens and orchards. The plan was one of uniform parallel streets, intersected at right angles. The Governor's own residence, standing on 300 acres, was to be on the middle of the houses facing the Delaware.

Waiting to greet him on arrival was a crowd of Friends, together with Swedish and Dutch refugees and a delegation of Indians. One of his first undertakings was to draw up a treaty of friendship with the Indians, in which he set out his hope that the two parties would live together in brotherhood and love. The treaty stood out from other treaties because it was kept. No drop of Quaker blood was ever shed by an Indian, and all Penn's promises were honourably observed. This was in contrast to other colonies where Indians were often unfairly treated. No breach of the peace occurred for over seventy years, when the Quaker government of the colony was finally dispossessed.

The population of the colony greatly increased, a result of Penn's policy of toleration, with immigrants from Germany, Holland and Scandinavia, the greater majority of them being Quakers. By the time of summer 1683 around 50 ships had arrived, carrying 4,000 immigrants. This figure included Germans from the Rhineland, who were given a block of 15,000 acres of land just west of Philadelphia, named Germantown. They formed a stalwart and valuable element of the population, who could always be relied upon to support Penn.

Remaining Years

After less than two years, however, Penn was forced to return to England to settle a dispute with Lord Baltimore regarding the colony's southern boundary. His time in England was meanwhile busily occupied with defending the Quaker cause and ministering at meetings. He was not able to return to Pennsylvania until 1699, but once again found it necessary to leave for home, to contest a bill being laid before parliament to change the status of the province into a Crown colony.

But he was never to return to Pennsylvania. His remaining years in England were soured by endless disputes and financial embarrassments. His health steadily declined and he died in July 1718. His remains were interred in the burial ground belonging to the meeting-house at Jordans, Chalfont St Giles (Buckinghamshire).

William Penn must be regarded as the greatest founder of the early American states. His holy experiment was an expression of faith in action,

30

1738 THE CONVERSION OF JOHN WESLEY

The Man Who Changed the Course of a Nation

If John Wesley had died in his thirty-fifth year he would never have been remembered; at most he would have been recognised as 'a sincere, a selfless, almost an heroic failure'. But in that year the earnest young cleric experienced a truly life-changing conversion that revolutionised his life. He travelled the length and breadth of the British Isles preaching the gospel, bringing about a moral and spiritual transformation hardly known since the days of the early Church.

Following the Puritan era, the Church in England had gone into gradual decline, affecting both the Established Church and the Nonconformist denominations. The eighteenth century eminent jurist, Sir William Blackstone, declared that after listening to every notable preacher in London he could not discover 'whether the preachers he had heard were followers of Confucius, of Mohammed or of Christ'. Beset by secularism, many had grown cold in their faith, while others had gone over to Unitarianism.

Possibly more threatening was the rise of Deism which also led many astray. Deism was a system of 'natural religion', which developed in the late seventeenth century. For a time it enjoyed considerable popularity, as it made no demands upon people. It discarded all that was mysterious and supernatural in the Gospels and reduced Christianity to what was 'natural' and 'reasonable'. The divinity of Jesus was denied and miracles were regarded as absurd.

With the foundations of Christianity undermined and biblical morality held cheap, the social structure of the land was falling apart. Whilst the wealthy enjoyed their luxuries, the working poor were untouched by the

253

gospel and neglected by the state. With the exception of a few charity hospitals, medical care was virtually non-existent and diseases such as smallpox, typhoid and cholera were responsible for a great number of deaths. Drunkenness was widespread, more so than at any other time in English history.[1] Gambling was also a national obsession, holding both rich and poor in its clutches. There was rioting, brutality and violence, and under a barbarous system of law adults and children alike could be hanged for some 160 offences.

Puritan Stock

John Wesley was born into a family of Puritan stock, and both his grandfathers were among the clergy ejected in 1662. His father, Samuel Wesley (1662–1735), had revolted against Nonconformity. Ordained into the Church of England, he was the Rector of the parish church of Epworth (Lincolnshire). His mother, Susannah, was a pious woman of remarkable strength of character. Every week she set aside time to instruct each of her children and to impart Christian habits, especially industry and prayer, and taught them to examine the state of their souls. She implanted in them the notion that they could only be saved by 'universal obedience, by keeping all the commandments of God'. This was a thought that later prompted Wesley to begin a search for salvation.

At the age of ten John was given a free place at Charterhouse School, London, and afterwards (in 1720) entered Christ Church College, Oxford. Such was his intellectual attainment that in 1726 he was elected a Fellow of Lincoln College, lecturing in Greek. His father persuaded him to be ordained; then for two years Wesley served as curate to his father before becoming a priest. It was around this time that he became more engrossed in his search for God and set out on a spiritual pilgrimage.

The Holy Club

In 1729 a group of three serious-minded young men at Oxford, led by Charles Wesley – who had followed his brother John to Christ Church – formed a religious society. Later that year they were joined by John who was soon accepted as leader. In their attempt to work out their own salvation, they believed it necessary to attain to holiness before God could accept

---

1. This was the gin age – the 'master-curse of English life' – when gin shops advertised 'Drunk for a penny, dead drunk for twopence'.
2. The government raised vast sums of money through lotteries, which financed the building of Westminster Bridge (1736) and the British Museum (1753).

them into heaven. Hence their desire to obey Christ's command: 'Be ye perfect, even as your Father which is in heaven is perfect' (Matt. 5:48).

To achieve their objective, the group pledged themselves to be regular in their devotions and to partake of Holy Communion once a week.[3] They fasted and vowed to be conscientious in their personal conduct. Four evenings a week they met to pray, study and discuss the Bible, and to give some account of their spiritual progress. They visited the prisoners in Oxford castle and cared for poor and needy families in the town. The group attracted great notoriety and soon became known as the 'The Holy Club', though the nickname that stuck was 'Methodists', presumably because of their methodical way of life.

Wesley's search for holiness was influenced in his thinking by William Law's book, *A Serious Call to a Devout and Holy Life*, which was a call to personal holiness. He embraced the challenge with all his powers, setting out his resolve in a letter to his father: 'My one aim in life is to secure personal holiness, for without being holy I cannot promote real holiness in others.' With this in mind, in 1735 he volunteered to become Chaplain to the English community in the colony of Georgia. It would also afford him an opportunity to preach to the Indians, a prospect that appealed to him. But his efforts to turn the community into a Holy Club, complete with sacraments and church discipline, caused considerable friction.

The mission was a disaster, and after two years he sailed for home, anxious to leave behind him the furore he had caused. Back in London (in February 1738) he was finally forced to admit that he had failed in his search. Writing in his Journal he confessed, 'I went to America to convert the Indians, but who will convert me?' Now convinced that he ought to stop preaching, there were two experiences that brought him through his spiritual crisis.

Saving Faith

In March he met a Moravian missionary, Peter Bohler, who encouraged him to continue preaching: 'Preach faith until you have it, and because you have it you will preach faith,' he urged. So Wesley continued his ministry, but still could not find peace – that is, not until the 24th May, when he came into a saving faith. In his Journal he describes how in the evening he went 'very unwillingly to a society in Aldersgate Street where one was reading Luther's preface to the Epistle to the Romans. About a quarter

---

3. This was most unusual; the common practice was to communicate only once a quarter.

before nine, while he was describing the change which God works in the heart through faith in Christ, I felt my heart strangely warmed. I felt I did trust in Christ, Christ alone for salvation; and an assurance was given me that He had taken away my sins, even mine, and saved me from the law of sin and death.'

This experience marked the turning-point in his search for salvation; he now knew that he was justified before God – by faith alone. He began to preach as never before, with conviction and power. The following Sunday he preached at St George's Church, Bloomsbury (London), on justification by faith. Not surprising, it caused some offence and he was told after the service that he would not be asked to preach there again. Soon branded an 'enthusiast',[4] such disapproval was repeated at a number of churches, so that doors were closed to him.

Open-air Preaching

The beginning of his lifelong ministry dates from March 1739, when the evangelist George Whitefield invited him to take over his work in Bristol among the coal miners of Kingswood. For some while Whitefield had been preaching to the men in the open air, and with much success. But he had arranged to visit America and wanted Wesley to carry on the work he had begun. 'You must come and water what God has enabled me to plant,' he wrote.

Wesley was at first reluctant, for he could not accustom himself to the thought of field-preaching. 'I could scarce reconcile myself to this strange way of preaching,' he recorded. '... I should have thought the saving of souls almost a sin, if it had not been done in a church...' But he went, and was soon preaching to huge crowds of miners as well as townspeople. Large numbers of them were saved, and at the end of a year he was able to report that a great transformation had taken place among the coal miners of Kingswood.

A natural leader and organiser, Wesley gathered the converts together in societies for building them up in their new-found faith. Meetings were held in private houses, though before long permanent society rooms were built. The first was in the Horsefair, Bristol, and the following year he purchased the derelict King's Foundery in the City of London for use as a chapel. Each society was divided into 'classes' of twelve, which provided a means of watching over the faith and morals of the members, and the

---

4. The term 'enthusiast' was one of ridicule, and denoted someone who was fanatical in their beliefs.

societies were in turn grouped into 'Circuits'. In 1744 he held a conference of his lay preachers, which became an annual event; it was not so much for discussion, but rather for him to give them his instructions.

Burning Heart

Not content simply to travel along the London-Bristol corridor, Wesley had a 'burning heart' to make the gospel more widely known. His hope was to 'reform the nation, particularly the Church of England, and to spread scriptural holiness over the land'. In 1741 he began his itinerant ministry, travelling to south Wales and the following year to Yorkshire. Many times he traversed the British Isles, basing his journeys on the Bristol-Newcastle-London triangle, with diversions into Scotland and Ireland; he also visited the colonies of North America as well. He preached wherever an opportunity arose, whether in a church or – more often – in the open air, despite being attacked by mobs or facing riots. Each year he travelled at least 4,500 miles – mainly on horseback – and preached some 5,000 sermons.

THE CAMBUSLANG REVIVAL

This Scottish revival serves as a reminder that other evangelists were also at work in Britain during the eighteenth century, as well as the Wesleys and George Whitefield (1714–1770), who was probably the more powerful of them all. The Cambuslang revival broke out early in 1742. For twelve months the minister, the Revd William McCulloch, had been preaching the gospel, and especially the need for regeneration. Whilst several people were converted, it was not until the Thursday evening meeting on 18th February that revival began, when some fifty people received counsel from the minister. Crowds from the surrounding areas began flocking to Cambuslang to hear the gospel. With the aid of local ministers, meetings were held daily and within the space of three months some 200 were converted.

McCulloch appealed to Whitefield for help. At his first meeting the evangelist preached to a crowd of more than 20,000 people; the following day was a 'Communion Sabbath' when another great crowd attended and of which Whitefield declared, 'Scarce ever such a sight was seen in Scotland'. A second Communion service was held in August when over 30,000 communicants were present to hear Whitefield preach again. McCulloch wrote afterwards, 'Not a few were awakened to a sense of sin ... (many) have declared ... that they had been ... filled with all joy and peace in believing.' Nine years after the revival the minister was able to report that he personally knew of about 400 people who had continued in the Faith, although there were probably other converts who were unaccounted for.

A loyal Anglican throughout his life, Wesley had no intention of breaking with the Established Church. But it was impossible to keep the 'new wine' within the confines of an 'old bottle' and a parting of the ways was inevitable. After his death[5] the Methodist movement became an independent system, forming the Wesleyan Methodist Church. However, a number of the societies were divided in opinions, chiefly concerning the matter of church government. In 1797 a small group of Methodists seceded from the mother Church to form the Methodist New Connexion, and in the first half of the following century further secessions followed.[6] Reunion was not achieved until 1932 when all the Methodist denominations came together to form the Methodist Church of Great Britain.

Transformation

The Revival[7] led to a moral and spiritual renewal throughout the land which touched all levels of society, especially the labouring poor. Many churches were also transformed, while clergymen entered into a renewed faith that brought a fresh zeal to their ministry – and an increase in church attendances. Some of the older Nonconformist denominations were considerably influenced by the revival, though with unequal results. The Congregationalists benefited most of all: their fervour was revived and their numbers rapidly increased. The Particular Baptists and the Presbyterians were affected, though to a lesser degree, while the Calvinistic Methodist Churches in Wales also evidenced strong growth. But the greatest impact was upon the Church of England. The rise of the Evangelical Party (the 'Low Church'), which became a strong and organised movement, revitalised a Church almost on its deathbed.

The Church is further indebted to Wesley in that he restored to the Catholic Faith two great biblical truths of the Reformation. Like Martin Luther, he reaffirmed the doctrine of justification by faith and the joyful assurance of the forgiveness of sins, through which it was possible to enter into a personal relationship with God. A second great truth was his emphasis on holiness, or Christian perfection. He did not regard this as conferring the title 'Saint' on certain distinguished divines, nor was it simply a matter of sinless perfection, for he realised that 'a man may be filled with pure

---

5. At this time (1791) the Methodist societies claimed 72,000 members in England, and 60,000 in North America, not counting the large number of adherents who attended the meetings.
6. These were the Primitive Methodists, the Bible Christians and the Wesleyan Reformers.
7. Often referred to as the Weslyan Revival, it would be more correct to call it the Evanglical Revival, for other evangelists – George Whitefield, Howell Harries and Daniel Rowlands were also involved.

John Wesley (1703-1791)

love and still be liable to error'. Rather it was the 'dedication of all our life to Him ...the giving to God of all our heart ...enabling us to walk as Christ walked...'

Social Concerns

Despite the demands of his preaching, Wesley found time to concern himself with a wide variety of social ills that required attention, and on the basis that 'faith without action was dead' he taught by example. He was involved in a wide range of social issues: education and literature, medical care for the poor, famine relief, and the slave trade among others. Over the years, the Evangelical Revival aroused within the nation a social conscience, evidenced by a greater concern for the underprivileged and the needy. Men and women engaged in great philanthropic causes that were to benefit the conditions of the masses. Among these were John Howard and Elizabeth

A pharmacy opened by Wesley in 1747

Fry, who worked to improve prison conditions, Hannah More who promoted popular education, Robert Raikes who founded the Sunday School movement, and William Wilberforce who fought hard and long to abolish slavery.[8]

The evangelical movement continued into the following century, when city missions were founded, free medical clinics opened, the great orphanages established, and agencies founded to care for the handicapped, the elderly and the homeless. It was from among the Methodists that the first leaders of the British Labour Movement were to be found. In 1834 three of the Tolpuddle martyrs transported to Australia were Methodist local preachers and the first Trade Union MPs were products of the revival.

There was also a great surge in foreign missionary activity among both Anglicans and Nonconformists, in part stimulated by Captain Cook's voyages of discovery in the Pacific. As never before, Protestants in Great Britain were stirred into action, signalling the beginning of the modern missionary movement. Societies were founded that were to reach out to the five continents, accessing regions so far untouched by the gospel. The Methodist Missionary Society (1786), the Baptist Missionary Society (1792), the Church Missionary Society (1799), were among the first to be established. Christian literature was provided by the Religious Tract Society

---

8. Wilberforce was a member of the 'Clapham Sect', a group of wealthy evangelical Anglicans who worked for social reform and the furtherance of the gospel.

(1799) and by the British and Foreign Bible Society – now the Bible Society – (1804). In America the Board of Commissioners for Foreign Missions was set up in 1810, and one of its first missionaries was Adoniram Judson of Burma.

By 1760 Methodism 'was easily the most highly co-ordinated body of opinion in the country, the most fervent, the most dynamic'. Yet because of the hostility of the Anglican hierarchy Wesley was forced to pursue his own course. The Methodist Church continued as a powerful force for good in England and America throughout the nineteenth century and, as one historian has claimed, saved the nation from the sort of revolution that had afflicted America in 1776 and France in 1789. And as Lloyd George admitted, 'John Wesley inaugurated a movement that gripped the soul of England (and) deepened its spiritual instincts'.

CHARLES WESLEY (1707–1788)

Charles, John's brother, was an Anglican minister and an evangelist. Remembered as one of the greatest hymn writers of all time, he wrote some 6,500 hymns and is regarded as the 'Poet of the Evangelical Revival'. That other great eighteenth century hymn writer, Isaac Watts, confessed that Charles' hymn, 'Come O Thou Traveller Unknown', was worth all the verses he himself had written (and that included 'When I Survey the Wondrous Cross'). The ministry of the two Wesley brothers complemented each other, for Charles' hymns reinforced the theology of John's sermons.

Hymn-singing was an essential element in Methodist meetings and a means for conveying scriptural truth. Wesley's hymns were also sung in evangelical meetings within the Established Church, as an alternative to the metrical psalms. Whilst many of these hymns are now lost in obscurity, the finest of his compositions are still sung around the world.

Charles Wesley came to faith on Whit Sunday, 1738, just three days before his brother. Only when John called to tell Charles of his own conversion did he learn the good news. He found Charles with a group of friends, and together they sang Charles' first ever composition, 'Where Shall My Wandering Soul Begin?' (Some authorities believe they sang 'And Can it Be?'.)

The two Wesleys together published four small volumes of hymns, with 'plain' tunes; later, some of the tunes were more stirring and others were 'annexed' from a variety of sources – psalm-tunes and favourite operatic tunes or arias and other tunes of the day. As Charles Wesley remarked, 'There is no reason why the Devil should have all the good tunes' – a remark later attributed to Rowland Hill and William Booth.

31

1740 THE FIRST GREAT AWAKENING PEAKS

Widespread Revival in the American Colonies

The initial surge of faith and fervour which led the early settlers to leave their homelands for the freedom of New England in time gave way to a decline in personal faith and church membership. Free from the threat of persecution and state interference, the Puritans set out to transform their settlements into veritable Bible commonwealths. In the four colonies where Puritan influence dominated they aimed to build a godly society based on the Scriptures, 'the onely rule to be attended unto in ordering the affayres of government'. Yet within two generations signs of a spiritual crisis arose which appeared to threaten the very life of the colonial Church.

The reasons for the erosion of religious faith during those years are not difficult to find. A growing number of immigrants had settled in the back-country, away from the influence of the churches. In the towns, people were becoming more prosperous as trade and commerce flourished, so that there was a lessening emphasis on church attendance and on biblical values. Christianity was degenerating into religious formalism, and the Puritan hope of a godly society was increasingly under threat.

Back in England, simply to associate with the Puritans had been accepted as an indication of a person's spiritual condition and, consequently, suitability for church membership. But in the New World some believers were uneasy about this procedure and wanted a different basis for acceptance. Under the leadership of Massachusetts, it was finally agreed only to accept into membership those who could testify to the saving grace of God in their lives, who gave their assent to Puritan doctrine and promised to live a godly life. Those who qualified were accepted into full membership, which gave them the privilege of bringing their infant children to be baptised and entitled male members to vote in the colony's public life.

Half-Way Covenant

Despite this apparent firm foundation, difficulties arose concerning the children of the earliest settlers. During the 1650s, more and more of these children were unable to testify to a conversion experience as their parents had known. Hence, though baptised as infants they were not allowed into full church membership. As they were not eligible to vote for town leaders, the number of church members was consequently in gradual decline. The problem persisted with next generation parents who wanted to have their children baptised, but unless they were converted their children were also refused baptism.

The situation presented church leaders with a dilemma: on the one hand they wished the church to continue as a believing church, at the same time they were anxious to keep as many as possible under the church's covering. At a meeting of Synod in 1662 it was recognised that 'Damned or saved, the children had to be made subject to the watch and ward of the church, or the Bible commonwealth was ruined.' In response, a compromise solution was devised, later called the Half-Way Covenant, whereby unregenerate second generation parents of moral standing could bring their children to be baptised. But neither they nor their children could attend the Lord's Supper until they had made a personal profession of faith.

Although some opposed the move and rejected it as a contradiction of Scripture, others wanted to go further and introduce a parish system whereby all inhabitants could receive baptism and even partake of the Lord's Table. One pastor, Solomon Stoddard (1643–1729), of the Congregational Church at Northampton (Massachusetts), believed it to be a 'converting ordinance' which could help a seeker understand 'the death and sufficiency of the death of Christ'. But the introduction of a compromise solution was a short-sighted step which failed to stem the tide of unbelief; rather, the problem was compounded.

Decay

By 1679 a 'Reforming Synod' held in Massachusetts contended 'that God hath a controversy with His New England People'. It was declared that there was 'a great and visible decay of the power of Godliness among many Professors in (the) Churches', with 'much Sabbath-breaking' and 'Sinful Heats and Hatreds'. A plea was made for 'a thorough and heart Reformation', with the prayer that God would 'pour down his Spirit from on High'. But the Half-Way Covenant continued in use and it was over thirty years before this prayer for revival was answered in the New England Church.

The first signs of revival were not in Massachusetts, but in New Jersey and among the Dutch Reformed churches. Theodore Frelinghuysen (1691–1747), a German educated in the Netherlands, and pastor of the Dutch Reformed Church, had experienced the 'heart-religion' of the German Pietist Movement. He ministered to Dutch settlers in the Raritan River Valley where he began to preach of the need for conversion. Before long, a work of revival took a strong hold of the Dutch churches; there were many conversions, accompanied by a deep sense of piety. Other pastors such as Gilbert Tennent (1703–1764), a Presbyterian of New Jersey, and Cotton Mather (1663–1727), a Congregationalist of Boston, also began to experience times of revival. Solomon Stoddard, pastor at Northampton for fifty-seven years, had reckoned on five 'harvests' – times of renewal – during his long ministry.

There was a great concern among many Evangelicals for the declining spiritual condition of the churches. Cotton Mather had declared that there was a 'general and horrible decay of Christianity among the Professors of it', while in 1734 Jonathan Edwards commented about the general state of the young people in Northampton that it seemed to be 'a time of extraordinary dullness in religion'. He went on to speak of their 'licentiousness ... lewd practices ... and frequenting the tavern', as well as their unseemly behaviour in church.

But this state of spiritual deadness was soon to change when a widespread time of revival broke out in the 1730s and 1740s, a period known as the Great Awakening. It began in 1734 in the town of Northampton, then after a brief period of declension emerged three years later on a larger scale, peaking in 1740. The Awakening was made up of a number of local revivals, largely under the influence of two leading figures: Jonathan Edwards (1703–1758), pastor of the Congregational Church in Northampton, a noted scholar and preacher, and George Whitefield (1714–1770), an ordained minister of the Church of England.

Jonathan Edwards

One of the greatest men in the history of the Church in America, Edwards was a theologian and scholar of repute. At the age of six he began learning Latin, and by the age of thirteen had acquired a working knowledge of the three classical languages – Latin, Greek and Hebrew. He graduated from

Jonathan Edwards (1703-1758)

Yale College in 1720, then spent a further two years studying theology. After a spell as a minister in a Presbyterian church in New York City he returned to Yale as a tutor, though was forced to resign two years later as a result of illness. In 1726 he became assistant pastor to his grandfather, Solomon Stoddard, at Northampton, and assumed full responsibility for the church upon his grandfather's death in 1729.

Outside of Boston, the Congregational church at Northampton was probably the largest and most influential within the colony. For twenty-three years Edwards devoted himself to the pastoral care of the congregation, especially to instructing them in the Word of God, and the church became 'a city set on a hill'. Anxious to bring his people into an experiential knowledge of God, he preached the gospel and appealed to his members to turn from sin – 'an offence against the majesty of God' – and to seek forgiveness and salvation in Christ.

In 1734 the mood of the town visibly began to change following a series of sermons Edwards preached on 'Justification by faith alone'. Through the winter of that year and into 1735 there arose among the people of the town a strong desire for godliness, with both young and old coming to a knowledge of salvation. In his account of the Awakening, *A Narrative of Surprising Conversions* (1737), he wrote that 'the Spirit of God began extraordinarily to set in and wonderfully to work among us; and there were very suddenly, one after another, five or six persons, who were to all appearances savingly converted, and some of them wrought upon in a very remarkable way'.

The town was manifestly transformed by this work of God, and in a period of 6 months there were over 300 conversions out of a population of 1200 people. Worship services were revitalised; the congregation gathered 'eager to drink in the words of the minister ... (and) the assembly in general were from time to time in tears while the Word was preached...' Edwards reported that the town seemed to be 'full of the presence of God. It never was so full of love, nor so full of joy, and yet as full of distress, as it was then. There were remarkable tokens of God's presence in every house.' Later, in November 1736, he recorded, 'I know of no one young person in the town who has returned to former ways of looseness and extravagance in any respect; but we still remain a reformed people, and God has evidently made us a new people.'

EDWARDS: THE LATER YEARS

It was not until the early 1740s that, along with other evangelical ministers, Edwards finally repudiated the Half-Way Covenant so favoured by his grandfather. When he placed the matter before his church it began a long drawn-out controversy, which ended in his being dismissed from the pastorate (in June 1750).

Within a short while Edwards accepted a call to be pastor of a small church at Stockbridge, a frontier hamlet of twelve white families, but where he was also able to minister to a tribe of Housatonic Indians. Although the work kept him busy, he created time for writing the treatises on which his fame now stands as America's foremost theologian. He devoted himself to defending the Calvinistic system against the 'rampant Arminianism' of his day. Among his works were 'Freedom of the Will' (1754), and 'Original Sin', 'The Nature of True Virtue', and his unfinished 'History of Redemption', all published after his death.

His intellectual gifts were recognised in 1757 when he was offered the presidency of the college of New Jersey (Princeton), in succession to his son-in-law, Aaron Burr. He had hoped to be able to continue his work on a series of volumes on the Arminian controversy, but following the advice of friends he accepted the offer and took up the position in January 1758. On the 13 February he was inoculated for smallpox, but died of the disease on the 27 March, in his fifty-fifth year.

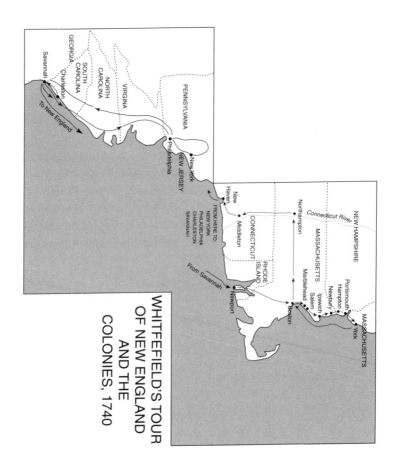

WHITEFIELD'S TOUR
OF NEW ENGLAND
AND THE
COLONIES, 1740

George Whitefield

The Awakening spread beyond Northampton, to western Massachusetts and all along the Connecticut River Valley, where more than thirty parishes were affected, to other parts of New England and southwards into Virginia. Although by 1736 the revival was in decline, it sprang to life again three years later with the arrival of George Whitefield. He planned to visit the colonies along the eastern seaboard in the hope of finding opportunities to preach. When he arrived at Philadelphia towards the end of October 1739, reports of his ministry in England had already gone before him. Newspapers had reported the success of his preaching in London and Bristol, both in churches and the open air, so that his visit was awaited with great expectation and the hope that the fires of revival might be rekindled.

Whitefield remained in America from the October of 1739 until December of the following year, during which time he made three tours around the colonies. Recognising the great need for the preaching of the gospel, he commented, 'I am persuaded that the generality of preachers talk of an unknown, unfelt Christ. And the reason why congregations have been so dead is because dead men preach to them.' Herein lies one of Whitefield's greatest concerns, for behind this comment was the realisation that many church ministers were unconverted and had been appointed simply on the basis of their formal orthodoxy and moral character.

Whilst readily welcomed by evangelical ministers, many of the Anglican clergymen bitterly opposed Whitefield and refused him the use of their pulpits. In which case he resorted to preaching in the open air, even over the winter months. He was a natural orator, with a clear and musical voice, and with a dramatic presentation that captured the attention of his congregations. His loud voice and clearly articulated words enabled him to make himself heard at a great distance when preaching in the open. The noted scientist, inventor and publisher, Benjamin Franklin, described how in Philadelphia he was able to hear Whitefield's message whilst standing towards the rear of a crowd of around 20,000 people.

CONVERSION OF GEORGE WHITEFIELD

Born at the Bell Inn, Gloucester, where his parents were the proprietors, Whitefield was in fact of an upper-middle-class family. Educated at St Mary's Crypt Grammar School, he planned to become an actor, but his 'early convictions of sin' caused him to consider becoming a clergyman. From the age of seventeen he began to take his religion more seriously: he partook of Holy Communion every Lord's Day, fasted during Lent, attended public worship twice daily and read devotional books.

At the age of eighteen, in 1732, he entered Pembroke College, Oxford, as a servitor (that is, one who waited upon the other undergraduates in return for tuition fees). Whilst the moral character of students at Oxford was generally in decay, Whitefield continued his pursuit of God with a renewed vigour, but with an emphasis on outward duties. He joined the members of the Holy Club in their practice of early rising, lengthy devotions and strict self-discipline, and shared with them the ridicule of the other undergraduates. The Holy Club members did all they could, Whitefield wrote later, 'to enter in at the strait gate', but they knew nothing of the new birth.

By the autumn of 1734 Whitefield was driving himself to even greater austerities in an attempt to bring 'the life of God' within his soul. At Lent, 1735, he passed the six weeks before Easter in a rigorous fast which dangerously weakened his body. Seriously ill and confined to bed, he finally recognised there was nothing more he could do. It was at this point that God stepped in, though what transpired is not known. There shone a ray of light into his heart: 'God was pleased to remove the heavy load,' he wrote, 'to enable me to lay hold of His dear Son by a living faith.' He had at last come to faith and experienced a new birth.

New England

In the September of 1740, the evangelist arrived in New England where he looked forward to ministering among the descendants of its Puritan founders. During his month's tour he preached daily to vast crowds, some of 8,000 or more. Always at the heart of his message he spoke of the necessity of the new birth and urged people to believe on the Lord Jesus Christ. After a successful week in Boston, he made a tour of several of the outlying towns – Salem, Ipswich, Newbury, Hampton and Portsmouth. Then, according to his preach and return method, he retraced his steps, visiting the same towns to find out how the work was progressing. When he returned to Philadelphia he was again greatly encouraged to find that the 'glorious work' begun in this province was also bearing fruit, which convinced him that the work was truly of God.

Wherever he went, Whitefield stirred up a deep interest in the gospel, so much so that a 'great and general revival of religion' broke out. Many were asking the question, 'What must I do to be saved?', and countless others sought out Whitefield for personal counselling. This hunger for God led to a great many people making a personal profession of faith.[1] So numerous were the converts throughout the colonies that there was an upsurge of interest in prophecy. With so many coming to faith, some

---

1. There were others labouring in New England at this time; they included William Robinson, Samuel Davies (Presbyterian) Daniel Marshall, Shubal Stearns (Baptist) and Devereux Jarrett (Anglican). Around 150 churches were affected by this awakening.

Christians thought that the millennium was approaching. It seemed possible to them that the revival might spread to other nations, even to the rest of the world, thus heralding the return of the Lord.

Impact

The Awakening was called 'Great' because of its widespread impact on the colonies, moving from Massachusetts into the middle and southern colonies, where many churches were renewed, and westwards into the back-country where later the Baptists and Methodists made considerable gains. It touched upper and lower classes of most Nonconformist denominations, and reached both Indians and slaves. Whitefield's tour of New England is said to have been the most sensational event in the spiritual life of colonial America. It is reckoned, from what is known of church registers, that around 50,000 new members were added to the churches in New England alone. Though the revival continued after Whitefield had left for England, by the following year it was beginning to abate.

The effect of the Awakening on the lives of the new believers, and in general on the social life of the colonies, was remarkable. It promoted a more active, a more individual form of religion, and there was kindled a love both for God and for one's neighbour among the people. Ordinary church members began to meet together for prayer and Bible study, and to encourage each other to lead godly lives. Personal quarrels were set right, there was more honesty in business and people generally took greater delight in the practice of their religion. For the next two centuries Puritan morality set the standards not only for the colonies, but later served as a basis for the foundation of the United States of America.

There was a renewed concern for evangelism, not simply for the white population, but also for Indians and slaves. David Brainerd (1718–1747) was foremost among a number of missionaries who engaged in evangelising the native Americans and was able to establish a number of 'praying towns' where Indians settled. And Samuel Davies (1723–1761) was among those who preached to the slaves. He had the joy of baptising about 150 adults, who were invited to share in church observances such as the Lord's Supper.

The Puritans placed much store against education. Already Harvard (1638) and William and Mary (1693) Colleges had been founded during the previous century. But as more young men were led into the ministry several more colleges were established: the College of New Jersey, Princeton (1746), Rhode Island College (later, Brown University) (1746), Queen's College (1766) and Dartmouth (1754).

For most of the next half century the land was in turmoil, from the French and Indian Wars, which began in 1754, then through the period of the American Revolution to the inaugural United States Congress of 1789. Throughout these years there was a general trend of secularisation when the churches again lost out. Even so, there were a number of local revivals throughout the colonies, from about 1795–1810 which has been recognised by some as another Great Awakening. This renewal provided the momentum for further waves of revival which continued through to the Civil War (1861–1865) and beyond.

An American addressing a British audience in 1832 declared, 'Revivals of religion have been gradually multiplying, until they have become the grand absorbing theme and aim of the American religious world.' Rightly so, and they continued through the remainder of the century. This period in United States history has justly been known as the 'Protestant century'.

32

1859 DARWIN'S *ON THE ORIGIN OF SPECIES* IS PUBLISHED

Theory of Evolution Rocks the Church

The publication of Darwin's book inaugurated an intellectual revolution unknown since 1517, when Martin Luther nailed his ninety-five theses to the door of the church of Wittenberg. Although the idea of evolution had been around for many centuries,[1] it was the explanation that lay behind Darwin's observations that proved of significance. Whilst many orthodox churchmen bitterly opposed the implications of Darwin's theory, which denied the belief in a Creator God, others of a more liberal persuasion were able to accommodate the new ideas.

Charles Darwin (1809–1882) was born into a well-to-do upper-middle-class family in Shrewsbury (Shropshire). He was the son of a doctor who had one of the largest medical practices outside London, and the grandson of Dr Erasmus Darwin, a well-known physician and naturalist, and of Josiah Wedgwood II of the famous pottery manufacturing family. Though his mother died when he was barely eight years old, he was cared for by his two adoring sisters and an older brother, and enjoyed the security of the large Darwin and Wedgwood clans.

At the age of nine the young Darwin was sent to Shrewsbury School where the renowned Dr Butler was headmaster. When he left after seven years he did not receive any special commendation: both his masters and his father considered him to be rather below standard in intellect. But as he

---

1. The earliest mention is to be found in the writings of the Greek philosophers, including Aristotle (384–322).

was 'doing no good' at school, at the age of sixteen his father sent him to Edinburgh to study medicine. He was unable to complete the course, as he found some of the lectures dull, anatomy disgusting and was ultimately repelled by watching surgery performed without anaesthetics.

When his father realised that his son had no inclination for medicine, it was proposed that he should become a clergyman, an idea not entirely unappealing to the young man. However, he thought it necessary first to study the Creed since he could not affirm a belief in all the dogmas, and felt he should polish up his Greek. During his time at Christ Church, Cambridge (1828–1831), he maintained a long-held interest in natural history. Through his close friendship with the Revd Professor John Henslow, a botanist, his excitement about science was encouraged, especially the study of geology. The two men became great friends and their frequent walks taught the student much more than he had learned from all his geology lectures.

The *Beagle*

After his graduation in 1831 it was the Revd Henslow who introduced him to Captain FitzRoy, Master of the survey ship *Beagle*.[2] On Henslow's recommendation, FitzRoy invited the twenty-two year old to take up the position of unpaid naturalist on the *Beagle's* second exploratory-scientific expedition around South America. The object was to complete the survey of Patagonia and Tierra del Fuego, commenced on a previous voyage, to survey the shores of Chile, Peru and of some islands in the Pacific, and to carry a chain of chronometrical measurements around the world. Darwin was delighted at the idea, though it was only after the Wedgwoods had persuaded his father to finance the trip that he was able to accept the invitation.

When the ship set sail from Devonport on 27 December 1831 Darwin took with him a few books, among them his Greek New Testament. At this point, it would seem that he was still orthodox in believing the biblical account of creation, and held to the view that God had separately created different species, each suited to their different environment. But on the ship he began his studies by reading a new book, *Principles of Geology*, by Charles Lyell, recommended by Henslow. The professor had warned him not to take too much notice of it: 'it is very interesting (but) it is altogether wild as far as theory goes'.

---

2. The EU Mars space lander was named Beagle 2 after Darwin's surrey ship.

Yet Lyell's thesis appealed to the young naturalist. The author argued that the earth's continents were not shaped by Noah's Flood, but by the action of the rains, the winds, earthquakes, volcanoes and other natural forces – forces still altering the earth. To Henslow, such ideas were heretical; to Darwin, they proved to be the beginning of a new and dazzling array of ideas that soon began to assail his mind.

As the ship sailed around the coasts of South America and Darwin saw the land masses of the Patagonia and the Andes mountains, he began to find himself in agreement with Lyell's conclusions. On a number of occasions he was able to make expeditions ashore, wandering through a forest, travelling into the interior either on foot or by boat, climbing mountains, and, in places, making contact with the natives. He never returned from an excursion empty-handed, but collected specimens and made observations. During the course of the five year voyage he filled eighteen small notebooks with records of his findings which, with his journal and his collections of specimens, were periodically returned to England for safekeeping.

The Galapagos Islands

In Septmber 1835 the Beagle reached the Galapagos Islands, over 500 miles off the coast of South America and just south of the equator. The 13 islands were formed of volcanic rocks of black basaltic lava, studded by numerous craters. It was here that Darwin first tentatively began to form his ideas of the origin of species.

As he walked across Chatham Island he met two gaint tortoises, each one weighing at least 200 pounds. (He later learned that no other species like them had developed anywhere else in the world.) On another island he encountered large numbers of lizards – the marine iguanas that inhabited the coastline and another variety that lived inland, though the two never mixed. Darwin observed that the two species agreed in their general structure and in many of their habits, yet were quite different.

What he later considered to be one of his most exciting discoveries was the existence of 'a most singular group of finches' – there were 13 different kinds of them, which showed differences in form and plumage but were basically alike. Darwin felt it was asking too much to assume that all 13 species were seperately created and still have so much in common. It was this conclusion that challenged his belief that all animals were created as they are and, together with his other observations on the islands, later convinced him of the reality of the evolution of living things.

After a stay of four weeks, the *Beagle* left the Galapagos Islands to

Cape Verde Is.

ATLANTIC OCEAN

Galapagos Islands

Callao

Salvador

Rio de Janeiro

Montevideo

Valparaiso

PACIFIC OCEAN

Buenos Aires

Tierra del Fuego

Falkland Is.

Cape Horn

The South American section of Beagle's round-the-world voyage

continue its circumnavigation of the globe, reaching Falmouth in October the following year. Despite his careful investigations, Darwin was not yet aware that he had made observations that were to prove important in the field of natural science. Back in England, he spent three months in Cambridge, where all his specimens were being catalogued by experts; he also began writing up his Journal.

Elected a Fellow of the Geological Society, he moved to London to complete his Journal and to begin writing up his findings, spending the next twenty years poring over the notes he had compiled on his memorable voyage. He also gave much time to reflecting on his ideas about the origin of species. Privately[2] he set down a list of questions and answers about the problem, gathering evidence for his theory of evolution.

Back home, he began to contemplate the idea of marriage. After drawing up a list of the pros and cons of matrimony, he proposed to his first cousin Emma Wedgwood, whom he married in January 1839. A devout Christian, Emma proved to be a devoted wife and mother, and under her management he was able to work peacefully at his books for the next forty years. The newly-weds moved into a house on Gower Street, London, though Darwin's continued ill-health[3] – which had first became apparent in 1837 – finally forced them to move into the country. They purchased Downe House,[4] in the village of Downe, near Biggin Hill (Kent), some sixteen miles from the city. The couple enjoyed few outings – with the exception of visits to the family and seaside holidays – and had to forego dinner parties and other social occasions. He was able to travel to London where he kept in touch with friends of the scientific fraternity.

Agnostic

Darwin's investigations had led him to give much thought to religion, until he finally realised that he could no longer accept a conventional belief in the Bible. He queried the history of the early chapters of the Old Testament, where he felt God to be a 'revengeful tyrant'. As for the New Testament, he rejected the supernatural element of the Gospels, nor could he believe that Christianity was a divine revelation. Above all he failed to understand why such a powerful Being should create a universe in which there was so much suffering. On the other hand, he found it impossible to conceive that such an 'immense and wonderful universe' – including man – was the result

---

3. He suffered from exhaustion, violent shivering and vomiting attacks, possibly the result of a tropical disease.

4. Downe House is today an English Heritage property and is open to the public.

of blind chance, and felt compelled to admit to a first cause which had an intelligent mind. Unsure of his beliefs, he concluded that he 'must be content to remain an agnostic'.

Reluctant to make his scientific discoveries more widely known – partly in respect for his wife's sentiments, but also fearful of the commotion he knew it would cause – he was finally persuaded by his friends Charles Lyell and T. H. Huxley to publish the work. *On the Origin of Species* appeared in November 1859, and the first edition of 1,250 books sold out immediately. By 1872 the work had run through six editions and had been translated into most European languages.

In his book, Darwin argued that the evidence he had collected showed that species had developed by natural selection, by adaption to their environment and by a gradual process of evolution. All the varied forms of life, he contended, had evolved over thousands of generations from lower forms of life. Given the struggle for existence everywhere, he concluded that 'favourable variations would tend to be preserved and unfavourable ones to be destroyed' – in short, only the fittest survived,[5] resulting in the formation of new species.

It was this suggestion of a mechanism for change that convinced biologists of the theory, for it showed how it was possible for evolution to have taken place. One further issue was on his mind. Though Darwin had decided not to discuss the origin of man in his book, he had added one significant sentence to his concluding chapter: 'Much light will be thrown on the origin of man and his history.' That single sentence caused the furore that he had feared.

THE DESCENT OF MAN

Published by Darwin in 1871, the *Descent of Man* sets out his theory that humans evolved from ape-like creatures. According to Darwin, 'man is constructed on the same general type or model as other mammals', which included his bones, the structure of his brain and his reproductive processes. All life is one, he concluded, because 'all life has arisen from one unremembered beginning'.

Whilst the gulf between man and the highest apes is immense, he insisted that the difference was only in degree. Animals could feel pain, pleasure and terror, had a memory, and could even reason, just as man could. And such faculties as maternal love, self-sacrifice, jealousy were not the exclusive property of man. The vast gap between the social instincts of an animal and those of

---

5. His idea of 'the survival of the fittest' was seized upon by the Nazis in support of their racist policy of the 1930s and 40s.

human beings was no argument, he claimed, just as he disregarded the idea of progression from primitive to civilised man. But he had continually to face the taunt, 'Where are the missing links? Why have none of them been found?'

Another unanswered problem faced Darwin, that man is no mere animal. The Bible teaches that man was made in 'the image of God', that he has a soul and is capable of a relationship with his Creator. Darwin's response was that man had risen from 'some primordial cell' through the fish, the amphibians and the mammals to one of an upright posture and a larger brain, with enough modifications to produce modern man – a pedigree, he admitted, that did not give man a 'noble quality'.

Mixed Reception

The book had a mixed reception, though it was not simply a matter of being rejected by the religious whilst being accepted by scientists: there were, in fact, scientists who dismissed Darwinism and evolution, and for good scientific reasons. But it was received with consternation among many orthodox churchmen – especially Evangelicals – who argued that the theory was inconsistent with the book of Genesis. It not only denied the idea of the creation of separate species 'after their kind', but implied that the world was not under the control of God; there were cruel forces at work which allowed only the fittest to survive and the weak to perish. It cut across other fundamentals of Christianity, too, which consequently damaged the faith of many ordinary Christians.

Criticisms of the theory were levelled at him from all sides, especially the press. The *Quarterly Review* magazine charged him with contradicting 'the revealed relation of the creation to the Creator', while another publication accused him of using 'absurd facts to prop up his uttterly rotten fabric of guess and speculation'. The *Athenaeum* magazine condemned him, describing 'the belief that man descends from the monkeys' as being 'wrought into something like a creed by Mr Darwin'. The Bishop of Oxford, Samuel Wilberforce, wrote in a review of the *Origin*, 'We have objected to the views … solely on scientific grounds… We think that all objections … savour of a timidity which is really inconsistent with a firm and well-intrusted faith.'

A now famous debate followed at a British Association of Science meeting, held in Oxford in June 1860.[6] Wilberforce, who was defending the authority of the Bible, claimed the superiority of knowledge by revelation over that obtained by scientific observation. As he concluded his argument,

---

6. Darwin was not present at the meeting, nor was the debate reported by a single London newspaper at the time.

he turned to his opponent, the scientist T. H. Huxley, and mockingly enquired whether it was through his grandfather or grandmother that he claimed descent from an ape?

Huxley was restrained in his reply, and suggested that if the question was would he rather have an ape for a grandfather or a talented man who used his skills to pour scorn on scientific debate, he would feel no shame at having an ape for an ancestor – but that he would indeed be ashamed of a brilliant man who plunged into scientific questions of which he knew nothing!

SCIENTISTS' VIEWS

Whilst many Christians were – and still are – opposed to Darwin's theory of evolution, atheists welcomed his work which refuted the idea of a Creator God and offered an acceptable explanation of how the world came to be. Science, they argued, was factual whilst the Bible was myth and could not offer a valid account of creation.

However, some believing scientists have contended that there is evidence for the view known as 'theistic evolution'. In 1870 Henry Drummond, Professor of Natural Science in the Free Church College (Theological Faculty), Glasgow, wrote that natural selection and evolution were facts and were not irreconcilable with the belief that God has created and sustains the world, a view still held today. J. C. Dearden, an Emeritus Professor of Medical Chemistry, has stated that he can see 'no particular problem in reconciling the evolutionary and Creationist approaches to the formation of the earth'. He points out that the description of creation in Genesis 'accords pretty well, in terms of chronological order, with that given by science'.

Emeritus Professor Douglas Spanner (University of London), a botanist, has taken the argument a stage further. He has suggested that 'Over the course of countless ages God, working in a way which science describes in terms of natural selection ... formed on earth a creature qualified anatomically, physiologically and psychologically for the final stage in His creative purposes. Into one member of this species the Creator breathed something of His Spirit, raising it to a quite new potentiality of responding to Himself. He transformed the ancestor into a man "made in His image."

Faith

For the last twenty years of his life Darwin continued writing books, moving from geology to zoology to botany. His last work appeared in 1881, just before his death. The prevailing view is that Darwin died an atheist, and that his drift from Christianity was sealed by his grief over the premature death of his ten-year-old daughter, Annie. But the truth appears to be rather different. Whilst he had wrestled for some time with the species problem before publication, he had not entirely rejected the idea of a Creator God.

At one point he confessed, 'I have never been an atheist in the sense of denying the existence of a God.' Nor had he completely severed his links with Christianity.[7] In fact, he came to faith some six months before he died, obviously the result of much heart-searching. Further, he wished he had not expressed his theory of evolution as he had done, for he was aware that some had falsely used his ideas.

That he came to faith was probably first recognised by Lady Elizabeth Hope,[8] wife of the First Admiral of the Fleet, Sir James Hope, and the leading figure of the temperance movement. Lady Hope had been asked to go and sit with the ailing scientist, and did so on a number of occasions. By then, Darwin was in the habit of reading his Bible; his favourite book was Hebrews – 'the Royal Book', he called it. It was obvious to his visitor that he was a converted man, and had a concern that others should hear the gospel. He even asked her to arrange an evangelistic meeting for his servants, tenants and neighbours in the summerhouse at the end of the garden. On his death he was buried in Westminster Abbey with full Christian rites, not because of his faith but rather because of his fame as a scientist of distinction.

Despite the evidence amassed by Darwin, creationists – those who stand by the biblical account in Genesis – have strong grounds for questioning the theory of evolution. Today's most widely accepted theory of the origin of the universe is that known as the 'Big Bang', a giant explosion caused by a mixture of gases. However, it seems unlikely that nothing can explode and create something, or that life can come out of non-life. Further, creation demands a Creator, and the wonder of creation is that all life and matter point to the work of a supreme and intelligent Deity. At the same time, the universe gives evidence of design and purpose, and therefore demands a Designer – an omnipotent Being able to bring order out of chaos.

Over the past 150 years a sense of alarm has given way to a more objective view of the theory. Evolution has become popular and is generally accepted by biologists; in educational institutions it is taught as fact, whereas Creationism is often ridiculed. But as evolution is only a theory, in the end both these positions are a matter of faith.

---

7. Since his travels on the *Beagle* Darwin had been an admirer of Christian missionary work, especially that of the South American Mission Society, which he supported financially for the last fifteen years of his life.

8. Some account of her visits to Darwin appeared in the *Christian Herald* and in the *English Churchmen*. See *Evidence for the Truth: Science*, by Dr E. K. Victor Pearce.

33

1900 THE BOXER REBELLION

The Massacre of Christians in China

In the long hot summer of 1900 some of the worst atrocities committed against Christians in the annals of modern missionary endeavour shattered the complacency of the Western world. A decree issued by the Empress Dowager of China urged provincial governors to 'exterminate the foreigners'. The call to kill was taken up by the Boxers, a Chinese secret society. Within the brief space of three months nearly 200 missionaries and children, as well as thousands of native believers, were brutally put to death.

During the nineteenth century there was an increasingly widespread feeling of discontent throughout the land, when China's ancient civilisation – once the greatest on earth – faced tremendous challenges for change. Political upheaval and a series of natural disasters combined to cause considerable unrest. The arrival of European superpowers intent on plundering China only served to aggravate the problems and trigger off the rebellion.

European Presence

There had been an effective European presence in China from the sixteenth century, when Portuguese traders entered Macao. They were followed by Dutch, Spanish and French commercial venturers, as well as the British East India Company, all anxious to gain a foothold in a potentially profitable market. By the beginning of the nineteenth century England was the most successful trading nation operating on the coast of China.

The British East India Company had built up a thriving trade in the drug opium, even though it was banned by the Chinese. The ensuing conflict between the two nations led to the Opium Wars (1840–42, 1858–60), when by the Treaty of Nanking (1842) China was forced to open up five 'treaty ports' for trading purposes.[1] Since the principle was followed that any privilege extended to one nation should be enjoyed by all, other European powers were able to take advantage of the arrangement.

Over the course of the century European nations extorted further concessions. A number of tributary states, two northern ports and various mining concessions were wrested from China. In fact, such was the exploitation that the possible partition of the land became the talk of Europe. This humiliation of China threatened to destabilise the ruling dynasty, creating anti-foreign feeling. Natural disasters – drought, famine and floods – compounded an already explosive situation. A severe famine in 1849 precipitated riots which triggered off a widespread rebellion (1850–1865), at a cost of twenty million lives. The rebels overran the most fertile provinces, pillaging and looting wherever they went. In 1877–1878 yet another great famine devastated the land, when nearly thirteen million people died.

The reintroduction of Christianity into China – one of the most resistant nations to the gospel – owed much to British military successes, a factor which did not enhance the cause of the gospel. By the terms of the Treaty of Nanking, both Protestant and Catholic missionary societies were permitted to set up mission stations in the treaty ports. Further concessions were gained by the Treaty of Tientsin (1858), by which the Chinese people were given religious liberty, allowing them to embrace Christianity. Missions were given the right to set up churches, open hospitals and schools, and to provide cemeteries. Foreign subjects were authorised to travel inland and provincial governors were ordered to ensure their protection.

> **EARLY CHRISTIANITY IN CHINA**
>
> Christianity was introduced into China in AD635 by Alopen, a Nestorian missionary, probably from Syria. Under the emperor, T'ai Tsung, China at that time was probably the most civilised empire in the world, where the exchange of ideas was welcomed. The emperor, Tai Tsung, studied the new religion and was favourably impressed. In 638 he issued a decree ordering that a church and monastery be built in the capital, Xian, and gave the missionaries the right to propagate their religion.
>
> Nestorian Christianity – a branch of the Faith which opposes the orthodox teaching about Christ – became widely established. Churches were erected and a large number of monasteries built, though the new religion was subject to much persecution. In 845 an unsympathetic Taoist emperor condemned seventy monasteries to be destroyed and ordered the 3,000 monks to return to secular

---

1. There were Canton, Amoy, Fuchour, Ningpo and Shanghai.

life. From that time the power of the Church began to dwindle and by the end of the tenth century there was no trace left of Nestorian Christianity.

Archaeological surveys have unearthed evidence of this early Christian presence. A Nestorian monument, known as the Siganfu (or Sxianfu) Stone, erected in 781, was discovered in 1625. It recorded the arrival of the missionaries and gave an account of the progress of the Church to that date. Recently, two statues depicting Jonah and the Virgin Mary have been discovered, and the site of a monastic complex – which could be the oldest Christian place of worship in China – has been unearthed.

Anti-foreign Feeling

Not surprisingly, Christianity stood in stark contrast to China's ancient religions, for the people were steeped in centuries-old religious beliefs and superstitions. Confucianism, which dated from the fifth century BC, was the religion of classical books and scholars, whilst Taoism, of an equal antiquity, was the religion of the common people. Buddhism, officially introduced from India in the year AD67, also attracted many adherents. But at the heart of Chinese religion was the practice of ancestor worship. The spirits of dead ancestors were believed to be capable of doing good or harm, and had to be propitiated by offerings and libations at either the domestic shrine or at an idol temple.

It was during the final decade of the century that the swell of anti-foreign feeling reached its peak. In 1895 China suffered a humiliating defeat at the hands of Japan, whilst Germany and Russia seized two northern naval bases. The introduction of railways and mining operations threatened not only jobs, but the very being of the nation. Further, two successive harvests caused widespread famine, compounded by a plague of locusts. Despite repeated fasts and sacrifices, the gods had failed to send rain. It was felt that the 'foreign devils' were the cause of the trouble and that their blood must be spilled.

The one incident that several observers held to have triggered off the rebellion was that of the concessions granted to Roman Catholic clergy. The Chinese government was persuaded to allow all Catholic clergy, from bishops down to the local priest, political status equal to their rank and the courtesies that went with it. Protestant missionary societies declined the privilege, as it was thought that to accept would have endangered the work of the gospel. There was considerable resentment following this move and Boxer fury was released.[2]

---

2. A number of escaping missionaries were saved from death by proving they were not Catholic priests.

Secret Societies

From the eleventh century a number of secret societies and political associations had exercised a powerful influence in China. Towards the end of the nineteenth century it was the Boxers[3] who captured the allegiance of the working classes and spearheaded the attack on the Westerners. The first mention of the Boxer rebels came in May 1898, when they were organised by Yu-hsien, the Governor of Shantung province. Believing that the gods must be displeased, anti-Christian resentment ran high and masses of country folk joined the rebellion. Chinese converts who refused to recant were tortured then brutally murdered. Villages, churches and chapels were destroyed and thousands made homeless.

On 31 December 1899 the rebels killed the first foreign missionary, the Revd Sidney Brook of the Society for the Propagation of the Gospel. For this, Yu-hsien was removed from office, but the rebellion quickly spread to other northern provinces. Warnings of an impending crisis were given by missionaries and friendly Chinese officials, but the British Minister in Beijing, Sir Claude MacDonald, did not judge the situation to be serious and hesitated to act.

The emperor had meanwhile been overthrown by his aunt, the Empress Dowager, a ruthless woman who for over fifty years had been the real power behind the throne. In a series of threatening edicts, issued in January 1900, she exhorted all governors and commanders-in-chief to combine to resist the 'enemy' and 'fight for the preservation of their homes'. By the decree she had sanctioned the actions of the Boxers.

Shansi Province

It was in Shansi province,[4] where much missionary work had been concentrated, that the greatest number of deaths was recorded. Shansi had a new governor – Yu-hsien, the demoted Governor of Shantung. When he turned a blind eye to the rebels' activities, the Boxers knew they were immune from interference. They went about with banners bearing the inscription, 'By Imperial command, destroy the religion'. When the governor ordered all native converts to deny their religion on penalty of death, several hundred native believers who disobeyed were executed.

---

3. The Chinese name of the society was *I Ho Ch'uan*, usually rendered as 'Righteous and Harmonious Fists', hence the term Boxers, a nickname first coined by missionaries.
4. A most amazing escape story is told by the Revd Archibald Glover, an Anglican clergyman, of his family's escape from Shansi and of a 1,000 mile journey to safety through rebel-held territory (*A Thousand Miles of Miracle in China*, Christian Focus Publications).

The worst massacre of the rebellion took place at Taiyuan, a provincial capital. When a mob set fire to the compound of the Baptist Missionary Society, they drove one lady missionary – Miss Edith Combs – into the flames; she was last seen kneeling as she burned to death. The remaining thirty-two missionaries and children, together with some Chinese believers and twelve Catholic clergy were rounded up and beheaded: the men first, followed by the women and children.

In June, at the northern town of Soping, members of the Swedish Holiness Union in co-operation with the International Missionary Alliance (now known as the Christian & Missionary Alliance), were holding their annual church conference. When the Boxers attacked they seized every member of the party and stoned them to death – nineteen missionaries, fifteen children and a number of Chinese believers. The massacre almost wiped out the small Swedish mission.[5]

> **STUDENT VOLUNTEERS**
> From around 1880 China became increasingly the focus of missionary endeavour and many outstanding young men were called to serve there. Men such as Dr Harold Schofield, a brilliant young graduate of Oxford and the 'Cambridge Seven' (which included C. T. Studd, the most famous England cricketer of his day). In America it was reported that 'the missionary spirit is rampant among the students', and among many who offered for China were three students from Yale – Horace Pitkin, Sherwood Eddy and Henry Luce.
>
> Much of this missionary enthusiasm was due to the influence of the American evangelist, D. L. Moody, who preached at a series of meetings at Cambridge University, and to Hudson Taylor, founder of CIM. As a result many young Cambridge graduates of wealth and high social standing volunteered for China in 1883–1884. In America, there was a similar groundswell of concern for China. In 1887, at the annual Northfield student conference, organised by Moody, the Student Volunteer movement was inaugurated. With the slogan, 'The Evangelisation of the World in this Generation', 100 young men signed a declaration of willingness to serve overseas. A student leader at Yale University declared that it was China that drew them all. The number of missionaries in China rose from 1,549 in 1877 to 2,785 in 1900, while ten years after the Boxer Rebellion the figure stood at 4,175.

Protection

Missionaries were often aided in their escape by Chinese Christians, as well as by sympathetic officials; in this way, many lives were saved that otherwise would have ended in tragedy. Even some of China's best statesmen

---

5. A Chinese evangelist managed to escape, but his wife and little daughter were killed. Only two missionaries, from another province, were left, and another was on furlough.

dared to challenge the Empress concerning her anti-foreign policy, while the Governor of Shensi province, H. E. Tuan, was the means of saving nearly 100 missionaries.

But there were many instances where others were offered protection, only to be betrayed. A party of six China Inland Mission (CIM) workers returning from leave to their station in Shansi were met by a group of soldiers whom they presumed were sent to escort them. The soldiers advised making a detour for reasons of safety. After a while they halted and withdrew their swords. The captain told the missionaries, 'You thought we came to protect you, but our orders are to kill you unless you promise to stop preaching your religion.' Because they refused, they were swiftly beheaded, including a seven-year-old boy. One Chinese believer escaped to tell the story.

MARTYR TESTIMONIES

Missionaries and their children faced the prospect of death with great courage and calmness, as is reflected in some of their last letters.

* from Mrs Duncan Kay, CIM, to their three children:
'I am writing this as it may be my last to you. Who knows but we may be with Jesus very soon. This is only a wee note to send our dear love to you all, and to ask you not to feel too sad when you know we have been killed... Try to be good children. Love God. Give your hearts to Jesus...'

* from Mrs Lizzie Atwater, American Board of Commissioners of Foreign Missions, to her sister:
'... I fear we shall not meet on earth.... I am preparing for the end very quietly and calmly. The Lord is wonderfully near, and He will not fail me... I just pray for grace to meet the terrible end bravely. The pain will soon be over, and oh the sweetness of the welcome above!'

* from Willie Peat (CIM) to his mother:
'The soldiers are just on us, and I have only time to say "Goodbye" to you all. We shall soon be with Christ, which is very far better for us. We can only now be sorry for you who are left behind and our dear native Christians... We rejoice that we are made partakers of the sufferings of Christ...'

These extracts are taken from *By Their Blood – Christian Martyrs of the 20th Century*, by James and Marti Hefley (Mott Media, 1979).

At Fenchow, northern Shansi, when the kind magistrate was replaced by one hostile to foreigners, the missionaries of the American Board of Commissioners of Foreign Missions and three CIM colleagues feared the worst. The new magistrate ordered them out of the town, accompanied by an armed guard under the pretence of protection. When they were beyond

The Kay family of CIM – the three elder children,
away at school and escaped death.

the town boundary, the guards turned on the missionaries and murdered them. In Chekiang province, during a period of persecution, many mission stations were attacked by Kiang-san, a secret vegetarian society. At the town of Ku-chau, the mission station was looted and destroyed and five missionaries and two children put to death.

Chihli province, the centre of the Chinese government, became the focus of some of the fiercest fighting. It was at the city of Paoting that the worst massacre outside Shansi province took place, and where the American (Northern) Presbyterian Mission, the CIM and the American Board of Commissioners had stations. The Boxers murdered two CIM workers outside the city walls, then closed off any way of escape. The Presbyterian compound was attacked and eight missionaries and four children, together with Chinese believers, were killed. When the mission house was set on fire, one missionary was seen walking along the verandah, holding the hands of his two sons as the flames spread around them.

Beijing

As the summer progressed the main body of Boxers moved rapidly towards the capital, Beijing. The aim was to annihilate the European population and the 5,000 native Christians, for the Empress had issued her worst ever decree. It consisted of one sentence: 'The foreigners must be killed; even if the foreigners retire, they must still be killed'.[6] Fearing the worst, missionaries and their converts flocked into the capital in the hope of finding protection. At last the diplomats realised the seriousness of the situation and sent a telegram pleading for troop reinforcements.

When the Boxers faced the European and American defences at the walls of Beijing on 20 June they were joined by troops of the Imperial Army. The defenders of Beijing held out for fifty-five days. During that time sixty-six foreigners were killed, and two adults and six babies died. On the 15 August an international rescue force finally arrived and broke the siege. The Empress fled Beijing; the Boxers were hunted down and thousands of them killed; and the Governor of Shansi province was captured and beheaded.

Letters and reports graphically recount the tremendous courage and faith shown by missionaries and by hundreds of Chinese believers during the rebellion. Of the 135 Protestant missionaries and 53 children who lost their lives, 159 were stationed in Shansi province or just across the border in Mongolia. The national breakdown of figures shows that 100 were from Britain and Commonwealth countries, 56 from Sweden and 32 from the United States – of these, 79 were associated with CIM and 36 with C & MA. The number of native Protestant Christians killed may have been as high as 30,000. Some 3,000 Roman Catholic converts, together with priests and nuns, were also murdered.

MARTYR POEM

AFRAID? OF WHAT?

Afraid? Of What?
To feel the spirit's glad release?
To pass from pain to perfect peace,
The strife and strain of life to cease?
Afraid – of that?

---

6. When the message was despatched to the south of China, two friendly officials altered the word 'kill' to 'protect', and for this they were cut in half.

Afraid? Of What?
Afraid to see the Saviour's face
To hear His welcome, and to trace
The glory gleam from wounds of grace?
Afraid – of that?

Afraid? Of What?
A flash, a crash, a pierced heart;
Darkness, light, O Heaven's art!
A wound of His a counterpart!
Afraid – of that?

Afraid? Of What?
To do by death what life could not –
Baptize with blood a stony plot,
Till souls shall blossom from the spot?
Afraid – of that?

Written during the Boxer Riots by E. H. Hamilton, of the American Presbyterian (South) Missionary Society, following the martyrdom of his colleague, Jack Vinson. Quoted by James and Marti Hefley in 'By Their Blood' (Published by Matt Media 1979), p 55.

Twentieth Century

As it turned out, the persecution in China – which continued throughout most of the twentieth century and is in evidence today – was but a foretaste of what was in store for the Church. During the years of the Second World War (1939–1945), both Nazi Germany and Japan were guilty of committing atrocities against Christians, whilst in countries under Communist rule believers were faced with attempts to eliminate all evidence of the Faith. And, unknown to many in the West, Christians in Asia, Africa, Latin America and the Middle East also faced persecution and martyrdom during those years.

More recently, attacks on the Church have been fuelled by the rise of Islamic militancy. The introduction of Islamic *Sharia* law, for Christians as well as Muslims, has led to civil war in southern Sudan and to violent clashes in northern Nigeria. Both countries have suffered a huge loss of life and a large number of churches has been destroyed. Indonesia has also witnessed brutal anti-Christian attacks, as Muslims waged a '*jihad*' (holy war) in a religious version of ethnic cleansing. And in Pakistan the religious authorities are rigorously enforcing the law, threatening the lives of both Muslims and Christians.

In the years of the early Church, persecution served only to spread the Faith rather than stamp it out. But Johan Candelin of the World Evangelical Fellowship has warned believers not to be sentimental about persecution. 'There is a dangerous misunderstanding common to many churches today, namely that persecution means growth...The truth is the other way round, growth brings persecution.' For the time being then, the Church in the West remains relatively unscathed, but who knows when this calm will one day be disturbed?

34

1948 THE REBIRTH OF THE STATE OF ISRAEL

The Jews Restored to their Ancient Homeland

In August 1897 the first Zionist conference was held in Basel, Switzerland, to consider the idea of establishing a homeland in Palestine for the Jewish people. At the conclusion, Theodore Herzl wrote in his diary: 'At Basel I founded the Jewish state. If I said this aloud, it would be greeted with worldwide derision. In five years, perhaps, and certainly in fifty, everyone will see it.'

Fifty years later, on 29 November 1947, the General Assembly of the United Nations voted for the establishment of a Jewish state in Palestine. For the first time after nearly 2,000 years of wandering and suffering, the Jewish people were to have their own land where – hopefully – they could live in safety and security.

Dispersion

Following the dispersion of the Jews from Israel in AD135, the land was occupied by successive waves of foreign invaders, though a remnant was always to be found in the land. Throughout that period Jews dreamed of the day when they would return to their homeland, a hope kept alive as they read the Scriptures in the synagogue and recited their prayers. And each Passover, which celebrated their great deliverance from Egypt, closed with the cry, 'Next year in Jerusalem!'

The return of the Jews to the land was in no small measure advanced by the support of British Protestants. Since the second century, the Church had viewed itself as the 'new Israel', claiming that God had rejected the Jews and that the promises regarding Israel now belonged to the Church. It was not until a renewed interest in the Scriptures, after the Reformation, drew the attention of Puritans to the many unfulfilled prophecies regarding Israel. They saw that God had not finished with the Jews and that one day the nation would come to a saving knowledge of Jesus as Messiah.

Equally important was the realisation that the Bible prophesied Israel's return to the land. The eighteenth century Evangelical Revival created an interest in this idea, when it was thought that God would use Britain to restore the Jews to their ancient homeland. One of the leading advocates of Jewish restoration was the Earl of Shaftesbury, who believed that their return would hasten the Second Coming of Christ. He worked tirelessly for the restoration of the land to the Jews, using his political and diplomatic offices for that purpose.

The nineteenth century witnessed the beginning of a return to the land, particularly from eastern Europe, which held the greatest concentration of Jews. From 1881 on, attacks ('pogroms') were made on Jewish settlements in Russia, when homes were looted and thousands of Jews killed. Around two million Jews left the country, and whilst the majority of them settled in the United States some found their way to Palestine.

Landmarks

Two important developments occurred around this time that are recognised landmarks in the progress towards setting up the modern State of Israel. In 1897 the Zionist Movement was founded under the dynamic leadership of an Austrian Jewish journalist, Theodore Herzl (1860–1904). Its aim was to secure a homeland for the persecuted Jews of Europe. Herzl was actively assisted by an Anglican clergyman, William Hechler, whose motivation was quite different to that of Herzl. For Hechler, his reading of prophecy had led him to conclude that the Jews would be returned to their homeland which would be followed by the Second Coming.

Then in 1917 a statement authorised by the British government affirmed its desire to assist the Jews in securing a homeland in Palestine. It was made in a letter written by Lord Balfour,[1] the British Foreign Minister, to the Jewish leader, Lord Rothschild. It declared: 'His Majesty's Government view with favour the establishment in Palestine of a national home for the Jewish people, and will use their best endeavours to facilitate the achievement of this object, it being clearly understood that nothing shall be done which may prejudice the civil and religious rights of existing non-Jewish communities in Palestine...'

A month later, when Britain captured Palestine from the Turks, the way appeared open for the implementation of this promise. At the San Remo Conference in 1922, Britain was given the mandate for setting up a Jewish national home in Palestine, a decision endorsed two years later by the League of Nations (the forerunner of the United Nations). However, in 1915 Britain had already given an undertaking to support Arab independence in Palestine after the defeat of the Turks, further complicating an already contentious issue.

REVD WILLIAM HECHLER (1845–1931)

The contribution made by William Hechler towards paving the way for a return of the Jews to their homeland has long gone unrecognised. Hechler, an Anglican clergyman, was from his early days steeped in Judaism and consequently developed a deep concern for the Jewish people. Born of a German father and British mother, he was ordained in 1873 and went out to Africa as a missionary. An attack of malaria the following year forced him to return home. Whilst recuperating in Germany he was invited to become tutor to the children of the Grand Duke of Baden. His position brought him into contact with many of Europe's royal families, including the future Kaiser William II of Germany, and he was enabled to press the claims for a Jewish homeland before some of Europe's most influential rulers. In 1885 he was appointed chaplain to the British Embassy in Vienna, a position which allowed him more time to pursue his interest in the Jewish people.

A serious student of prophecy, Hechler reckoned the Jews would return to their homeland in 1897. After reading Herzl's book, *The Jewish State*, he joined forces with the author to promote the Zionist cause by persuading the Sultan of Turkey to allow Jewish immigration to Palestine. He was able to arrange a meeting in 1898 between Herzl and the Kaiser in Jerusalem. When he failed to secure German support for the cause he next looked to England for help, which came in the form of the Balfour Declaration.

After the First World War when the Jews failed to emigrate to the Promised Land in the great numbers he had anticipated, Hechler repeatedly warned his Jewish friends of an extensive massacre of Jews in Europe – a prophecy tragically fulfilled. Hechler maintained his interest in Zionism to the end of his life and died poor and neglected in the Mildmay Hospital, London.

Arab Attacks

At first the Arabs were agreeable to the idea of a Jewish homeland in Palestine. But as they began to sense that it would be a threat to their own independence, the prospect for peace vanished. Fearful of being overwhelmed by Jews, from 1920 onwards Arab attacks on Jewish towns and settlements resulted in the deaths of many Jews. The main source of the trouble arose from the appointment by the British of Haj Amin El Husseini as the Grand Mufti of Jerusalem,[2] who used the Islamic religion to stir up the Arabs.

---

1. The author of the Declaration was, in fact, a secret Jew and Assistant Secretary to the British War Cabinet.

2. During World War II Husseini moved to Berlin and supported Hitler.

When the British refused permission for Jews to defend themselves, a Jewish defence force, the *Haganah*, was formed. In a vain attempt to placate Arab unrest, the British government partitioned Palestine. Some 78 per cent of the land – which had been promised to Israel – was made over to Abdullah Hussein, who was installed as King of the Arab nation of Trans-Jordan (now Jordan). This left a mere 22 per cent of Palestine to be shared between the remaining Arabs and Jews.

Despite the conflict, Jews continued to make their way back to the land. By 1929 the number of immigrants totalled 150,000, while a further 250,000 left Europe for Palestine following the rise to power of Hitler in 1933. Serious anti-Jewish attacks followed in 1936, when the Arab High Committee called a general strike which paralysed much of the country's economy. Of the one million Arabs in the land in 1939, many of them had only recently immigrated from Egypt and other parts of the Middle East. Attracted by the new, improved economic climate in the land, Arab immigrants for the most part settled in areas where Jews were already living and better work opportunities were available.

Dispute

Several attempts were made to settle the dispute between Jews and Arabs. The Peel Commission, set up in 1937, proposed that the remaining 22 per cent of the land should be divided into separate Arab and Jewish states, but the Arabs turned down the plan. Despite its promise of a homeland, in 1939 a British government White Paper proposed severe restrictions on Jewish land purchases and immigration, limiting the annual total to 15,000 for a period of five years. It also called for the establishment of an independent Arab-dominated state in Palestine within ten years.

Again, the Arabs refused to entertain the idea of a Jewish presence. They repeated their demand for an end to immigration and a halt to the sale of land to Jews, insisting that all Jews who had 'invaded' Palestine since the 1880s should leave. The League of Nations rejected the proposals as incompatible with the British mandate. But the war intervened and the League of Nations was discontinued. The British went ahead and placed its restrictions on the Jews.

Meanwhile, the Nazis were pursuing their policy of the 'Final Solution' – the extermination of the Jews. A meeting of nations in 1938, called by the United States, met at Evian-les-Bains, on the southern shore of Lake Geneva, to discuss the problem of Jewish refugees. Only three nations – the Dominican Republic, Holland and Denmark – offered to take in more

The British Mandate, 1920

The British Mandate, 1922

Some 78% of the Mandate was made over to the Arabs with Abdullah Hussein as King of Transjordan.

refugees.[3] Because no one seemed bothered about the Jews, Hitler felt free to go ahead with his own solution. Thousands of lives could have been saved if only Britain and other Gentile nations had been more sympathetically inclined.

By 1945 many of the remaining Jews were desperate to leave Europe and the Holocaust behind, and emigrate to Palestine. A plea to the British Prime Minister, Winston Churchill, to allow the 100,000 Jews in Allied refugee camps into Palestine, was turned down, for he refused to exceed the annual quota.[4] Yet another enquiry was set up, in which Hebert Morrison, a sympathetic British Cabinet Minister, proposed the division of the Holy Land into separate areas, consisting two-fifths Arab, a similar amount British, and one-fifth Jewish, each one under the British High Commission. The Arabs rejected the plan as did the Jews, who pointed out that it did not meet the commitment of the Balfour Declaration.

An Anglo-American Commission recommended in 1946 the setting up of a bi-national state under British control, but the new Labour Foreign Secretary, Ernest Bevan, turned down the idea, afraid of offending the Arabs with their vast oil resources. As the British were still intent on implementing the 1939 White Paper, to set up an independent Arab state, the Jewish resistance movement began a policy of destruction, blowing up bridges and railways in an effort to force the hand of Britain.

United Nations

Weary of the situation and the high cost of the war in terms of both lives and finance, in February 1947 Britain gave the problem over to the newly-formed United Nations. A UN committee representing ten nations recommended partitioning the land into separate Jewish and Arab states, with Jerusalem and its suburbs as an international zone under UN control. Whilst the Arabs yet again turned down the plan, the outcome can only be seen as the handiwork of God. When the plan was brought before the UN General Assembly on 29 November 1947, a two-thirds majority was needed for its acceptance. The partition plan was approved by thirty-three votes to thirteen, with ten abstentions (including Britain).

The timing of the vote was providential. It came just at the moment

---

3. Shortly afterwards the British government relented and agreed to receive 10,000 Jewish children between the ages of two and seventeen from Germany, Austria and Czechoslovakia. This rescue became known as the 'Kinderstransport'.

4. Many were returned to refugee camps in Europe, whilst others were detained in prison camps on Cyprus.

when many nations were sympathetic to the Jewish cause. The horrific memory of the Holocaust had appalled the world, and the sight of Jews fleeing Europe in order to find a homeland of their own touched the hearts of many. Added to this, the United States had a new pro-Zionist president, Harry S. Truman, a southern Baptist, who threw all his weight behind the plan and was able to persuade other nations to do the same. The Soviet Union, hopeful that the new Jewish state would have a socialist government, also gave its support.

The UN decision was a signal for the Arabs to intensify the battle for the land. On 2 December, aided by armed forces from Lebanon, Iraq and Syria (and later joined by Egypt and Trans-Jordan), Arab terrorists launched further attacks. David Ben-Gurion, the Jewish leader, ordered the Haganah[5] onto the offensive, which reclaimed some of the ground lost to the Arabs. The British failed to intervene in the fighting, and by the time the new state was declared over 1200 Jews had been killed in Arab attacks.

By now the United Nations was having second thoughts about the formation of a Jewish state, but hesitated about what course of action to take. The Soviet policy towards Israel changed to one of anti-Zionism. And in America, the onset of the Cold War forced Truman to listen more to his State Department's advice (which had foreseen disaster for the West if the motion were passed). If the British withdrawal had been delayed for even a few months, the outcome would have been quite different. Commenting on these events, historian Paul Johnson remarked, 'Israel slipped into existence through a fortuitous window in history which briefly opened for a few months in 1947–48. That ... was luck; or providence.'[6]

State of Israel

Before the UN could take any action, however, the new State of Israel came into being. It was proclaimed in Tel Aviv, the temporary capital, at the Museum on Rothschild Boulevard, on 14 May 1948, in the presence of the National Council. The assembly sang the new national anthem, The *HaTikvah* ('the hope'), accompanied by the Palestinian (now Israel) Symphony Orchestra, and Ben-Gurion – who became Israel's first Prime Minister – read out the Scroll of Independence.

'By virtue of our national and intrinsic right,' he announced, 'and on the strength of the resolution of the United Nations General Assembly, we

---

5. A defence organisation set up in March 1921
6. A History of the Jews, Paul Johnson, p. 526

hereby declare the establishment of a Jewish state in Palestine, which shall be known as the State of Israel.' The ancient name of Israel was chosen, the name used by Jews from Bible times (cf. Matt 2:20), rather than Palestine, which was associated with foreign conquerors. A provisional government was formed, which was immediately recognised by America and Russia. Next day the British left the land and Arab armies from five nations launched an attack.

Ruins of one of over 40 synagogues destroyed by the Jordanian army during their occupation of the Old City of Jerusalem, 1948-1967

Against all odds – humanly speaking – the invaders were gradually repelled, but at the cost of 6,000 Israeli lives. The Arab nations failed to dislodge the new state and, with the exception of Iraq, signed an armistice with Israel early in 1949, though all five nations remained in a formal state of war with Israel. When the fighting ended, the Arabs were left with rather less territory than had been awarded them by the UN Commission. Whereas originally they had been allotted western Galilee, most of central Palestine and the Gaza strip, they now had Judea and Samaria (the West bank), the Gaza strip, plus East Jerusalem (the Old City), captured by Jordanian troops.

Prophecy
The re-birth of Israel must rank as the greatest event in the history of the Church, linked as it is with the fulfilment of prophecy given over 2,500

years ago, and looking forward to the Second Coming of Messiah. Israel's return to the land was foretold by the prophets. Jeremiah (23:7–8) speaks of the Lord bringing back his people 'out of the land of the north and out of all the countries where he had banished them', whilst Isaiah (11:11) foretells of the Lord 'reaching out his hand a second time to reclaim the remnant.' These scriptures have been wonderfully fulfilled since 1948, and the Jewish population of the land has risen from 650,000 in 1948 to over five million today, gathered from over a hundred nations around the world.[7]

THE HEBREW LANGUAGE

Hebrew, the language of the Old Testament writers, was already in use when Moses and the Israelites came out of Egypt. Following the return from the Babylonian exile, the Aramaic language – which is closely related to Hebrew – was introduced into Israel and was spoken until at least the first century. However, since the discovery of the Dead Sea Scrolls (in 1948) it has been recognised that Hebrew continued in use alongside Aramaic, and it was more than likely the spoken language of Jesus. (See *Understanding the Difficult Words of Jesus*, by David Bivin and Roy Blizzard Jr. Published by the Centre for Judaic-Christian Studies.)

After the destruction of Jerusalem (in AD70 and again in 135) Hebrew as an everyday language fell into disuse until the end of the nineteenth century, though it continued to be employed for Jewish worship and literature. That it was revived was largely due to the vision of one man, Eliezer ben Yehuda (1858–1922), a Lithuanian educated at the Sorbonne in Paris, who emigrated to Israel in 1881.

Ben Yehuda believed that if the Jews were to have their own homeland, then they must recover the use of their own language by which they could be knit together. He spent his lifetime in searching out and listing Hebrew words lost over the centuries, and adding new ones based on Hebraic linguistic patterns. He also began to compile a dictionary, which was not completed until long after his death. In 1948 Hebrew became the official language of the new state of Israel. Today, all new immigrants to the land are given a crash course in the language to help them integrate into Israeli life.

It was also prophesied that the nation would be born in a day (Isa. 66:8), which was the case when the UN voted to create a Jewish state, an event without precedence. Other scriptures prophesied that Israel would return to the land in unbelief (Ezek. 36:24–27), then God would give them a new heart and put his Spirit in them. Whilst in 1948 there were no known Jewish believers in the land, that has now changed. Since the mid 1960s the number of Messianic Jews in Israel has risen from 300 to around

---

7. This figure includes over a million Russian Jews who have arrived since the fall of Communism in the former USSR.

7,000, meeting in more than 80 congregations and house groups, a large number of them from a Russian background.

The birth of the new state has also given rise to developments that have seen a loosening of long-held prejudices between Jews and Christians. Jewish interest in Jesus has noticeably increased, especially since the 1967 Six Day War, so that some Jews are now able to speak of 'our Jesus', recognising him as one of the greatest Jews ever. In addition, there have been numerous books written by Jews about Jesus, something that previously would have been unthought of.

For Christians, there has been an increasing awareness that the roots of our Faith are Jewish – that our God, our Saviour and our Scriptures came to us from the Jews. There has also been a genuine desire on the behalf of many Gentile Christians to put right the long centuries of prejudice and anti-semitism and be reconciled to the Jewish people.

In the fifty years since Israel was re-established the nation has been forced to fight for its very existence. It has been involved in four further wars against Arab armies, as well as an internal battle – the Palestinian *intifada* ('uprising') – against terrorist groups, all of whom are still intent on driving Israel into the sea. But God's promises remain firm: he has not rejected his Chosen People, and his commitment to the covenant made with Abraham, Isaac and Jacob still stands firm, serving as a reminder that God is faithful to his promises.

35

1960: BENNETT RESIGNS & THE CHARISMATIC MOVEMENT ADVANCES

Neo-Pentecostal Renewal Spreads

One of the most remarkable features of the twentieth century Church has been the growth of the Pentecostal movement. From an insignificant beginning, it now claims some 600 million adherents around the world, and after Catholicism and Protestantism is recognised as the 'Third Force' in Christianity. While initially it resulted in the founding of a number of Pentecostal denominations, from 1960 the onset of the Charismatic renewal movement among the Anglo-Catholics of California permeated all branches of Christendom, especially in countries of the Developing World. With its emphasis on the gifts of the Spirit, it brought both numerical and spiritual growth.

Contrary to what critics have suggested, the charismatic[1] renewal movement is thoroughly orthodox and is the on-going experience of the early Christians, known since the Day of Pentecost. In fulfilment of Jesus' promise (Acts 1:5), the first disciples were baptised with the Holy Spirit at Pentecost (Acts 2:1–13) and straightway began to speak 'in other tongues'. The Greek word used here is *glossolalia*, meaning tongues or languages. In verse two it suggests that the disciples burst into ecstatic utterances, whereas verse 11 refers to speaking in languages they had not learned. We later read that they received other spiritual gifts and were also empowered to perform 'great signs and miracles'.

The gifts of the Spirit experienced within the Charismatic movement

---

1. From the Greek *charismata*, 'gifts of grace'. See 1 Cor 12–14, Rom 12 and 1 Pet 4:10.)

are among those listed by the apostle Paul in his correspondence with the churches in Corinth and Rome. The gifts were given by God primarily for the whole Church, for serving and strengthening the body of Christ, but also for the conviction and conversion of unbelievers. Some, however, have argued that gifts such as tongues, prophecy and healing were only temporary and for the apostolic period; once the Church was founded, they were no longer needed. Nevertheless, there is documentary evidence that the gifts continued to be used in the Church over the first few centuries. Since then, spiritual gifts seem to have disappeared from sight. But the promises of God have not changed and the gifts are still available today.

Origins

The origins of the modern movement can be linked to the teaching of John Wesley, who revived the doctrine of holiness, or Christian perfection, known among the Puritans. Holiness was reckoned to be a gift from God and a second work of grace following conversion; it was also linked to the Second Coming of Christ. The teaching took hold among Methodists and spread across the Atlantic to other mainstream Protestant denominations. Holiness churches were established where the idea that holiness as a long-term struggle was replaced by the teaching that, following conversion, it could be claimed as a 'second blessing'. It was identified with the baptism of the Holy Spirit, by which the believer is endowed with power for witness and service.

By the end of the nineteenth century there was an increasing desire in some sections of the Church for holiness and for Holy Spirit baptism, and it was in this context that the modern Pentecostal movement had its beginning. In America, a Methodist evangelist, Charles Parham, opened a Bible college in Topeka, Kansas, in the autumn of 1900. The first exercise he set his students was to examine the biblical evidence for the baptism of the Holy Spirit. After three days they concluded that it was a recognised biblical experience accompanied by speaking in tongues. At their watchnight service that New Year's Eve, 'a mighty spiritual power filled the entire school'. As they were praying a number of the students received the baptism of the Holy Spirit and began to speak in tongues. Though the news was received with scepticism, by 1906 around a thousand people in the United States had received the blessing.

But it was the revival at Azusa Street, Los Angeles, in 1906, that more than anything focused the Christian public's attention on the issue of Holy Spirit baptism. Under the ministry of a black preacher, the Revd W. J.

Seymour, hundreds were baptised in the Spirit and spoke in tongues. News of the work spread far and wide and attracted a large crowd of visitors from all over North America, Europe and beyond, who then carried the message back to their own churches. Despite the evidence of changed lives, the movement proved controversial; opposition to the revival set in and church leaders turned hostile.

Between 1906 and 1911 a number of Churches were founded, including the predominantly black Church of God in Christ, as well as the Church of God and the Pentecostal Holiness Church. In 1914 many of Parham's followers joined with Pentecostal converts to form the Assemblies of God, now the largest Pentecostal denomination. In Wales, the Apostolic Church was formed in 1916, while the Elim Church and Assemblies of God were established in the early 1920s.

AZUSA STREET REVIVAL

An unknown Black preacher, the Revd W. J. Seymour was invited to preach at the (Nazarene) Holiness Church in Los Angeles. When it was realised that he believed in the baptism of the Spirit with speaking in tongues, the invitation was withdrawn. He moved to 312 Azusa Street, in a predominantly black district, where he rented a livery stable that had once been a lumber yard and had been used as a Methodist chapel. God worked mightily, and within a month Sunday attendance had risen to well over a thousand. News of the meetings spread throughout the country and to other parts of the world, reaching as far away as India, China and Japan. Furthermore, racial barriers were broken down as Black and White Christians worshipped together, unsegregated.

It would be fair to say that the twentieth century Pentecostal movement actually began in Azusa Street and that it owes its birth to the African people of America. Alexander Boddy, an Anglican clergyman from Sunderland, who became the leader of the movement in England, writing of the Azusa Street revival, said, 'It was something very extraordinary that White pastors from the south were eagerly prepared to go to Los Angeles, to have fellowship with them and to receive through their prayers and intercessions the blessing of the Spirit.'

The Azusa Street revival lasted for about three years, with meetings sometimes continuing through the night. As in Bethlehem, a stable became the birth-place of a truly international revolution.

Growth

Over the years the Pentecostal movement has continued to grow and large numbers of converts have been added to their churches. Like early Methodism, the movement appealed mainly to poorer people, so that Third World countries such as Brazil, Chile, Zaire and Indonesia all enjoyed tremendous growth. Nevertheless, the movement did not take hold in Britain as it had done in America; whilst growth was hindered by two world wars, critics such as F. B. Meyer, A. T. Pierson and Oswald Chambers did little to allay the suspicion with which Pentecostals were held.

Starting in the 1950s, however, a renewed interest in Holy Spirit baptism began to develop in America and Canada, and three men in particular were to the forefront of this revolution. David du Plessis, a South African who was the Executive Secretary of the World Conference of Pentecostal Fellowships, was led by God to become involved in the World Council of Churches (WCC). He became an 'ambassador extraordinary' for the WCC and was widely used of God to represent the Pentecostal movement in ecumenical circles.

Around the same time, Demos Shakarian, a Pentecostal businessman of Arminian extraction, founded the Full Gospel Business Men's Fellowship International (in 1952), which did much to spread the message and further helped prepare the way for the Charismatic renewal.[2] As the momentum of the movement gathered pace, the quietness was shattered by events taking place in a thriving Anglo-Catholic church at Van Nuys, a few miles north of Los Angeles. When the rector, the Revd Dennis Bennett, announced that he had been baptised in the Holy Spirit and had spoken in tongues, he caused an uproar in his church. What had been a low-key experience among those who had known the baptism was brought out into the open and became front-page news, even in the secular press.

New warmth

As a boy of eleven, Dennis Bennett had experienced conversion at a young people's meeting. He recalls that 'his heart had glowed with a new warmth and happiness, when for the first time he felt the presence of God'. At the age of twenty-six he entered theological college to train for the ministry, but was fed with 'extreme liberal humanism' which rejected basic truths such as the divinity of Jesus, the virgin birth and miracles, and weakened his hold on the things he had been taught as a boy. He soon fell away from his personal relationship with God and became more concerned about study and church work.

In 1951 Bennett was ordained into the Episcopalian (Anglo-Catholic) Church, with its strong emphasis on the sacraments. Before long he began to feel a dryness of spirit creeping upon him. The work at his church, St Mark's, was flourishing: the congregation had grown to 2,500 and there was a staff of four clergymen. Yet, though people in his church were being

---

2. See Shakarian's biography, *The Happiest People on Earth*, published Hodder.

helped, rarely were their lives changed. It was in this frame of mind that he learned of a couple who had been 'fired-up' with some kind of experience of the Holy Spirit. Speaking to them, he realised that they had found something of what he had lost. He began to re-examine the New Testament and the Prayer Book concerning the work of the Holy Spirit and came to the conclusion that this young couple had received something quite valid when they spoke in tongues.

After three months of searching, Bennett prayed to receive the baptism of the Spirit, though stressing that he did not want the tongues! As he did so, without being carried away he found that he was beginning to speak in a new language; there was no compulsion or embarrassment — the new words simply flowed from his lips. For over three months he said nothing to his congregation about his experience, though some noticed the change and enquired after his secret. Over the course of the following four or five months, around seventy of his parishioners were baptised in the Spirit. News began to get around, rumours circulated and opposition began to build up, until he finally felt he had to tell the church of his experience.

Resign!

On Sunday morning 3 April, 1960, Passion Sunday, at all three morning services he shared what had happened to him. All went well until the end of the second service, when one of his assistants snatched off his vestments, threw them on the altar and stalked out of the church, crying, 'I can no longer work with this man !' Outside, one man stood on a chair shouting, 'Throw out the damned tongues-speakers !' And when one of his vestrymen told him bluntly, 'You should resign,' he was ready to do so. At the third service he did just that; and he walked away from the parish he had served for seven years.

News of the events hit the headlines of the local newspapers and then swept the country through reports in *Time* magazine and *Newsweek*. But what happened that Sunday morning at St Mark's proved to be a crucial turning point, for it brought into the open a movement that had been under cover for some years. No longer was baptism in the Spirit a subject to be kept private, and many people across the historic denominations who had had enjoyed a similar experience now felt able to declare their position.

When Bennett was invited to become vicar of St Luke's, Seattle, he took over a mission church which had made no noticeable impact on the community for fifty years. He accepted the challenge. Under his ministry people were filled with the Holy Spirit, church attendance multiplied, and a new sense of love and unity pervaded the congregation. As the Holy Spirit attracted widespread news coverage, Bennett received invitations from across North America and Europe to share his experience. Catholics and Protestants alike were anxious to discover how their faith might be rejuvenated and how receiving the gift of God could give them a spiritual uplift.

GIFTS OF THE SPIRIT

Beyond the New Testament there have been few references made over the centuries by Christian writers to the use of spiritual gifts. Justin Martyr (c100–c165) testified that there were men and women who possessed the gifts in his day, and Irenaeus (c130–c200), Bishop of Lyons, writing towards the end of the second century, mentions the use of the gifts of healing, prophecy, visions and speaking in 'all kinds of languages'. He even speaks of raising the dead. By the fourth century the gifts seem to have fallen into disuse, and both Augustine (354–430), the Bishop of Hippo in North Africa, and Chrysostom (c347–407), Bishop of Constantinople, argued they had only been given for the launch of the Church and were therefore no longer necessary.

It was not until the Reformation that once again there was the occasional mention of spiritual gifts. They were apparently part of Martin Luther's Christian experience, and some Puritans recognised the validity of the blessing. Speaking in tongues was known among the first Quakers, while the gifts of the Spirit were in evidence among the Huguenots of France.

In the nineteenth century, there were a number of believers in the historic Churches who, after the teaching of Wesley, caught a fuller vision and preached both holiness and the baptism of the Holy Spirit. Men such as Charles Finney, D. L. Moody and R. A. Torrey influenced churches both sides of the Atlantic to seek spiritual gifts, while in Britain proponents of the message included William Booth of the Salvation Army, Evan Roberts, the Welsh revival leader, Alexander Boddy, an Anglican clergyman from Sunderland, and Smith Wigglesworth[3], the Pentecostal evangelist.

England

Prior to 1960, the Pentecostal movement in England had aroused little interest and news of events in America had so far received scant attention. It was a visit to California in 1962 by Dr Philip Hughes, editor of the quarterly theological journal *Churchman* that helped publicise the renewal movement. In an editorial Hughes wrote warmly of what he had discovered, disarming the prejudices of many British Christians and opening the door for a new work of God.

Visitors such as the Revd Frank Maguire of Los Angeles, Larry Christenson and David du Plessis addressed well-packed congregations in

---

3. See the author's *70 Great Christians*, p263.

the UK, and magazine articles appeared that welcomed their message. Under the leadership of Tom Smail, formerly Vice-Principal of St John's College, Nottingham, and Michael Harper, formerly curate at All Souls Church, Langham Place, London, the Fountain Trust was set up in 1964 which for sixteen years promoted the Charismatic renewal. Supported by such eminent Christians as Campbell McAlpine and Arthur Wallis, meetings were arranged at London's Westminster Hall that attracted large gatherings, where many believers received the baptism of the Spirit.

The Revd Michael Harper, General Secretary of the Fountain Trust,
set up in the 1960s to further charismatic renewal.

The Charismatic renewal affected the complete sprectrum of Christianity and included all classes of people. Catholic, Orthodox and Protestant churches, as well as the house-church movement, were touched by the Spirit. In America it spread to the so-called 'drop-out' generation, and in the 70s groups such as the Jesus People made an impact on the British scene.

Many can testify to the new lease of life they have experienced, as both individuals and churches received a second blessing. Though there has been an emphasis on the more spectacular gifts, other gifts have been released and people converted to Christ. Church services have been enlivened by exuberant worship, and fellowship between believers has been revitalised and crossed denominational boundaries. Unlike the movement at the beginning of the century, neo-Pentecostalism has not resulted in breakaway groups forming new denominations; rather it strengthened the historic churches from within, giving them a new lease of life. While it has not amounted to the kind of revival some had hoped for, many churches have known numerical growth at a time when others were on the decline.

Division

By the early 1990s there was a feeling in some circles that the renewal movement was running out of steam, only for the Christian world to be startled in 1994 by what became known as the 'Toronto Blessing'. Although a Holy Spirit movement from which many people benefited, it was characterised by a number of manifestations not normally associated with the baptism of the Spirit, causing a sharp division of opinion.

It is essential for Charismatics that this renewal is not lost, but rather that it continues to develop and come to maturity. This object can be achieved only if the Scriptures are given a more central place in both worship and teaching, and the balance within the Trinity is restored, giving the Father his rightful place. And as in all movements of God, that which believers have received should be shared with others, so that the love of God is expressed in more practical terms.

That the Charismatic movement has made a considerable impact on the Church makes it impossible for critics to write it off. It is no longer an unusual phenomenon that can be expected to go away. As one commentator has written, 'As long as the practice (i.e. baptism in the Spirit) remained within the Holiness and Pentecostal churches, it could be ignored. But now both clergy whose excellence of training cannot be overlooked, and sophisticated laity in the major denominations, have spoken not only for the personal value of the experience, but of its theological significance.'[4] The gifts of the Spirit, however, are not simply for 'personal value'; they are for building up the Body of Christ and for reaching the unsaved.

---

4. Morton Kelsey, quoted by Michael Harper, *As At the Beginning*, p95.

36

1974 INTERNATIONAL CONGRESS ON WORLD EVANGELISATION

'Let the Earth Hear His Voice'

In the eighteenth and nineteenth centuries America and Britain experienced a series of revivals which completely revitalised Western churches. The movement climaxed in the second half of the nineteenth century, following what has been recognised as the greatest revival in modern times. It began in New York in 1857; within two years it had set alight the eastern states of America and profoundly affected the British Isles. In the initial two years of the movement over two million people were converted and admitted into church membership.[1] The result was evidenced by the founding of missionary societies and Bible colleges, schools and hospitals, together with many other humanitarian agencies.

With the establishing of new foreign missions it was recognised that there was a need for a meeting of minds to share matters of common interest and concern. To this end a series of conferences were held between the years 1860–1900, culminating in the World Missionary Conference at Edinburgh in 1910. The conference met under the slogan of 'The evangelisation of the world in this generation', the watchword adopted in 1876 by the Student Volunteer Movement (later to become the Student Christian Movement).

Under the chairmanship of John R. Mott, an American Methodist converted under D. L. Moody, the emphasis of the conference was on uniting together to evangelise the world. Sadly, the Archbishop of Canterbury, Randall Davidson, would only permit Anglican participation on the condition that doctrinal debate was not included. Hence topics such as the

---

1. See *The Second Evangelical Awakening*, by J. Edwin Orr.

content of the gospel and the theology of evangelism were not raised. Even so, in his closing address Mott urged the need for the Church to develop a plan for the evangelisation of the whole world.

PRAYER MEETING REVIVAL

The 1857 revival, known as the Second Great Awakening, heralded a break with tradition in that it was led not by clergy but by laymen, who called people together to pray. It originated in New York when Jeremiah Lanphier gave up his business to become city missionary to the Dutch Reformed North Church on Fulton Street. He started a midday prayer meeting for city workers to join him in calling upon God. Soon, similar prayer meetings were being held all over the city and beyond, praying for the conversion of the unsaved. Revival broke out, and by May of the following year some 50,000 people in New York alone had come to the Lord. In the years 1857–58 around one million people in the eastern states of America were converted and joined Protestant churches.

In the British Isles, Ulster (Northern Ireland) was the first to experience revival, early in 1859. One young man gathered three others together to pray for revival, and before long revival fell upon the land, affecting southern Ireland as well. When reports of the awakening reached Scotland it aroused fervent interest. Revival soon swept the country, and the years 1859–60 were times of tremendous blessing. The revival in Wales may well have been independent of that in Ulster, though every county enjoyed a great work of God.

The revival in England began almost unnoticed in the summer of 1859, in Northumberland, and gradually progressed southwards, affecting all denominations. In London, special services were held throughout the capital, including ones at St Paul's Cathedral and Westminster Abbey. It was reckoned that over one million people were converted in the British Isles during the years 1859–61.

Under the work of evangelists such as C. G. Finney, D. L .Moody, William Booth and H. Grattan Guinness, the movement continued through the remaining decades of the century.

Enemy Within

The Edinburgh conference was successful in that it broke down old barriers and encouraged a further desire for fellowship and co-operation, and marking the emergence of the ecumenical movement. But the failure to give consideration to the theology of mission later proved it to have been a misguided decision, for it failed to further stimulate the churches' missionary vision. There was yet another enemy within the Church, which for some while had been infiltrating universities and theological colleges. Known as theological liberalism (or modernism), it was a movement that emanated from within the Church to seriously challenge the authority of the Bible.

The threat of liberalism was given an impetus by the publication in 1859 of Darwin's controversial book, Origin *of Species,* [2] in which the author

---

2. See chapter 32.

appeared to deny the accuracy of the Bible and the existence of a Creator God. Around the same time there were critics, mostly German theologians, who also cast doubt upon the validity of the biblical text. They concluded that the early books of the Old Testament and many of the New Testament epistles were historically unreliable. Their conclusions denied the inerrancy of the Scriptures and undermined the faith of many ordinary churchgoers.

Social Gospel

A further, more serious development was that of the teaching commonly known as the social gospel, a mis-leading development which undermined the gospel of salvation. A product of liberal thinking, it was argued that if God is the Father of all men, then all men are brothers; consequently, each one must care for the welfare of all. This led to focusing attention on social, moral and political issues at the expense of evangelism, and ignored the need for man's redemption. The idea was that the kingdom could be built on earth simply by moral effort, social reform and political action, and in this way society could be changed to conform to biblical standards.

Hopes of maintaining any achievement gained at the Edinburgh Conference were hindered by the progress of liberalism. It permeated mainline churches and continued as a threat to missionary endeavour beyond the Second World War (1939–1945). Following the war there were a number of international Christian conferences held where this teaching was given prominence. When the World Council of Churches[3] (WCC) was formally constituted at Amsterdam in 1948 as a 'fellowship of churches which accept our Lord Jesus Christ as God and Saviour', there was hope that the gospel of salvation might be restored. But this was not the case. It seemed that there was a greater desire to keep up an appearance of unity rather than to maintain the cause of the gospel.

An effort was made to rectify the matter at the WCC Assemblies at Delhi (1961) and again at Uppsala (1968), where the idea was put forward that the gospel was a restructuring of society and a reconciliation within humanity rather than reconciliation with God. Attempts were made by some delegates to strike the right balance between evangelism and social concern, but their voices were muted. Although the final declaration was clearer about the need for conversion to Christ, the turning point did not appear as a religious choice, for it declared there were those who 'unknowing served the "man for others"'.[4]

---

3. See *The Lion Book of Christian Thought*, (p. 242ff), Tony Lane.
4. Ibid.

Recovery

Despite these drawbacks there were signs of a recovery amongst Evangelicals. As far back as 1928 the Inter-Varsity Fellowship of Evangelical Unions had been founded, which served as a rallying point in the universities. Further encouragement was provided in 1939 by the International Fellowship of Evangelical Students, which was set up under the leadership of Dr Martin Lloyd-Jones, while in 1946 the Inter-Varsity Christian Fellowship began to hold missionary conferences for students every three years. These events were an expression of a biblically-based theological movement that emerged in the early 1940s and was aimed at restoring the Bible to its rightful position in the Church as the Word of God.

It was during this decade that the American evangelist, Billy Graham, came to the fore and was before long recognised as the greatest evangelist since the days of D. L. Moody. His obvious anointing as a gospel preacher and his gift of leadership helped re-establish evangelism as an essential element in Christian thought and teaching. He became the friend of Presidents and Prime Ministers alike, not only in the West but in the Far East as well, and was increasingly acknowledged as an international statesman.

As he travelled the world, Graham discovered that there were Christian leaders who had become discouraged with evangelism; others ignored it altogether, as social, political and economic issues were deemed more important. Determined to find a way forward, he invited a select group of evangelical leaders from various parts of the world to meet with him to discuss the situation. It was agreed that there was a desperate need for some means of stimulating the work of world evangelism. The outcome was a gathering (in 1960) of thirty-three Christian leaders from twelve countries who met informally in Montreux, Switzerland, to discuss the problems and opportunities for preaching the gospel. This was the first of a number of conferences held during the next three decades to further the cause of the gospel.

Berlin Congress

Recognising that there was a great need to train evangelists for their work, a congress was held in Berlin[5] (in 1966) to encourage this work. The success of the congress led to a series of regional conferences, in Singapore (1968),

---

5. Two of the delegates were members of the Auca tribe of Indians from Ecuador, where in 1956 they and their fellow tribesmen had killed five American missionaries who had attempted to reach them with the gospel.

Minneapolis (1969), Bogota (1969) and in Amsterdam (1971), as well as one in Kansas City (1970) for Black evangelicals, plus a European Congress on Evangelism (1971) which drew 1,000 delegates from thirty-six countries. This latter conference was given over to a thorough examination of the theology and practice of evangelism, and the challenges facing the churches of Europe.

To maintain the momentum of the Congress it was felt necessary to organise a further such gathering, especially as there was so much theological confusion within the WCC. There was a growing presence of an element within the Church which held to universalism, the idea that because God was a God of love then ultimately all would be saved. And mission was described in terms of reconciliation within humanity rather than reconciliation with God, which was regarded as of secondary importance. There were Evangelicals within the WCC who opposed this trend, though they were in the minority.

THE ECUMENICAL MOVEMENT

For Protestants, the origins of ecumenicism go back to the end of the eighteenth century and the beginning of the modern missionary movement. Following the Evangelical Revival, inter-denominational foreign and home missions were founded which helped draw Evangelicals together. In the second half of the nineteenth century unity was further expressed in a series of missionary conferences, beginning with Liverpool in 1860 and culminating in the Edinburgh conference of 1910. An International Missionary Council was planned to follow, though it was not set up until 1921, after the First World War. Several theological differences emerged and it finally integrated with the World Council of Churches in 1961.

Faith and Order was another off-shoot of Edinburgh, and was aimed at bringing about some form of church unity. It met in Lausanne in 1927 and again at Edinburgh in 1937, where it declared, 'We humbly acknowledge that our divisions are contrary to the will of Christ. We pray God in his mercy to shorten the days of our separation and to guide us by his Spirit into fulness of unity.' A further movement, Life and Work, was concerned with relating the Christian Faith to political, social and economic problems. It met at Stockholm in 1925 and again at Oxford in 1937.

Proposals were put forward that the two movements should become one body, to be called the 'World Council of Churches'. An advisory conference was arranged to work out a constitution, though the inaugural meeting was delayed until 1948. At an assembly at Amsterdam, 351 delegates from 147 different (Protestant) Churches affirmed that 'The World Council of Churches is a fellowship of churches which confess the Lord Jesus Christ as God and Saviour according to the Scriptures...' Roman Catholic participation in the movement began in 1960.

In 1973 at the Bangkok conference of the WCC Commission on World Mission and Evangelism, salvation was defined largely as a struggle for economic justice and for human dignity, and a struggle of hope against despair.[6] There was obviously an urgent need for a simple, biblically-based statement that expressed the true nature of evangelism, which knit together the two elements of evangelism and social justice. It was largely this concern that provoked the need for a further international congress, which was already being planned for 1974 to focus on the unfinished task of world evangelisation.

Lausanne

Under the theme of 'Let the Earth Hear His Voice', 2,700 official delegates, together with 1300 observers and guests from over 150 countries, gathered in Lausanne, Switzerland, for the International Congress on World Evangelism (ICWE).[7] Fifty percent of the participants were from the Third World, but there were none from the USSR or from mainland China. It was described by *Time* Magazine as 'possibly the widest-ranging meeting of Christians ever held'. Included among the delegates were many key evangelical leaders, as well as others with valuable specialisms and knowledge.

In his opening address, Billy Graham traced the succession of other similar gatherings dealing with missions and evangelism over the previous two decades, and went on to stress the urgent need to develop evangelistic strategies. Among his hopes for the Congress was that it would 'frame a biblical declaration on evangelism' and 'challenge the Church to complete the task of world evangelisation'. He also drew attention to the need to 'state the relationship between evangelism and social responsibility'. For the next ten days the congress gave itself to a daily programme of worship, prayer, Bible study and planning for world evangelism. However, the Congress failed to tackle the matter of the relationship between evangelism and social action, which had to be remedied at a later congress.

A final document was issued, known as the Lausanne Covenant. It was called a covenant rather than a declaration, not in the biblical sense of the word, but in the ordinary sense as of a binding contract, for its intention was to express a commitment to world evangelism. The Lausanne Covenant

---

6. Since Bangkok there has been a more balanced position on this subject within the WCC.
7. For a report of the Congress, see *Making Christ Known*, edited by John Stott (Paternoster Press), which contains the text of the Lausanne Covenant, together with reports from later conferences within the Lausanne Movement.

Billy Graham (b. 1918)

is a summary of evangelical belief, and contains a commitment to pray and work for the evangelisation of the world. Before the close, the delegates further decided to form a permanent committee to maintain the on-going vision and work of the Congress. To this end, a Strategy Working Group and a Lausanne Theology and Education Group were set up.

A number of follow-up conferences were held, in Nairobi (Africa), India, Hong Kong, Singapore and even Cuba. The one in Nairobi was a Pan-Africa Assembly which brought together Christian leaders from all across the continent, despite racial and political differences. Then between 1977 and 1982 six consultations were held to study various aspects of evangelism, which covered – among others – The Gospel and Culture, Muslim Evangelisation and An Evangelical Commitment to a Simple Lifestyle.

Sacrificial Service

A Consultation at Pattaya (Thailand) in 1980 was given over to a study of seventeen 'people groups', focusing on how to reach particular people for

Christ. Among the groups included were refugees, Jewish people, Muslims and nominal Christians of both Protestant and Catholic persuasion. It was at Pattaya that it was finally proposed that a world conference should be organised to deal with the thorny question of the relationship between evangelism and social responsibility. Although the Lausanne Covenant had included two paragraphs entitled 'The Nature of Evangelism' and 'Christian Social Responsibility', the two had not been linked except by the statement that 'in the Church's mission of sacrificial service, evangelism is primary'.

A move to correct the omission was made at a conference held two years later, at Grand Rapids (USA) in 1982, when a group of fifty delegates met together to work out a biblical basis for this unresolved issue. The subject was looked at in the light of Scripture and 'from every conceivable angle'. Despite the feelings of apprehension expressed by some delegates beforehand, in its final report the conference affirmed that there was an inalienable link between evangelism and social action.

It declared that they were linked by a threefold relationship: (1) that social action is a 'consequence' of evangelism, (2) that it is a 'bridge' to evangelism, and (3) that it is also a 'partner' of evangelism. Even so, in making this affirmation it was acknowledged that evangelism had priority because of its relationship to people's eternal destiny.

Meanwhile, plans were going ahead for a second International Congress on World Evangelisation, which took place in Manila (in the Philippines) in July 1989. Lausanne II was attended by over 3,000 delegates from 170 countries, and included representatives from Eastern Europe and the Soviet Union, though once again not from mainland China. The aim was to consider further the unfinished task of the Lord's Great Commission (Matt 28:19), to 'make disciples of all nations'.

A final document, the Manila Manifesto, was drawn up and was accepted by the overwhelming majority of the delegatus. The Manifesto is a rather more expansive version of the Lausanne Covenant, and each of its twelve paragraphs has important additions beyond those of its predecessor.[8] The Manifesto concludes by declaring that 'the whole Church is called to take the whole gospel to the whole world, proclaiming Christ until he comes, with all necessary urgency, unity and sacrifice.'

---

8. It is for this reason that the Lausanne Committee ruled that the two documents must always be published together.

Way Forward

The impact of these conferences has contributed greatly to the goal of world evangelisation. One of the most significant developments was that Third World Christian leaders and evangelists emerged as those more than able to play a prominent part in the task of evangelisation; indeed, they were already fully committed. At the 1974 Congress some fifty percent of the speakers and the Planning Committee were from the Third World, and several hundred evangelists were delegates to the other conferences and consultations. These evangelists received encouragement and training, and new movements and strategies were launched that assisted them in reaching out with the gospel. In Bolivia, for example, one tribe which had twenty churches in 1974 had increased to one thousand churches by 1980.

Though the relationship between evangelism and social responsibility was finally worked out at Manila, liberal theology continues to weaken the cause of the gospel. Many churchmen condemn attempts to evangelise peoples of other religions on the grounds that they already have their own beliefs. And although Christianity may claim that Jesus is God's fullest revelation to mankind, it is argued that other religions have their own way of salvation and do not need the gospel. Again, others suggest that all religions are of equal value and are simply different expressions of the same thing, a view that tends much towards the idea of a one world religion.

For nearly two millenia the stronghold of Christianity has been in the West, from where the gospel went out to all the world. Today, whilst the West flounders in a sea of apparent indifference, Christianity is growing in the Southern and Eastern areas of the globe, especially in regions where believers are suffering persecution. And though the world Christian community has risen to two billion, it still leaves two-thirds of the world yet to be evangelised. The task of evangelism gets harder as the opposition from other religions and from secularism mounts apace. But the promises of the Lord are sure, just as the command to take the gospel to all nations remains in place.

Christian Focus Publications

publishes books for all ages

Our mission statement –

STAYING FAITHFUL

In dependence upon God we seek to help make His infallible Word, the Bible, relevant. Our aim is to ensure that the Lord Jesus Christ is presented as the only hope to obtain forgiveness of sin, live a useful life and look forward to heaven with Him.

REACHING OUT

Christ's last command requires us to reach out to our world with His gospel. We seek to help fulfill that by publishing books that point people towards Jesus and help them develop a Christ-like maturity. We aim to equip all levels of readers for life, work, ministry and mission.

Books in our adult range are published in three imprints.

Christian Focus contains popular works including biographies, commentaries, basic doctrine and Christian living. Our children's books are also published in this imprint.

Mentor focuses on books written at a level suitable for Bible College and seminary students, pastors, and other serious readers. The imprint includes commentaries, doctrinal studies, examination of current issues and church history.

Christian Heritage contains classic writings from the past.

For a free catalogue of all our titles, please write to

Christian Focus Publications, Ltd
Geanies House, Fearn,
Ross-shire, IV20 1TW, Scotland, United Kingdom
info@christianfocus.com